The Alcuin Club: Promoting the Study of Liturgy

Founded in 1897, the Alcuin Club seeks to promote the study of Christian liturgy and worship in general with special reference to worship in the Anglican Communion. The Club has published a series of annual **Collections**, including *A Companion to Common Worship*, volumes 1 and 2, edited by Paul F. Bradshaw; *The Origins of Feasts, Fasts and Seasons in Early Christianity* by Paul F. Bradshaw and Maxwell E. Johnson (SPCK 2011) and, by the same authors, *The Eucharistic Liturgies: Their Evolution and Interpretation* (SPCK 2012); also *The Cross and Creation in Christian Liturgy and Art* by Christopher Irvine (SPCK 2013), *Eucharistic Epicleses Ancient and Modern* by Anne McGowan (SPCK 2014), *Dean Dwelly of Liverpool: Liturgical Genius* by Peter Kennerley (Carnegie Publishing 2015), *Ancient Christian Worship* by Andrew B. McGowan (Baker Academic 2016), and *The Rise and Fall of the Incomparable Liturgy: The Book of Common Prayer 1559–1906* by Bryan D. Spinks (SPCK 2017). The **Alcuin Liturgy Guide** series aims to address the theology and practice of worship, and includes *The Use of Symbols in Worship*, edited by Christopher Irvine, two volumes covering the celebration of the Christian Year: *Celebrating Christ's Appearing: Advent to Christmas* and *Celebrating Christ's Victory: Ash Wednesday to Trinity*, both by Benjamin Gordon-Taylor and Simon Jones, and most recently *Celebrating Christian Initiation* by Simon Jones. The Club works in partnership with the Group for the Renewal of Worship (GROW) in the publication of the **Joint Liturgical Studies** series, with two studies being published each year. In 2013 the Club also published a major new work of reference, *The Study of Liturgy and Worship: An Alcuin Guide*, edited by Juliette Day and Benjamin Gordon-Taylor (SPCK 2013).

Members of the Club receive publications of the current year free and others at a reduced rate. The President of the Club is the Rt Revd Dr Stephen Platten, its Chairman is the Revd Canon Christopher Irvine, and the Secretary is the Revd Dr Gordon Jeanes. For details of membership and the annual subscription, contact The Alcuin Club, St Anne's Vicarage, 182 St Ann's Hill, Wandsworth, London SW18 2RS, United Kingdom, or email: alcuinclub@gmail.com

Visit the Alcuin Club website at: **www.alcuinclub.org.uk**

Alcuin Club Collections 93

The Pilgrimage of Egeria

A New Translation of the *Itinerarium Egeriae*
with Introduction and Commentary

Anne McGowan
and
Paul F. Bradshaw

LITURGICAL PRESS
ACADEMIC

Collegeville, Minnesota
www.litpress.org

Cover design by Ann Blattner.

1   2   3   4   5   6   7   8   9

Library of Congress Cataloging-in-Publication Data

Names: McGowan, Anne, 1979– translator, writer of added commentary. |
    Bradshaw, Paul F., translator, writer of added commentary.
Title: The pilgrimage of Egeria : a new translation of the Itinerarium Egeriae
    with introduction and commentary / Anne McGowan and Paul F.
    Bradshaw.
Other titles: Itinerarium Egeriae. English.
Description: Collegeville, Minnesota : Liturgical Press, 2018. | Translation of:
    Itinerarium Egeriae. | Includes bibliographical references and index.
Identifiers: LCCN 2017061424 (print) | LCCN 2017058900 (ebook) | ISBN
    9780814684450 (ebook) | ISBN 9780814684214
Subjects: LCSH: Egeria, active 4th century–5th century—Diaries. | Christian
    pilgrims and pilgrimages—Middle East—Diaries—Early works to 1800. |
    Jerusalem—In Christianity—Early works to 1800. | Jerusalem—Description
    and travel—Early works to 1800. | Liturgies, Early Christian. | Church
    year—Early works to 1800. | Middle East—Description and travel—Early
    works to 1800. | Church history—Primitive and early church, ca. 30–600.
Classification: LCC DS104.5 (print) | LCC DS104.5 .I813 2018 (ebook) | DDC
    263/.042569442—dc23
LC record available at https://lccn.loc.gov/2017061424

Contents

Preface

With the aim of making this late fourth-century diary of a pilgrimage to the Holy Land more easily intelligible, earlier English translations have—to a greater or lesser extent—rendered Egeria's Latin into English somewhat freely. Her facility in the language does not match that of classical authors, her grammar and syntax are often far from accurate, and her style is highly colloquial. As others have suggested, she probably wrote as she talked. Our translation has aimed to be rather more literal, though without insisting on this in absolutely every instance lest the meaning should become entirely lost. It is hoped that this arrangement will capture the author's style sufficiently so as to convey more of her own personality, even at the cost of demanding more of the reader. Brackets indicate where words have been supplied to aid the sense, and inclusive language has been adopted where appropriate.

We have retained the Latin names the author uses for liturgical seasons, *Pascha*, *Quadragesima*, and so forth, and the method of designating the days of the week that was used in the Western church at the time: the Lord's Day, the second/third/fourth/fifth/sixth day, and the Sabbath. We have also kept the Roman method of reckoning the divisions of the day. The period of daylight was divided into twelve equal hours, and nighttime similarly. Thus, the first hour of the day could be said to correspond approximately to 6–7 a.m., the third hour approximately to 8–9 a.m., and so on. But this is only very approximate because the actual duration of an hour varied throughout the year as the periods of daylight and darkness increased and decreased in length in the course of the changing seasons.

We have included a very substantial introduction covering both early pilgrimage as a whole, especially travel by women, and the many liturgical rites of Jerusalem that Egeria described, as well as a verse-by-verse commentary alongside the translated text. Both of these draw on the most recent scholarship that was not available to those who prepared earlier English translations. Just as is the case with research on liturgical developments, so too studies of the origins and varieties of religious travel and of ascetic and monastic practices in late antiquity have led in recent decades to a renewed appreciation of the diversity and local particularities of such activities. We refer to the possibility of Egeria's relationship with an ascetic or monastic community in the Introduction on pp. 6–7, but a full account of how consideration of sources not normally included in "mainstream" monastic literature and the application of new critical methods to ancient texts might help to situate Egeria within the emergent phenomenon of religious communities of women lies beyond the scope of our book.[1]

It is hoped that the range of background information to the author's journey and her participation in the worship of the Jerusalem church that we have provided will furnish both the novice to the subject and the more experienced student or scholar with what they need in order to understand more fully this fascinating insight into Christian life and piety in that formative period.

Anne McGowan
Paul F. Bradshaw

[1] The interested reader might begin by consulting the works we have listed in the section on "Early Ascetic and Monastic Life" in the Select Bibliography on pp. 211–12.

Acknowledgments

The cover illustration and Figure 1, a map of the eastern provinces of the Roman Empire, is courtesy of *The Oxford Classical Dictionary*, digital edition [http://classics.oxfordre.com/page/maps/], ed. Sander M. Goldberg (New York: Oxford University Press, 2015); the superimposition of Egeria's route and the major places she visited is our own work.

Figure 2 is reproduced by permission from Jan Willem Drijvers, *Cyril of Jerusalem: Bishop and City* (Leiden: Brill, 2004), 215.

Figure 3 is reproduced from a redrawing of an original by Virgilio C. Corbo, *Il Santo Sepolcro di Gerusalemme* (Jerusalem: Franciscan Printing Press, 1981), vol. 2, Plate 3.

Figure 4 is adapted from a drawing by Kenneth John Conant, "The Original Buildings at the Holy Sepulchre at Jerusalem," *Speculum* 31 (1956): 17, Plate III d.

Our thanks are due to Matthew Tatro for his invaluable assistance in the digital manipulation of these figures.

Except where otherwise noted, all translations of ancient sources are our own work.

Abbreviations

AL	The Armenian Lectionary
BCE	Before the Common Era
Brodersen	Kai Brodersen, *Aetheria/Egeria, Reise ins Heilige Land*, Sammlung Tusculum (Berlin: De Gruyter, 2016)
CE	Common Era
ET	English translation
Gingras	George E. Gingras, *Egeria: Diary of a Pilgrimage*, Ancient Christian Writers 38 (New York: Newman Press, 1970)
JLS	Alcuin/GROW Joint Liturgical Study
LXX	The Greek Septuagint translation of the Old Testament
Maraval	Pierre Maraval, *Journal de Voyage (Itinéraire)*, Sources chrétiennes 296 (Paris: Cerf, 1982)
NPNF	*Nicene and Post-Nicene Fathers of the Christian Church*
Wilkinson	John Wilkinson, *Egeria's Travels*, 3d ed. (Warminster: Aris and Philips, 1999)

The abbreviation of titles of books of the Bible follows the format adopted in the *New Revised Standard Version*, and the numbering of the Psalms is that of the Hebrew text rather than the Septuagint/Old Latin.

INTRODUCTION

The written record of one woman's prayerful engagement with holy places and holy people encountered on her multiyear journey through Palestine, Egypt, Syria, Mesopotamia, and Asia Minor around the turn of the fifth century has attracted the attention of scholars in many disciplines. Her writing merits a footnote (and often much more) in standard discussions of the development of Christian worship, monastic life, the archaeology of the Holy Land, the Latin language, the *itinerarium* as a literary genre, and the phenomenon of religious travel in late antiquity.[1] More recently, this early Christian author has attracted attention as a religious educator and biblical interpreter whose writings helped other women more vividly visualize the world of the Scriptures.[2] As her original readers might have used her words to glimpse hallowed terrain, living saints, and sacred celebrations they had not seen themselves, so we who read her words from a great temporal distance can still see the projection of a holy world refracted through her text. Some might even be inspired to follow in her footsteps.[3]

---

[1] The spheres of liturgy, archaeology, and pilgrimage have received the most attention but have rarely been considered together. See, for example, the critique in Martin D. Stringer, *A Sociological History of Christian Worship* (Cambridge: Cambridge University Press, 2005), 69.

[2] See Marion Ann Taylor, "Introduction," in *Handbook of Women Biblical Interpreters: A Historical and Biographical Guide*, ed. Marion Ann Taylor and Agnes Choi (Grand Rapids, MI: Baker Academic, 2012), 18.

[3] This travelogue and its author have, for example, inspired an online network documenting Mediterranean pilgrimage monuments (http://www.egeriaproject .net/) as well as some contemporary pilgrimages, including the one described

The Identity of This Diary and Its Author

1. The Manuscript

Only one incomplete eleventh-century manuscript preserves this anonymous account of a western European woman's journey to the Holy Land and surrounding region, although eleven short quotations from the text surfaced in a ninth-century manuscript from Toledo in 1909 and two further fragments were published in 2005.[4] It is bound together with some works of Hilary of Poitiers (*De mysteriis* and fragments of a hymnal) in Codex Aretinus 405, and was once housed in the more famous library at the Benedictine Monastery of Monte Cassino before finding its way to the library of the Pia Fraternità dei Laici in Arezzo, Italy, sometime after 1532.[5] It was rediscovered in the modern era by the Italian historian and archaeologist G. F. Gamurrini in 1884,[6] who published it in 1887, and again in a corrected version in 1888.[7] Since then there have been a number of further editions and translations into several languages, one of the most recent editions being that by Pierre Maraval, on which we have based our translation.[8]

---

in Lawrence R. Farley, *Following Egeria: A Modern Pilgrim in the Holy Land* (Chesterton, IN: Ancient Faith Publishing, 2014).

[4] See Appendix C, pp. 207–8 below.

[5] Maribel Dietz, *Wandering Monks, Virgins, and Pilgrims: Ascetic Travel in the Mediterranean World, A.D. 300–800* (University Park, PA: Penn State University Press, 2005), 44. She remarks that this transfer was somewhat ironic given the criticism of monastic wandering in the opening chapters of the *Rule of Benedict*.

[6] See G. F. Gamurrini, "I misteri e gl'imni di s. Ilario vescovo di Poitiers ed una peregrinazione ai luoghi santi nel quarto secolo," *Studi e documenti di storia e diritto* 5 (1884): 81–107; Gamurrini, "Della inedita peregrinazione ai luoghi santi," *Studi e documenti di storia e diritto* 6 (1885): 145–67; Augusto Campana, "La storia della scoperta del Codice Aretino nel Carteggio Gamurrini–De Rossi," in *Atti del Convegno Internazionale sulla Peregrinatio Egeriae, nel centenario della pubblicazione del Codex Aretinus 405 (già Aretinus VI, 3)* (Arezzo: Accademia Petrarca di lettere arti e scienze, 1990), 77–84.

[7] G. F. Gamurrini, *S. Hilarii tractatus de mysteriis et hymni et S. Silviae Aquitanae peregrinatio ad loca sancta*, Biblioteca della Academia storico-giuridica 4 (Rome: Cuggiani, 1887); Gamurrini, "S. Silvae Aquitaine: Peregrinatio ad loca sancta," *Studi e documenti di storia e diritto* 9 (1888): 97–147.

[8] Pierre Maraval, *Journal de Voyage (Itinéraire)*, Sources chrétiennes 296 (Paris: Cerf, 1982).

The work carries no indication of its title, if there ever were one, nor of its author, nor any explicit reference to her place of origin or the date of the journey. It falls into two distinct halves, the first being a travel diary proper (chapters 1–23) and the second a detailed description by the same author of the daily services and liturgical year at Jerusalem (24–49). The abruptness of the transition between the two parts, together with the second half being out of the chronological sequence of the journeying, suggests that they were originally separate documents that were united by someone else, conceivably even the recipients to whom they were addressed. As it stands, the manuscript is made up of three quires or quaternions (gatherings of four folded sheets forming eight folios or sixteen pages), which would originally have resulted in a total of forty-eight pages. Unfortunately, however, the middle of the three has lost its outer sheet, reducing it to six folios or twelve pages. This accounts for the two major breaks in the text, between 16.4 and 16.5 and within 25.6.

In addition, the beginning and end of the document are obviously missing. If the extant manuscript did once have another complete quaternion preceding it, we could be lacking quite a substantial part of the original. It is quite possible that some account of the beginning of the author's journey from home to Constantinople and then to Jerusalem, with a more extensive description of the "Holy City and its environs," occupied the beginning of the original text,[9] and we will consider that further in the section on her route below (pp. 15–20). On the other hand, what might have comprised the conclusion of the manuscript is unclear, as the author seems to have nearly finished her description of the liturgical year at Jerusalem at the point where the extant manuscript breaks off in mid-sentence.

2. *The Author and Her Status*

For a manuscript known to the modern world for not much more than a century, this woman's letters recounting her journeys have generated an immense secondary literature. Much of the early controversy surrounded the identity of the author. Three main theories attracted substantial numbers of adherents,[10] and while consensus

---

[9] Gingras, 16.
[10] For a helpful overview, see Gingras, 2–7.

settled decades ago on Egeria as the most probable name of the traveler, aspects of some of the other theories continue to haunt, perhaps
subconsciously, some of the discussions about her social status.
Gamurrini, the person who reintroduced this text to the world from
its obscure repository in an Italian library, hypothesized that the
author was Silvia of Aquitaine (330–406), based on a reference to a
woman named Silvania mentioned in the *Lausiac History* of Palladius
as someone who went with him to Egypt ca. 388. Silvania was the
sister-in-law of Flavius Rufinus, which would have given her imperial connections by association, since Rufinus was a prefect of Theodosius I, who ruled as emperor from 379 to 395.[11]

Another early theory connected the document to Galla Placidia
(388–450), a woman with even more direct imperial connections as
the daughter of Theodosius I and Galla and the sister of Honorius
and Arcadius.[12] Since she had been a victim of a kidnapping and
forced marriage to the Visigothic King Athaulf in the early fifth century, this theory brought the added appeal of drama and intrigue.
Maribel Dietz remarks, "It was perhaps the romantic leaning of the
nineteenth century that led some scholars to believe that she was the
author of the mysterious travel account."[13] The common link of a
Theodosian connection underlying these first two theories is poten-
tially attractive insofar as it would place the author within an established line of imperial women travelers to the Holy Land, including
most prominently Helena (Constantine's mother) and Eudocia (Theodosius II's wife)—even though the author herself does not mention
Theodosius (or any other political figure, for that matter) in her account. A Theodosian link is also sometimes used as corroborating
evidence for the author's place of origin (since Theodosius had Spanish roots), date (since Theodosius was emperor during the closing
decades of the fourth century, when the narrative is commonly dated),

---

[11] Palladius, *Hist. laus.* 142. Gingras, 2, notes that Gamurrini had been misled
by a Latin translation of Palladius that referred to this woman as Silvia and
presented her as the imperial minister's sister.

[12] See C. Kohler, "Note sur un manuscript de la Bibliothèque d'Arezzo," *Bibliothèque de l'École des Chartres* 45 (1884): 141–51.

[13] Dietz, *Wandering Monks, Virgins, and Pilgrims*, 45.

and/or social status (since imperial connections would presumably have facilitated a journey of the length and scope described).[14]

The third prominent candidate was the *sanctimonialis* ("holy" or "religious" person)[15] who was the subject of a letter written by a Spanish monk, Valerius of Bierzo (or Vierzo), to his fellow monks at a Galician monastery toward the end of the seventh century for their spiritual edification.[16] Marius Férotin in 1903 was the first to identify the "most blessed Egeria" named in the opening lines of the letter with the author of the travel diary,[17] a conclusion accepted as virtually certain today. Manuscript copies of Valerius's letter present her name in various ways, including Etheria (Aetheria), Echeria, Eiheria (Aeiheria), and Egeria. Convinced that "Egeria" must have resulted from a scribal conflation of Aetheria (or Etheria), a name attested in Spain and Gaul, with Egeria the Roman nymph, Férotin presented the woman's name as "Etheria," even though this spelling occurs only once in one manuscript. The oldest manuscripts favor the spelling "Egeria," and this is the version that most scholars have settled on since the middle of the twentieth century.[18] Further support for "Egeria" appears in the manuscript tradition. The *Liber glossarum* includes an excerpt from chapter 15.3 of the text of the travels as we have it accompanied by a marginal note identifying the author as

[14] See ibid., 47; Gingras, 8–9. E. D. Hunt, *Holy Land Pilgrimage in the Later Roman Empire AD 312–460* (Oxford: Clarendon, 1982/New York: Oxford University Press, 1984), 164–65, not only speculated that she might have been part of the circle of this Spanish-born emperor, but even implied that she might have traveled east with him as he went to Constantinople at the end of 380!

[15] In later Latin usage this term came to designate a monk or nun; however, it is unclear whether it had acquired this degree of specificity when Valerius wrote: see Catherine Sider Hamilton, "Egeria," in *Handbook of Women Biblical Interpreters*, 180.

[16] An introduction, the Latin text, and a French translation of this letter are presented by Manuel C. Díaz y Díaz in Maraval, 321–49; ET of the text in Wilkinson, 200–204. For more on Valerius, see Dietz, *Wandering Monks, Virgins, and Pilgrims*, 183–84, and the annotated bibliography in Ursicino Domínguez del Val, *Estudios sobre Literatura Latina Hispano-Cristiania I, 1955–1971*, Corpus Patristicum Hispanum 2 (Madrid: Fundación Universitaria Española, 1986), 245–48.

[17] Marius Férotin, "Le véritable auteur de la 'Peregrinatio Silviae,' la vierge espagnole Éthéria," *Revue des questions historiques* 74 (1903): 367–97.

[18] See Gingras, 4–7, and Wilkinson, 167–68, for summaries of the debate.

Egeria.[19] Abbey library catalogues from the twelfth century include the *Itinerarium Egerie abbatisse* (St. Martial, Limoges) or *Ingerarium Geriae* (Celanova, Galicia) among their holdings.[20]

Valerius's letter goes on to describe Egeria's journeyings and even implies that she *may* have returned home eventually and had some ongoing influence there—if this is what can be read behind the ideas that she "had fulfilled all her faithful desires" and that she "will return to that very place where in this life she walked as a pilgrim"— and that she merited praise among the early saints from his region. Valerius aims to present Egeria as a model of virtue (in the form of a "weak woman" at that!) for his monks to follow in their hope of one day attaining heavenly glory. While Egeria might have agreed with him that *part* of "her purpose was to pray and find edification," some of Valerius's other comments, such as the claim that "she sought healing for her own soul," do not fit as easily with Egeria's stated purposes, at least in the surviving text, but may fit better with evolving conceptions of pilgrimage as late antiquity blended into the early medieval period.[21] Valerius does not discuss or even allude to her liturgical descriptions of Jerusalem.

Speculations about Egeria's identity are also tied to proposals about whether she was an ascetic and/or monastic woman. [22] Because she speaks of those to whom she is writing as her "revered sisters" (3.8; 12.7; 20.5), it has often been concluded that she was a member

---

[19] Various versions of this manuscript, which is thought to have originated in either France or Spain ca. 750, list: Egerie, Egeriae, and Egene.

[20] Wilkinson, 168.

[21] English quotations from Wilkinson, 200-204. For more on the development of the concept of pilgrimage and disjunctions between motivations for religious travel in late antiquity and later paradigms of the purposes of pilgrimage, see below, pp. 27–45.

[22] She has been portrayed as "an untutored, fragile young nun, a sturdy old abbess with royal connections and classical training, and a pious slut" who went out of her way to spend time with men; this pithy summary is from Mary B. Campbell, *The Witness and the Other World: Exotic European Travel Writing, 400–1600* (Ithaca: Cornell University Press, 1991), 20. Passing references to Egeria as a "loquacious nun" in works focused on other topics, as in Leonard R. Palmer, *The Latin Language* (London: Faber & Faber, 1954; reprint ed., Norman, OK: University of Oklahoma Press, 1988), 149, have also perpetuated this association.

of a religious order, even an abbess.[23] However, the term "sisters" is open to a wide variety of interpretations: it could designate a natural, biological tie to these other women; it could be a term of endearment, recognizing the recipients of her letter as her "sisters" in Christ through the bonds created by the Christian community as an alternative family; or it could be a way to designate fellow members of a more or less organized form of communal religious life entered into by a group of women. Nevertheless, the most frequent presumption is that it does indicate that Egeria was a participant in some form of established religious community, and that she was addressing her account to women who shared a common way of life and intense interest in the Scriptures and the church's liturgical life.

Those who contest this conclusion question how it would be possible for a woman in religious community to absent herself from her sisters for several years on an open-ended journey of indeterminate length and ever-expanding terrain. Writing from Constantinople, Egeria felt compelled to inform her sisters by letter about the reasons for her ongoing absence (23.10), but apparently did not perceive (or perhaps, at such great distance, realistically feel) great pressure from them to return home according to a predetermined schedule. Nor did she indicate any obligation to seek permission from a superior for more time away as she planned further travels to Ephesus and other parts of Asia Minor, suggesting that she did not have ties to the sort of stable, institutionalized, rule-bound community that is commonly associated with monastic life in the West, especially in later periods.[24] Furthermore, how would a religious woman have funded such a journey?

In addition to questions of a logistical nature, concerns about Egeria's spiritual goals (or lack thereof) have also been raised. For example, Hagith Sivan notes that although Egeria recounts many "meetings with monks," her writings would not prove particularly

---

[23] The title in the St. Martial catalogue entry noted above suggests some tradition of the author as an abbess, and Gingras, 146, n. 39, identifies another "less certain" reference to the author as an abbess in Monte Cassino's library catalogue from 1532.

[24] For more on the diverse expressions of an ascetic vocation open to women in late antiquity, see Susanna Elm, *'Virgins of God': The Making of Asceticism in Late Antiquity* (Oxford: Oxford University Press, 1994).

edifying for fellow monastics wishing to learn more about religious life in the East, since she "transmits neither their miracles nor their edifying conversations." Sivan also finds her pilgrim piety lacking in the ascetic emphasis of some of her Western contemporaries, like Paula and Melania, concluding that Egeria "is best perceived as a layperson, a member of a group of pious and devout women who decided to follow aristocratic precedents of pilgrimage to the East."[25] Maraval similarly suggested that she came from a circle of women that inclined toward a monastic way of life but could not be described as a formal religious community.[26]

Andrew Palmer challenged Sivan's arguments. He pointed out that Egeria seemed to have a closer relationship with the deaconess Marthana, in charge of a convent of nuns at the shrine of St. Thecla (23.3), than with anyone else that she met, suggesting to him that the two of them shared an equality of status. He claimed that her "consuming interest" in seeing monks and nuns was a sign of her own religious vocation (although, as we shall see later in this Introduction, such visits were in fact a standard feature of early pilgrimages), suggesting that her apparent lack of interest in monastic patterns of life may have been because she had covered all that in another part of her diary no longer extant. He also argued that she was a member of a religious community on the grounds that she really was having to justify her extension of her journey to her sisters (17.1–2; 22.1–2); that the expense of such a long absence would not necessarily have been crushing; and that her amazement at the silk and gems in the churches of Jerusalem (25.8-9) did not speak of a familiarity with affluence.[27]

Others, too, have found supporting evidence for Egeria's ascetic and/or monastic status in her descriptions of the people she met along the way. Gingras noted that she was especially interested in "the monastic milieu, seeking out the monks even in more remote

---

[25] Hagith Sivan, "Who Was Egeria? Piety and Pilgrimage in the Age of Gratian," *Harvard Theological Review* 81 (1988): 59–72, here at 67, 71. See also Sivan, "Holy Land Pilgrimage and Western Audiences: Some Reflections on Egeria and Her Circle," *Classical Quarterly* 38 (1988): 528–35.

[26] Maraval, 23–27.

[27] Andrew Palmer, "Egeria the Voyager, or the Technology of Remote Sensing in Late Antiquity," in *Travel Fact and Travel Fiction: Studies on Fiction, Literary Tradition, Scholarly Discovery and Observation in Travel Writing*, ed. Zweder von Martels (Leiden: Brill, 1994), 39–53, here at 41–45.

areas such as the Sinai peninsula and the eastern frontier of the empire."[28] Paul Devos observed that she emphasized the monastic connections of certain bishops she met, which for him was a point of support for her own monastic connection.[29] Stephen Davies argued that Egeria's journal in fact *did* betray a broad interest in ascetic matters, concluding therefore that Egeria likely belonged to some form of monastic community, "either a formally organized monastery for women or a loose ascetic society of wealthy women on the order of Paula, Melania, and company."[30] Julie Ann Smith noted that Egeria's descriptions of the great liturgical feasts in Jerusalem seem to draw an us-vs.-them distinction between ordinary laypeople and the sort of group to which Egeria and her sisters may have belonged. Egeria was impressed by the great crowds, and noted specifically the presence of lay men and women as well as monks. Smith proposed that she "would not need to comment on this lay participation if she were a laywoman herself."[31] Dietz also commented that the ability of Valerius of Bierzo "to recognize Egeria as a nun reveals that, at least in the seventh century, a Spanish cleric did not see any inconsistency between a relatively itinerant lifestyle and a monastic profession."[32]

Still others have theorized that Egeria was a consecrated virgin who belonged to a religious community that was not exactly monastic in the fully developed sense of the term but quasi-monastic or peripherally monastic, particularly because the letter of Valerius refers to her revisiting the region "with holy virgins." Perhaps she should be called a canoness or a protocanoness rather than a *monacha*. Drawing on references in Palladius's *Lausiac History* (ca. 420), Patricia Wilson-Kastner notes that "loosely organized communities of virgins

[28] Gingras, 8.

[29] Paul Devos, "La date du voyage d'Égérie," *Analecta Bollandiana* 85 (1967): 165–94, here at 169–75. However, Sivan, "Who was Egeria?" 68, countered that the rarity of monastic bishops in the West ca. 400 would have made this conjunction of vocations noteworthy enough in its own right for a Western traveler.

[30] Stephen J. Davis, *The Cult of Saint Thecla: A Tradition of Women's Piety in Late Antiquity* (Oxford: Oxford University Press, 2001), 59, n. 93.

[31] Julie Ann Smith, "Sacred Journeying: Women's Correspondence and Pilgrimage in the Fourth and Eighth Centuries," in *Pilgrimage Explored*, ed. Jennie Stopford (Woodbridge/Rochester, NY: York Medieval Press, 1999), 41–56, here at 47.

[32] Dietz, *Wandering Monks, Virgins, and Pilgrims*, 48.

who were not monastics, although they were pledged to a life of prayer and virtue," did exist in the East and West; women in these communities were not necessarily subject to the same restrictions as the more organized sort of monastic life that coalesced around figures like Paula or Macrina. As with Sivan, part of her argument is based on the general *lack* of specificity of Egeria's commentary on the lives of the monks she meets: "She speaks in general ways about their virtue, but never discusses their rule or organization, and spends her time noting their learning in the Scriptures. Although we possess no firm evidence, it seems likely that Egeria's community with its liturgical concern is at least the ancestor of the communities of canonesses which gave such noble service to the church before being absorbed into women's monastic orders." [33]

Of special concern is the question of whether Egeria's demonstrated interest in capturing significant aspects of liturgical life in Jerusalem for the benefit of her sisters has any bearing on the question of her religious status. She seems to have immersed herself in the full range of liturgies in Jerusalem, including the daily night offices prayed primarily by monks and virgins, although nonmonastic laypeople were certainly welcome at these services too (see 24.1). Numerous commentators and scholars have suggested that Egeria's attentiveness to the details of the liturgy, her awareness of certain similarities and differences between the forms of celebration in Jerusalem and the way things are done "as with us" at home (for example, 38.1; 39.1), and her efforts in many instances to capture a sense not just of the liturgical *ordo* but also the sensory surround and emotional experience of the liturgy suggest that she was a monastic rather than an ordinary layperson.[34] Sivan, on the other hand, proposes that "interest in liturgy" simply typifies the sort of events that are likely to captivate the interest and imagination of pilgrims, particularly since "the liturgy of the holy places was developed within the context

---

[33] Patricia Wilson-Kastner, "Preface," in *A Lost Tradition: Women Writers of the Early Church* (Washington, DC: University Press of America, 1981), xix. In Palladius's account, the size of these women's communities varies from about 50 to 400; "One should also note that although the focus of Palladius' *History* is on Egypt, these communities seem to extend over Asia Minor and even into the West" (ibid., xvi).

[34] See, for example, Gingras, 8; Dietz, *Wandering Monks, Virgins, and Pilgrims,* 53.

of pilgrimage and for pilgrims" and thus liturgy would have "formed the main component of the exclusive Christian environment in which Egeria appears to move and which stands in marked contrast to realities in Palestine of the late fourth century."[35]

The devotional and pious undertones of Egeria's pilgrimage are also cited as further support that Egeria was a monastic woman. She visited places not just to see noteworthy sites for herself, but in order that she might pray at specific locations associated with important moments in salvation history. Her typical *modus operandi* was to read an appropriate passage from the Scriptures or from another relevant text (such as the acts of the martyrs) associated with the site in question (see the section of this Introduction on worship in the holy places below). While this particular pattern of devotional activity might not be open to the average Christian of this age, does a devotional interest by itself substantiate a claim of monastic affiliation? Part of the issue may be that there is relatively little surviving literary evidence of the devotional activity that might have been typical for nonelite and nonliterate Christians of this era, although recent studies that draw on material evidence are beginning to provide a fuller picture of the rich varieties of devotional life that may have existed outside the orbit of the church's official liturgical prescriptions.[36]

What no one seems to have commented on is that Egeria never mentions saying daily prayers herself or joining in any regular hours of prayer with others while traveling, but merely praying at sacred sites and participating in the Eucharist. Would not a member of a regular monastic community have engaged in some daily pattern of prayer all the time and at least have mentioned it once or twice? Only in Jerusalem does she describe the public services of the monastic communities in the Church of the Holy Sepulcher, and even then says nothing of any hours of prayer or other devotions that those communities might have observed on their own.

Theories that Egeria was a woman of high social status and considerable means traveling with a large entourage have retained a subtle attraction, even if no direct links can be drawn between her and the Theodosian regime. Long-distance travel in late antiquity was fraught with probable hardships, and Egeria seems to have been

---

[35] Sivan, "Who Was Egeria?" 69.

[36] For example, see Kimberly Diane Bowes, *Private Worship, Public Values, and Religious Change in Late Antiquity* (Cambridge: Cambridge University Press, 2008).

undeterred by any significant ones—or at least they are not even deemed worthy of her mention. Furthermore, she was accompanied by a military escort on one particularly perilous leg of her journey (7.2) and benefited from the attention of holy men and women, including bishops, without seeming particularly surprised. She seems to have followed her own agenda, eager to take advantage of opportunities to visit more places she learned about along the way. She never expressed fears that her funds were beginning to run low and she seems to have had no difficulty privileging piety over penury. Furthermore, seeking external clues corroborating the presence of a high-status Western woman traveler on such an extended trip to the Holy Land, some have identified Egeria as the anonymous woman lambasted by Jerome (347–420) in a letter to Furia ca. 394 for her ostentatious exhibition on her "foolish" journey.[37]

Although the ability to travel so far for so long, as well as her ability to read and write, suggests that Egeria was probably not from the lowest socioeconomic class, there are no indications within her own report of her travels that her social or economic status was particularly high either. She gladly benefited from the hospitality of those she encountered, primarily monastics, but she was just as likely to have been one of them rather than one "above" them. She described traveling by mule or donkey and on foot rather than via coach or carriage. [38] Military escorts, especially in dangerous regions, were not reserved solely for the most wealthy or well connected. She seemingly had fellow travelers, since she often referred to "we," but nothing resembling a true "entourage." The energy and enthusiasm underlying the narrative "suggest that she was youngish, or at least not elderly," but she never indicated her age.[39] "What is known incontrovertibly about her is that she was wealthy enough to afford a three-year journey and to hire mules and a retinue, and important enough to be greeted by bishops everywhere she went."[40]

[37] Jerome, *Ep.* 54.13. See Germain Morin, "Un passage énigmatique de S. Jérôme contre la pèlerine espagnole Eucheria?" *Revue bénédictine* 30 (1913): 174–86; Gingras, 146, n. 45; Dietz, *Wandering Monks, Virgins, and Pilgrims*, 47, n. 16; but cf. Elm, '*Virgins of God,*' 274, n. 71, who suggests it was instead Melania.

[38] Dietz, *Wandering Monks, Virgins, and Pilgrims*, 48.

[39] Smith, "Sacred Journeying," 47.

[40] Hamilton, "Egeria," 180.

3. Her Education and Literary Style

Closely related to the matter of Egeria's social status is that of her education. Based on her writing style (rather inelegant when judged by the standards of late antique classical education) and her apparent lack of familiarity with classical literature and even Christian writings beyond the Scriptures and some hagiography, Sivan concludes that she did not receive the level of education that a classic aristocratic young lady could have expected in this period and was therefore more likely to have been a middle-class person than a proper aristocrat.[41]

She was certainly well versed in the contents of the Bible and able to quote from it at some length and with considerable accuracy, which has led some to conclude that she must have been carrying a copy of a Latin translation with her as she went.[42] It has to be admitted, however, that her understanding of Scripture was entirely at the literal level rather than that of allegorical exegesis. She presents the events of the Old Testament and the places associated with them that she visited largely in historical and geographical terms without displaying any of the typological interpretations that were current in early Christianity. In short, she may not have been badly educated, but her learning does not appear to have been particularly sophisticated.

Egeria's Latin is somewhat idiosyncratic,[43] but likely adequate nonetheless to achieve her purposes and satisfy the interests of her intended readers. As far as we know, she did not have in mind any audience beyond the immediate recipients of her writing, and thus it is not a fair comparison to place her everyday conversational style alongside more polished prose intended for wider dissemination. She misspells some words and tends to be imprecise with her

---

[41] Sivan, "Who Was Egeria?" 66–67. However, Egeria's focus on a small selection of sacred texts "could represent indifference to as easily as ignorance of other literary texts": see Victoria Erhart, "*Itinerarium Egeriae*: A Pilgrim's Journey," in *Women Writing Latin: From Roman Antiquity to Early Modern Europe*, ed. Laurie J. Churchill, Phyllis R. Brown, and Jane E. Jeffrey (New York: Routledge, 2002), 1:168.

[42] For an example of a substantial quotation, see 10.1; and also see 10.7, where the use of a copy of the Scriptures by the travelers for their acts of worship is explicitly mentioned.

[43] For studies of her Latin style and vocabulary, see the relevant section in the Select Bibliography, p. 210.

grammar—but is not therefore to be caricatured as uncultured. She is a Latin speaker, and the cadences of the spoken language come through in her writing.[44]

Her prose style and descriptions are rather simplistic and even a bit dull by modern standards; many find her account rather tedious in its seemingly straightforward litany of details. For example, Peter Dronke laments: "Every stranger she meets is presented as an image of the identical plaster saint. There is never a mishap, and gradually one almost begins to long for one. If only Egeria had told of even one monk or bishop who was not gracious but rude, even one who was not a walking textbook of sacred geography but had told her pious fibs that she saw through, the vivacity of the work would have gained immeasurably."[45]

Others have highlighted the careful attention Egeria devotes to crafting her details into an idealized structure that is not exactly a narrative framework featuring plot and drama, but one that seeks to convey the *experience* of her expedition to her audience of sisters. It is primarily their interests and concerns that give form and shape to her account, which is written for *them* rather than for the sake of preserving her own reflections or reminiscences for herself or for an imagined readership in future generations. "It seems safe to assume that her method neither shocked nor bored her readers and that it can be held to reflect a state of mind and a conception of geography and the physical world that were commonly and contentedly shared."[46] Nevertheless, aspects of her own personality shine through: "What comes through Egeria's account most vividly is the immense excitement she feels in meeting various holy men and women, in traveling to biblical and historical sites, and in observing the local customs."[47]

Leo Spitzer provides one of the more charitable scholarly readings of the frequent redundancies and apparent grammatical peculiarities, considering Egeria's style as one of "hieratic decorum" consistent with the genre of Christian pilgrimage literature and even a precursor

---

[44] Gingras, 44.

[45] Peter Dronke, *Women Writers of the Middle Ages: A Critical Study of Texts from Perpetua (203) to Marguerite Porete (1310)* (Cambridge: Cambridge University Press, 1984), 21.

[46] Campbell, *The Witness and the Other World*, 23.

[47] Dietz, *Wandering Monks, Virgins, and Pilgrims*, 49.

of the style deployed by medieval vernacular epics.[48] The repetitions emphasize what Egeria *saw* or *what was shown to her* by others, attending to what happened in *this* place or *that* place (and "according to the Scriptures," in cases where this applied). The details Egeria includes and repeats "are all destined to detain the pious reader—a second pilgrim as it were—and to fix his [*sic*] attention on particular stations."[49] Egeria's account is constructed in such a way that the actions of holy people are emphasized rather than the identities of the people themselves (as everyone who facilitated any aspect of the journey or provided information or interacted with Egeria in any way, save solely for the deaconess Marthana, remains unnamed). Egeria does not typically dwell on extensive pragmatic descriptions of the sites she visits either, but rather focuses on their significance as revelations and manifestations of the holy in this world.[50] Thus a valley might be flat or a place beautiful, but these qualities are connected to the sacred happenings that unfolded there more so than in qualities naturally inherent in the places themselves. In this sense, Egeria's account is an idealized one with particular motivations, and consequently she is not aiming to reproduce a classical style or adhere closely to its conventions—and should not be judged according to these standards.

4. Her Route

Because a considerable portion of the manuscript is missing, no information is provided about her itinerary to Jerusalem from her home in the West (wherever that was—see the next section of this Introduction), apart from implying that she had crossed the River Rhône on the way (18.2). On her return journey to Constantinople she mentions that she had also passed through Chalcedon and the provinces of Bithynia, Galatia, and Cappadocia on her outward route

[48] Leo Spitzer, "The Epic Style of the Pilgrim Aetheria," *Comparative Literature* 1 (1949): 225–58, here at 248.

[49] Ibid., 233–34.

[50] For example, Spitzer proposes that Egeria's account operates with the following sort of logic in introducing the places *where* this or that happened: "I am mentioning this place / This place was pointed out to me *for* it has significance . . . and even perhaps, with the pattern: This place existed, *for* it had significance" (ibid., 241–43, emphasis in the original).

(23.7), but that is all. At one point in her narrative she does say that it had been a full three years since she arrived in Jerusalem (17.1), and most of this time appears to have been spent in the city, from which she obviously derived her detailed account of the regular services and of its liturgical year in what is now the second half of the text (chapters 24 to the end). She also refers, however, to a visit to Egypt she had made earlier (7.1), and in her discussion of the region around Tathnis in Egypt, where Moses was said to have been born, she comments, "I had already known those places, as I said above, that is, when I had been in Alexandria and the Thebaid" (9.5; see also 9.1), an apparent reference to the part of the manuscript that is now absent.

This visit seems to be confirmed by the letter of Valerius of Bierzo mentioned above (pp. 5–6), which provides an overview of her journeys, although not quoting directly from her text. According to him, Egeria had visited "many different provinces and cities," "congregations of holy monks in the Thebaid," and "*all* the provinces of Egypt," seeming to corroborate her asides and suggesting that he may have had access to a more extensive text of her travels than the one known to us from the Arezzo manuscript. Valerius focuses on Egeria's visits first to Egypt, then to Sinai (where the extant manuscript begins), and finally to her scaling the heights of various mountains—Nebo, Pharan, Tabor, Eremus, and the Mount of Elijah—without dwelling on her extensive stay in Jerusalem, save for the merest mention that "she reached what she had longed for, the much-desired and most holy places of the birth, passion, and resurrection of the Lord."[51]

Further attestation concerning Egeria's journeying prior to the point where the Arezzo manuscript begins comes from Peter the

---

[51] Quotations from Wilkinson, 201, emphasis added. Sivan, "Who Was Egeria?" 60, comments on Valerius's obsession with mountains as representing "obstacles that, in spite of a feminine fragility so lovingly dwelt upon by Valerius, she had surmounted through her devotion and piety." As a text on a woman ascetic written by a man and addressed primarily to an audience of other men, Valerius's letter typifies the dominant portrayal of female ascetics in the extant literary record. As Elm, *'Virgins of God,'* 382, comments, "this by no means rules out that these texts do indeed reflect, to a certain extent, what ascetic women did and thought. Yet . . . most of our texts were written to delineate, evaluate and elaborate male modes of action and self-perception via the rhetorical medium of the female."

Deacon's *Liber de locis sanctis* (Book of the holy places), prepared in 1137. Peter served as librarian at Monte Cassino (which certainly had at least one copy of Egeria's travels at some point, since Codex Aretinus 405 had its home there into the sixteenth century).[52] He relied on three major sources for his compilation: the Venerable Bede's eighth-century book on the holy places, which supplies the basic structural framework; an anonymous travel guide to Jerusalem from the early twelfth century; and excerpts from Egeria's work. When Gamurrini discovered the Arezzo manuscript in the late nineteenth century, he recognized the overlap between the conclusion of Peter the Deacon's book and material from the first seven chapters of the newly resurfaced woman's travel diary. In addition, however, some of the material prior to these obvious quotations from Egeria's text may well come from a fuller version of the manuscript. As George Gingras noted, "although Peter the Deacon does add considerable information to his borrowings from Bede, he slavishly follows the structure of the latter's text until he begins to speak about places in Egypt connected with the Exodus of the Hebrews. . . . These passages blend smoothly into those extracts that can unmistakably be identified as borrowings from Egeria."[53] Therefore, it is reasonable to assume that Peter the Deacon's reflections on Egypt and discussion of the trek from Clysma to Sinai probably reflect the basic trajectory of Egeria's earlier itinerary even if they do not preserve all of her words or details.[54] On the other hand, as it is not easy to know where material has been drawn from Egeria's diary and where it comes from another source, we feel obliged to treat it with some caution and have not included excerpts from that work in our translation.[55]

---

[52] See above, p. 2, n. 5.

[53] Gingras, 16.

[54] Peter the Deacon, *De locis sanctis*; critical edition in *Itineraria et alia geographica*, ed. Paul Geyer et al., Corpus Christianorum Series Latina 175 (Turnhout: Brepols, 1965), 91–103. Wilkinson, 86–106, translates annotated extracts from *De locis sanctis* to provide perspective on what Egeria might have written although he reorders the contents to privilege Egeria's work rather than Bede's in the sequence of the descriptions.

[55] For just one example of the difficulty of using Peter's work as a source for Egeria's text, see Philip Mayerson, "Egeria and Peter the Deacon on the Site of Clysma (Suez)," *Journal of the American Research Center in Egypt* 33 (1996): 61–64.

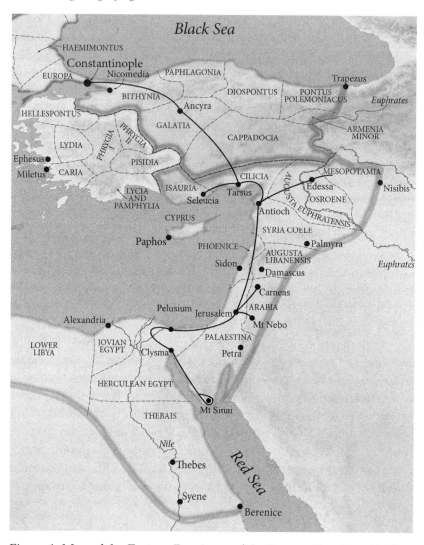

Figure 1: Map of the Eastern Provinces of the Roman Empire with the
Approximate Route of Egeria's Journeys

Nevertheless, with that caveat, this source could indicate that in
that missing part of her diary Egeria described places that were within
a day's journey from Jerusalem to which she made excursions while
residing in the city, including Bethlehem, Hebron, Anathoth, and the
tomb of the prophet Amos at Tekoa. There may also have been a visit

to Galilee.[56] Both Valerius and Peter also provide information apparently derived from the first part of her expedition to Sinai just prior to the beginning of the extant portion of her manuscript. She seemingly traveled south via Pelusium on the Mediterranean coast and then Clysma (also mentioned at 7.1) at the head of the Red Sea, where the Israelites were believed to have crossed when being pursued by the Egyptians (Ex 14:21-31). Following what was said to be their Exodus route, she continued south through the desert on the eastern side of the sea and eventually reached Pharan (also mentioned at 1.4), where she set off on the last leg of the journey between mountains to Sinai, during which the extant manuscript now begins.[57]

In it, Egeria first describes the ascent of Sinai (1–3), where she encountered monks living there and presbyters assigned to various churches and was shown sites associated with the giving of the Law. From there she went on to Mount Horeb, where Elijah was said to have fled from King Ahab (4.1-4). The return journey to Pharan involved a visit to the site of the burning bush and other places associated with that part of the Exodus journey (4.5–5.12). After two days' rest there, Egeria continued on to Clysma, where after a further rest she turned west for several days in order to see the places through which the Israelites had passed on their way from Rameses to the Red Sea, before returning via Pelusium back to Jerusalem by the way she had come (6.1–9.7). It is interesting to note that she made no attempt to trace the route of the Exodus in its chronological order, as she visited Sinai before going to the site of the burning bush and after that to places associated with the period before the crossing of the Red Sea.

Some unspecified time later, she undertook another journey from Jerusalem, this time a shorter one to Mount Nebo, from which Moses was said to have viewed the Promised Land before his death (Deut 32:49-50). Traveling via the cities of Jericho and Livias, she was, as usual, shown what were said to be the sites of various biblical events along the way (10–12). A third excursion from the Holy City was made to the tomb of Job at Carneas, a journey of eight days, stopping on the way at Sedima, thought to have been Salem, the city of

[56] See Wilkinson, 88–93, 95–101.
[57] See ibid., 101–6, 201–2.

Melchizedek, and at Aenon, where John the Baptist had baptized, as well as at Tishbe, from which Elijah came (13–16).

Eventually, Egeria resolved to set out from Jerusalem on her journey back to her home, but made a detour to Edessa on the way to visit the tomb of the Apostle Thomas (17–19). From there she went on to Carrhae, said to be the city of Abraham, where she also visited the tomb of a saintly monk and martyr, Helpidius, whose feast day it happened to be, before returning to Antioch to resume her journey homeward (20–21). She stayed at Antioch for a week, gathering together what was necessary for the journey, but after leaving there and passing through Tarsus, she once more made a detour, this time to visit the shrine of St. Thecla, three days' journey away, before returning to Tarsus to rejoin her route (22–23.6). After another three days there, she finally set off for Constantinople. On arriving in that city, she recorded that her plan was then to go to the shrine of the Apostle John at Ephesus and possibly other places (23.7-10). But there her narrative ends, and so we do not know if she accomplished this or ever returned home.

5. Where Was Her "Home"?

As with her name, the traveler's likely place of origin has also generated multiple theories. Current consensus places her in northwestern Spain, and more specifically in the province of Galicia, typically because of Valerius's letter. Most of the other theories situate Egeria in west central Europe, although Italy and Britain have also been suggested.[58] Gamurrini's identification of the author as Silvia of Aquitaine contributed to a search for clues of French or Gallic connections among the earliest modern contributors to the debate, looking primarily to Aquitaine or to Gallia Narbonensis. For example, Karl Meister pointed to certain aspects of the style of the Latin as a clue to the Gallic regional origins of the author, to her passing comparison between the Euphrates and Rhône rivers (18.2), and to a more extended reference in Peter the Deacon's work to the waters and fish of the "Italian Sea" as collective evidence that Egeria was most likely from the Mediterranean region of southern Gaul. Furthermore, as-

---

[58] For a review of the major theories, see Gingras, 10–11.

suming that the author was a religious woman, Meister observed that monastic centers were more widespread in southern Gaul than in the remote regions of Galicia before the middle of the sixth century.[59]

A variation of this theory has been revived recently by Hagith Sivan, who also accentuates the Rhône River as "the sole allusion to a western site in the entire narrative," suggesting that "one is usually inclined to draw comparisons with what is most familiar and what immediately comes to mind."[60] Since the Rhône was the waterway that connected the interior regions of Gaul to the Mediterranean Sea, Egeria may well have crossed this river at some point during her travels if she was from Spain or Gaul. Classical Latin authors had similarly referred to the "fast-flowing" qualities of the river, but Egeria is likely drawing more on her personal experience since evidence of her familiarity with this sort of Latin literature is otherwise unattested.[61] Of course, such a reference would be most meaningful to the *readers* of the account if they either had direct knowledge of this river as well or if Egeria had made some comments about it in a previous section of her narrative (now lost) describing the journey from her homeland to the Holy Land. In a further variant of this theory, Clifford Weber presented a detailed case that she originated from the area of Mont St. Michel in Normandy.[62]

The emphasis on Egeria's Spanish origins is closely connected to the significance of Valerius's letter as indicating a possible geographical overlap between Valerius and Egeria, an issue first raised by Férotin and reinforced by others. Latinists have also raised potential points of convergence between Egeria's language and the Latin developing on the Iberian peninsula. Much has also been made of Egeria's portrayal of her encounter with the bishop of Edessa, in

---

[59] Karl Meister, "De itinerario Aetheriae abbatissae perperam nomini s. Silviae addicto," *Rheinisches Museum für Philologie* 64 (1909): 337–92, here at 363–68. More recent studies suggest that Galicia (at least before the eleventh century) was not as isolated as had often been presumed and that monasticism flourished there from the late fourth century influenced by intellectual and physical links extending throughout the Mediterranean world: see the overview and references cited in Dietz, *Wandering Monks, Virgins and Pilgrims*, 160.

[60] Sivan, "Who Was Egeria?" 64.

[61] Wilkinson, 131, n. 2.

[62] Clifford Weber, "Egeria's Norman Homeland," *Harvard Studies in Classical Philology* 92 (1990): 437–56.

which the bishop remarked that she had come from "the farthest distant lands" (19.5). This idea seems to be reinforced by Valerius's statement that Egeria came from "the far western coast of the ocean," which could be a reference to the province of Galicia.[63] Proponents of Egeria's Spanish origin find this data compelling; skeptics contend that for a relatively remote Eastern bishop who likely encountered long-distance travelers infrequently, *any* part of the West would have seemed like a far country and thus no precise information can be gleaned from such a statement.[64] Dietz draws attention to the possible significance of the words in Egeria's account as *her* representation of what the bishop said, reflecting her own awareness of the great distance between Edessa and her homeland.[65] This may be the most that can be concluded with any certainty, but there seems to be no pressing reason to rule out Spain as a possible starting point for Egeria's journey. Might it also be significant that the manuscript fragments of her work that have been found all come from Spain, suggesting its wide diffusion there?

6. The Date of Her Journey

The internal evidence of the manuscript has provided modern commentators with rather clear absolute parameters about the possible time range when Egeria might have made this multiyear excursion. She noted that she was unable to visit Nisibis because it was under Persian control and off limits to Roman visitors (20.12); this makes the year 363, the year that this city fell into Persian hands, the earliest possible date for this portion of her journeying. On the other hand, she did visit Antioch, staying for a week at one point (22.1), which would not have been possible after 540, the year when the

---

[63] Other Iberian authors, including Idatius and Isidore of Seville, seem to use similar terminology: see Zacarías García Villada, "Le lettre de Valérius aux moines de Vierzo sur la bienheureuse Aetheria," *Analecta Bollandiana* 29 (1910): 377–99.

[64] See, for example, Sivan, "Who was Egeria?" 64, who raises doubts as to the likely extent of Valerius's true knowledge of Egeria's origins.

[65] Dietz, *Wandering Monks, Virgins and Pilgrims*, 46. Furthermore, if Egeria was from Spain, she would not have been the sole Spanish traveler from this period to journey east. Other Spanish visitors to the Eastern Mediterranean included the poet Prudentius, Hosius of Córdoba, Avitus of Braga, Orosius, and Bachiarius (ibid., 158).

Persians destroyed that city. This span of 177 years, however, is quite large. Consequently, scholars have tried to date the journey more precisely based on other references to particular people, places, and liturgical celebrations within the document, coming to various conclusions ranging nearly throughout this whole time period, but largely settling on a date in either the late fourth or early fifth century.[66]

Much has been made over the title "confessor" that Egeria associates with the bishops of Batanis, Edessa, and Carrhae (19.1; 19.5; 20.2). If by confessor she means someone who suffered during the persecution of Christians but not to the point of martyrdom, the most likely episcopal candidates that she might have met who fit this description (Abraham in Batanis, Eulogios in Edessa, and Protogenes in Carrhae) would have been bishops simultaneously in these locales only between the years of 381 or 382 and 387, with other evidence suggesting Egeria visited Carrhae no earlier than the spring of 382 and Edessa no later than 386.[67] Since Christian persecution in the Roman Empire had ended early in the fourth century, it would be unlikely to find many such confessor bishops much later than this. However, it is not certain that Egeria did use confessor in this sense, and other possibilities have been raised, such as a category of monk devoted to celebrating the divine office—a usage that might have been familiar to her in the West.[68] If Egeria did not necessarily connect confessors and persecution, this would remove a dating constraint based on the usage of this term alone.

In 1967, Paul Devos developed the former line of argumentation most extensively, relying on the sequence of Eastern (and particularly Syrian) bishops and the dates of Easter in various years to propose that Egeria must have made this Syrian sojourn in the spring of 384, after spending time in Jerusalem roughly between 381 and 384.[69]

---

[66] For an overview of these theories, see Gingras, 12–15.

[67] For the development of the details of these arguments, see Gamurrini, *S. Hilarii tractatus de mysteriis*, xxvii–xxix; Anton Baumstark, "Das Alter der *Peregrinatio Aetheriae*," *Oriens Christianus* 1 (1911): 32–76.

[68] See A. Lambert, "*L'Itinerarium Egeriae*, vers 414–16," *Revue Mabillon* 28 (1938): 49–69.

[69] Devos, "La date du voyage d'Égérie." See also Agustín Arce, *Itinerario de la virgen Egeria (381–384)*, 2d ed. (Madrid: Biblioteca de Autores Christianos, 1996), xxiv.

Egeria states that she was in Jerusalem for "three full years" and afterward visited Edessa en route to Constantinople (17.1), arriving at Carrhae on the eve of an important local feast commemorating the martyrdom of St. Helpidius (April 23 or 24; see 20.5). Since Egeria never seems to have been pressed for time (if her regular contemplation of various side journeys is any indication), it seems reasonable to presume that she would have stayed in Jerusalem to celebrate Easter there before departing for places farther east. Considering her report that the distance between Jerusalem and Edessa was twenty-five staging posts (17.2), Egeria's typical traveling pace of about one stage per day, and her comments that she stopped along the way for one full day in Hierapolis (18.1) and three days in Edessa (19.3) in addition to the day required for travel between Edessa and Carrhae, Easter must have been relatively early in the year she made this journey to enable her to get to Carrhae for the feast of St. Helpidius on April 23. Between 382 and 386, the only year in which Easter falls in March is 384 (March 24), and it is no earlier than April 5 (in 386) in any of the other years in this range. Therefore, Devos concluded that Egeria must have made her journey to Syrian Mesopotamia in late March and April of 384, visiting the three confessor bishops along the way, thus placing Egeria's travels between ca. 381 and 384, which is now the dating that most scholars accept.[70] Egeria's references to the Imbomon (the supposed site of Christ's ascension) in Jerusalem as a "place" but never a "church" (see 31.1; 35.4; 39.3; 43.5) may corroborate a relatively early date for the text by suggesting that Egeria visited Jerusalem *before* the work at this location sponsored by Poemenia (which occurred at some point between 379 and 392) transformed the site into a church.[71]

Before and since, several alternative chronologies have been proposed based on other details in the account that would push the date toward the very end of the fourth century, into the early fifth century, or in some cases even later than this. Some are based on architectural

---

[70] See Maraval, 27–36. However, E. D. Hunt, "The Date of the *Itinerarium Egeriae*," *Studia Patristica* 38 (2001): 410–16, did not rule out the possibility that the visit could still have been in the 390s.

[71] Jerome, *Comm. in Zeph.* 1.15f. See Paul Devos, "La 'Servante de Dieu' Poemenia d'après Pallade, la tradition copte et Jean Rufus," *Analecta Bollandiana* 87 (1969): 189–208, here at 206; Wilkinson, 15, 171.

developments in the post-Constantinian era. Bellarmino Bagatti associated a reference in the eighth-century Jerusalem lectionary to Archbishop John of Jerusalem as the founder of a church on Sion as referring to John II (386/7–417), arguing that Egeria, who mentions a church at Sion, must have been in Jerusalem after 387.[72] However, it seems that Cyril of Jerusalem was already aware of a church on Sion as early as 348, and the lectionary reference may even point back to John I (ca. 117–119).[73] Germain Morin contended that St. Thomas's remains were moved from a shrine near the city of Edessa to a church within its walls in 394. Reading Egeria's somewhat ambiguous Latin at 19.2 as a reference to visiting a unified church *and* shrine (although her words could just as plausibly indicate a visit to the church *and* the shrine of St. Thomas as two separate points of interest), Morin concluded that Egeria must have visited Edessa after 394.[74] Finally, some have proposed that the complex Egeria experienced at St. Thecla's shrine near the city of Seleucia (23.2, 4) seems much too developed for the late fourth century, considering that most of the other churches in the area date no earlier than the mid-fifth century—although St. Thecla's cult is ancient and there was clearly an earlier church building on the site of the shrine itself.

Other arguments for a date after the 380s rest on textual grounds or on attempts to link aspects of Egeria's text with external evidence. For example, if Egeria is the same woman Jerome critiqued in his letter to Furia,[75] Egeria's travels would probably have taken place ca. 393–396, based on the most likely dating of that letter. Egeria's probable or possible quotations from the Scriptures and perhaps other texts as well have also been raised as having potential bearing on the dating of her writing. Joseph Ziegler claimed in 1931 that Egeria quoted, sometimes word for word, from Jerome's Latin translation of Eusebius's *Onomasticon*, which was completed after 390, and that Egeria's direct quotations or recognizable paraphrases from the Scriptures are quite similar to Rufinus of Aquileia's translation of Origen's

---

[72] Bellarmino Bagatti, "Ancora sulla data di Eteria," *Bibbia e Oriente* 10 (1968): 73–75.

[73] Cyril of Jerusalem, *Baptismal Catecheses* 16.4; Wilkinson, 170.

[74] Morin, "Un passage énigmatique," 179; see also Wilkinson, 170–71.

[75] See above, p. 12, n. 37.

Homilies on the Old Testament (from the year 404).[76] In the course of recounting her meeting with the bishop of Edessa, where she received a copy of King Abgar of Edessa's legendary letter to Christ and of Christ's reply to Abgar, Egeria mentioned that she already had "copies of them at home" (19.19). Presumably the copies Egeria already had would have been in Latin, and a source that was widely distributed and that Egeria might have encountered in the West could have been in Rufinus's translation (from 403) of Eusebius's *Ecclesiastical History* (which had included a Greek translation from the Syriac "originals").[77]

Other proposals for a later date tried to explain why Egeria appeared to celebrate Christ's ascension in *Bethlehem* rather than in Jerusalem on the fortieth day of the Easter season (see 42) by identifying a convergence between an ascension celebration on the fortieth day after Easter and the feast of the Dedication of the Church of the Nativity—which coincided on May 31, 417, according to a Georgian liturgical calendar.[78] More recent scholars, however, generally reject the assumption that the festival in Bethlehem that she described was in fact of the ascension.[79]

Still other theories rest on small details about church life disclosed in the text. If the Marthana at St. Thecla's shrine mentioned in Basil of Seleucia's *Life and Miracles of St. Thecla* (completed in or before 448) is the same as Egeria's deaconess acquaintance Marthana (who seems to be written about in the past tense in Basil's work), this would suggest that Egeria wrote before 448, although this connection would provide an outer limit rather than an indication of the earliest possible dating of the text.[80] The late date of 533–540 was proposed early in the last century by Karl Meister, who drew on his philological background to argue that certain historical facts and the general portrayal of church life (such as the level of monastic development and the

---

[76] Joseph Ziegler, "Die *Peregrinatio Aetheriae* und das *Onomastikon* des Eusebius," *Biblica* 12 (1931): 70–84; idem, "Die *Peregrinatio Aetheriae* und die hl. Schrift," *Biblica* 12 (1931): 162–98.

[77] So Gingras, 13.

[78] See, for example, E. Dekkers, "De datum de 'Peregrinatio Egeriae' in het feest van Ons Heer Hemelvaart," *Sacris Erudiri* 1 (1948): 181–205.

[79] See below, p. 97.

[80] See Gingras, 14–15.

elaborate fasting practices) would more conceivably reflect an early sixth-century context than the world of the late fourth century.[81] His theory attracted early adherents but is not widely accepted today because of the strength of other evidence pointing to a significantly earlier date.

Pilgrimage in Early Christianity

1. Travel and Travelers in Late Antiquity

The fourth and fifth centuries witnessed a surge in travel and migration relative to earlier and later periods.[82] Many travelers moved from one place to another in the course of conducting official business, either imperial or commercial. Others were uprooted involuntarily as the movement of Germanic tribes in northern Europe threatened the stability of urban centers and prompted some to become migrants who traveled long distances in search of safer dwelling places. People and frontiers also shifted on the Roman Empire's eastern edges amidst ongoing conflicts with the Persians. In Roman North Africa, Vandal invasions precipitated significant displacement of peoples in the fifth century.[83] Those who took to the roads and water routes primarily out of religious motivations would have comprised the minority of the total number of travelers but an increasingly significant contingent with the growing influence of Christianity in the Mediterranean world; the expansion of travel in general and travel among Christians (undertaken voluntarily or involuntarily) also paved the way for new possibilities and interpretations of the spiritual significance of this physical movement.[84] Nonetheless, there

---

[81] See Meister, "De itinerario Aetheriae," 341–63; Gingras, 12–13.

[82] On late antiquity in general as a period of postclassical vibrancy, the range of which extended from ca. 150 to 750 (thus overlapping with the early medieval period), see Peter Brown's classic study, *The World of Late Antiquity: From Marcus Aurelius to Muhammed* (London: Thames and Hudson, 1971).

[83] See Mark W. Graham, *News and Frontier Consciousness in the Late Roman Empire* (Ann Arbor: University of Michigan Press, 2009) for perspectives on how communication from the edges of the empire shaped the worldview not only of travelers but even of those who remained in place.

[84] In addition to travel that could be classified as spiritual wandering and/or a primitive sort of pilgrimage, Christians traveled under ecclesial auspices to convey themselves to and from church councils, as exiles in the wake of various

were numerous logistical challenges common to travel in late antiquity that would have had an impact on all categories of travelers no matter what their initial inspiration, and Egeria attests to some of them in her correspondence.[85]

Although she rarely emphasized the challenges and hardships she faced on her journey, her mention of military escorts in Egypt underscores the perils travelers could encounter on Roman roads plagued by robbers endemic to certain areas, who took advantage of the relative isolation of travelers and the terrain. For example, in 7.2 she writes about desert staging posts between Clysma and the city of Arabia featuring "monasteries with soldiers and officers, who always led us from fort to fort"; another imperial escort leads Egeria's group from Migdol to another fort "according to the custom" (7.4). The soldiers, "who in the name of Roman authority had afforded us assistance while we journeyed through dangerous places," are dismissed once the group reaches Arabia and the relative security afforded by a public highway (9.3).[86]

Most travelers sought safety in numbers by traveling in groups whenever possible, and religious travelers were no exception.[87] Egeria used plural pronouns like "we" and "us," suggesting that she may have joined up with a larger traveling entourage at some points, although her implicit travel companions do not seem to have included a spouse, other members of her immediate family, close friends, or any of the "sisters" from her community. She does, however, mention

---

theological controversies, and as missionaries called to spread the Gospel first throughout the Mediterranean basin and eventually to more distant lands: see Dietz, *Wandering Monks, Virgins, and Pilgrims*, 24–27.

[85] For a more extensive overview of the practical and spiritual aspects of travel in late antiquity, see "The Culture of Movement" in Dietz, *Wandering Monks, Virgins, and Pilgrims*, 11–42. See also Michael McCormick, *Origins of the European Economy: Communications and Commerce, A.D. 300–900* (Cambridge: Cambridge University Press, 2001); Lionel Casson, *Travel in the Ancient World*, 2d ed. (Baltimore: Johns Hopkins University Press, 1994); and Albert C. Leighton, *Transport and Communication* in *Early Medieval Europe, AD 500–1100* (Newton Abbot: David and Charles, 1972).

[86] For what Egeria's use of military escorts may indicate about her socioeconomic status, see above, p. 12, and the commentary on 7.2.

[87] See Hunt, *Holy Land Pilgrimage in the Later Roman Empire*, 76–82; Bernhard Kötting, *Peregrinatio Religiosa* (Münster: Regensberg, 1950), 363–81; John Wilkinson, *Jerusalem Pilgrims before the Crusades*, 2d ed. (Warminster: Aris & Phillips, 2002), 36–37.

various "holy guides"—including monks, presbyters, and the occasional bishop—who provided assistance and accompaniment along the way; if Egeria was a woman with ties to a religious community, it would not have been unusual for someone in her situation to travel alongside clergy and/or male ascetics.[88]

Typical travelers of the era conveyed themselves by land using their own feet; if animals were used on the roads they were generally mules or donkeys. In making her journey by donkey or mule, and sometimes on foot (as in her ascent of Mount Sinai, 3.2), Egeria was thus representative of common travelers of the time. Horses were more costly to obtain and maintain and were therefore used mainly by members of the military and those whose official business allowed them to transport themselves and their messages more efficiently using the Roman *cursus publicus,* the state-run service providing replacement horses and vehicles at staging posts along the various main routes of the empire.[89] Camels were highly effective for transporting travelers and goods through regions without roads, such as deserts and mountainous areas. Egeria encounters camels in the Sinai and is astonished by their navigational ability.[90]

Beyond inns accessible to the general population, religious travelers had a range of additional options for lodging. Their proliferation suggests that religiously motivated journeys were becoming increasingly common from the late fourth century onward.[91] Hostels were set up in areas under Roman jurisdiction, particularly in and around the Holy Land. Jerome and Paula founded a hostel in Bethlehem, for

[88] See Dietz, *Wandering Monks, Virgins, and Pilgrims,* 49–50; Elm, *'Virgins of God,'* 274. On Egeria's guides, see 1.2; 10.3; 13.2.

[89] Official business might have included bishops traveling to church councils; Eusebius remarks that Constantine allowed some bishops "the right to use the public post, [and gave] to others a generous supply of pack-animals" (Eusebius, *Vita Constantini* 3.6.1; ET from Averil Cameron and Stuart G. Hall, *Eusebius: Life of Constantine* [Oxford: Clarendon Press, 1999], 123). Prescriptions in the Theodosian Code indicate that the system was frequently abused; in particular, travelers with some means might use their money to gain access to this system through simple bribery or the purchase of an illegal post warrant.

[90] See 6.2. For more on the system of Roman roads and travelers' means of conveyance in late antiquity, see Dietz, *Wandering Monks, Virgins, and Pilgrims,* 17–22; Wilkinson, *Jerusalem Pilgrims,* 28–55.

[91] On pilgrims' accommodations while traveling, see Casson, *Travel in the Ancient World,* 300–29.

example, as did Rufinus and Melania the Elder in Jerusalem. Semi-eremitic groups within the orbit of local holy sites, such as the various groups of monks Egeria encountered in Egypt and Marthana's monastery near St. Thecla's shrine at Seleucia, comprised other prominent sources of shelter. A charism for monastic hospitality likely coincided with opportunities for these communities to obtain financial support from travelers.[92]

The period between the fourth and sixth centuries also seems to have been a particular high point for religious travel among women. While it is not possible to determine exact numbers or their percentage as a proportion of all religiously motivated travelers, a number of factors seemingly converged to make such travel both possible and desirable for women in a way it had not been before and would not remain for long. For women adopting an ascetic or monastic lifestyle, cloistered communal life was not yet the norm. Sociopolitical conditions in most of the Eastern Roman Empire were relatively stable during this period; coupled with the explosive growth of Christianity during the fourth century and the growing renown of certain holy places and holy people, it was uniquely feasible for many women like Egeria to undertake journeys to the Holy Land and surrounding regions not only to see the famous holy places but also to rub shoulders with living holy ones and many other fellow travelers along the way. For women who wanted to express their religious devotion by journeying—whether this took the form of imperial patronage (like Constantine's mother Helena), site-specific visits to holy places, and/or monastic wandering (whether temporary or more perennial)—there were few social pressures beyond family and finances standing between them and their spiritual desire for travel.[93]

Based on the women whose stories we know more intimately from their own correspondence or external documentation of their journeys, a certain profile of these women religious travelers begins to emerge. The majority were widows or unmarried virgins.[94] Some

[92] See Smith, "Sacred Journeying," 42.

[93] Dietz, *Wandering Monks, Virgins, and Pilgrims*, provides an excellent survey of the varieties of religious travel among women; many of the examples cited below are drawn from her account.

[94] See Gillian Cloke, *"This Female Man of God": Women and Spiritual Power in the Patristic Age, AD 350–450* (London/New York: Routledge, 1995), 82–89 (on

already had more freedom than the average woman of the age by virtue of their status as imperial women or members of the aristocracy. Many traveled with other women in their families or with close female friends as a sort of extension of their natural family ties. These units might have included mothers and daughters (such as Paula and Eustochium), grandmothers with their granddaughters, or biological sisters.[95] Fabiola traveled with friends. Egeria does not seem to have been accompanied by any of the "sisters" with whom she corresponded, but her letters to them provided a sort of vicarious connection to a female community that was invited to participate in the journey to some degree. Female travelers also seem to have gravitated toward other devout women in similar situations whom they met while traveling. Egeria, for example, seems to have formed a special connection with the deaconess Marthana; and a number of women who did not return to their homeland founded or joined women's religious communities.[96] Others founded *xenodochia* (hostels) to provide hospitality to other travelers like themselves and other

---

the order of widows); Elm, *'Virgins of God.'* Some prominent exceptions to this general trend include the married women Melania the Younger and the empress Eudocia; however, the life circumstances of each at the time they traveled afforded them an atypical amount of liberty within their relationships. Melania was in a chaste marriage (and accompanied by her husband), whereas Eudocia was exiled from Constantinople and not living with her husband: see Dietz, *Wandering Monks, Virgins, and Pilgrims*, 108, n. 5.

[95] For more on the role of families and extended family units in late antique female monastic life, see Jo Ann McNamara, "Muffled Voices: The Lives of Consecrated Women in the Fourth Century," in *Medieval Religious Women: Distant Echoes*, ed. John A. Nichols and Lillian Thomas Shank (Kalamazoo, MI: Cistercian Publications, 1984), 11–29; Anne Ewing Hickey, *Women of the Roman Aristocracy as Christian Monastics* (Ann Arbor, MI: UMI Research Press, 1987); Vito Antonio Sirago, *Cicadae Noctium: Quando le donne furono monache e pellegrine* (Soveria Mannelli: Rubbettino, 1986). The family-based women's monastic movement gathered around Macrina (sister of Basil of Caesarea and Gregory of Nyssa), her mother, and other women with connections to this family provides a sort of parallel example from Asia Minor: see Elm, *'Virgins of God,'* 78–105.

[96] Dietz, *Wandering Monks, Virgins, and Pilgrims*, 108–9. Pelagia of Antioch seems to be unique in joining a *male* monastery on the Mount of Olives, although she reportedly did so disguised as a man: see ibid., 147; and *Holy Women of the Syrian Orient*, ed. Sebastian P. Brock and Susan Ashbrook Harvey, The Transformation of the Classical Heritage 13 (Berkeley: University of California Press, 1987), 40–62.

charitable services to those in need (such as the ill and the elderly).[97] These traveling women were in contact with men, especially male monastics, during their journeys; however, "generally men played roles such as spiritual adviser, local guide, or holy man to be visited."[98]

While the extent of Egeria's correspondence is unique for a late antique woman traveler, the multiple women who appear in sources from this period as religious travelers suggest that Egeria was not an anomaly and likely would not have been perceived as such by her contemporaries.

> While it is accurate to say that both women and men traveled for religious reasons in this period, the conjunction of travel, monasticism, and patronage seems to have been particularly appealing to women. . . . This culture of monastic travel comes to an abrupt end, particularly for women, by the ninth century with the emergence of a more fully cloistered monastic experience for women. An Egeria or Melania would be hard to imagine in the Carolingian period. Even royal or imperial travel by women—such as the voyage of the Byzantine princess Theophano to the Ottonian court for her wedding to Otto II—was considered exceptional and extraordinary in the tenth century.[99]

The connections between travel and monastic life for women in this time period are likely more than coincidental. Monasticism provided a socially acceptable way for women to devote their lives to spiritual pursuits while renouncing marriage, granting them a relative freedom to focus on other opportunities like travel, which in turn brought them into contact with holy people—including women similar to themselves. In an age especially concerned with identifying orthodoxy and heresy, which played out particularly surrounding the sacraments of baptism and Eucharist, traveling women may have

---

[97] Melania the Elder founded not only monasteries but also a *xenodochium* on the Mount of Olives. Euphemia, a widowed woman attracted to monastic life, founded a *xenodochium* with her daughter in the city of Amida. Both of these instances suggest the perception of a close connection between monastic life and an itinerant lifestyle among some women in this time period: see Dietz, *Wandering Monks, Virgins, and Pilgrims*, 121–22, 138, 144.

[98] Ibid., 109.

[99] Ibid., 8.

been less controversial in some ways than traveling clergy, since women were excluded from ministering these sacraments to others. "From Egeria's incomplete account of her travels, there are no hints that her orthodoxy or identity were ever questioned."[100]

2. What Constituted a Pilgrimage?

If a pilgrim is someone who travels to a sacred place for religious reasons and a pilgrimage is the journey of such a person, the common contemporary understanding of pilgrimage seems to correspond with who Egeria was and what she was doing. By her own account, religious motivations played a prominent role in inspiring and extending her voyage; for example, her exchange with the bishop of Edessa suggests that her long journey was made "for the sake of piety" (19.5). The question remains, however, whether pilgrimage is the most appropriate designation for what Egeria was doing when her travels are viewed against the context of late antiquity, which included quite a broad range of possibilities for religiously motivated travel. At the time Egeria wrote, the Latin terms *peregrinatio* and *peregrinus*, often translated as "pilgrimage" and "pilgrim," respectively, did not yet carry the more specific implications concerning *religious* travel and traveler (particularly in connection to a journey to a precisely identified holy place) that they would come to acquire sometime during or after the seventh century.[101] Rather, a *peregrinatio*

---

[100] See ibid., 57–58; quotation from 58. This contrasts markedly with the situation of Orosius, an Iberian priest, who in 414 sought refuge in North Africa from barbarian invasions in Spain; while there he was in contact with Augustine of Hippo. Around this same time, a decree from Pope Anastasius (399–401) insisted "that no cleric from overseas should be received unless he had a certificate signed by five bishops, because at that time Manichaeans were discovered at Rome." See *The Book of the Pontiffs (Liber Pontificalis)*, ed. and trans. Raymond Davis (Liverpool: Liverpool University Press, 1989), 31, as quoted in Dietz, *Wandering Monks, Virgins, and Pilgrims*, 57, n. 49.

[101] Dietz, *Wandering Monks, Virgins, and Pilgrims*, 28, credits Augustine's allegorical use of *peregrinus* and *peregrini* to denote the "religious travel" of the Christian soul through this world en route to the heavenly Jerusalem with doing much to popularize the concept. Gregory the Great, *Registrum epistolarum VIII, Ep. 2*, applies this term to literal travel to holy places. For more on Augustine's use of this terminology, see Gillian Clark, "Pilgrims and Foreigners: Augustine on Travelling Home," in *Travel, Communication and Geography in Late Antiquity*, ed. Linda Ellis and Frank L. Kidner (Aldershot/Burlington, VT: Ashgate, 2004), 149–58.

(a relatively rare term in late antique literature) could be understood as a more generic journey undertaken for a multitude of potential purposes, and *peregrinus* could be applied to anyone who was a "traveler" or merely a noncitizen of the locale and thus a "foreigner" or "stranger." Egeria does not use the term *peregrinatio* at all, and both of her references to *peregrinus* as a concept could have the more general application rather than a specifically religious one: she notes that one of the qualities of the holy bishop of Arabia who met her traveling group at Rameses is "receiving strangers very well" (8.4), and elsewhere she says, "If someone is a stranger, unless they have testimonies from those who know them, they do not so easily come to baptism" (45.4).

The contemporary scholarly understanding of pilgrimage was profoundly shaped in the twentieth century by the anthropological work of Victor and Edith Turner on pilgrimage, which extended Victor Turner's previous work on the liminal stage of rites of passage to consider aspects of other life situations, including pilgrimage and monasticism, as intentionally "liminoid" in an analogous way.[102] For the Turners, a pilgrimage entails a journey from a "Primary Centre" comprised of the pilgrims' regular social context to a specific "Sacred Centre," with this sacred locale becoming the prominent focus of the pilgrimage. Although the ultimate purpose of journeying may be to engage the supernatural through rituals and other interactions while at the sacred site, the place itself as a destination assumes a primary role in the Turners' understanding of pilgrimage. The pilgrimage is concluded by the return journey to the Primary Centre, where pilgrims are reaggregated into their original community. As they share their experiences with those at the Primary Centre, the pilgrims who have been changed by their journey exert the potential to bring about change in their communities of origin.

Between the time of their departure from and return to the Primary Centre, pilgrims voluntarily enter a "semi-liminoid state," in which "symbolically, all attributes that distinguish categories and groups

---

[102] Victor W. Turner and Edith L. B. Turner, *Image and Pilgrimage in Christian Culture: Anthropological Perspectives* (New York: Columbia University Press, 1978), esp. 1–39 (on "Pilgrimage as a Liminoid Phenomenon"). See also Victor Turner, *The Ritual Process: Structure and Anti-Structure* (London: Routledge and Kegan Paul, 1969).

in the structured social order are . . . in abeyance."[103] The normal
social strictures accompanying such designations as gender and social
class no longer apply (at least with the same degree of intensity),
enabling pilgrims to form a bond of *communitas* with one another
forged around their shared experiences, as they are all freed tempo-
rarily from many of the dynamics of authority structures, locales,
and temporal associations that had tended to govern their daily lives
back home at the Primary Centre. This state of temporary liminality
may be associated with distinctive ways of dressing and/or acting
that serve as additional means of marking the characteristic status
that pilgrims assume. For the Turners, pilgrimage constitutes "the
quintessence of voluntary liminality."[104] Its defining characteristics
include the intention to travel to a particular place for a limited time
to engage the rituals appropriate to that destination.

Historians and others have found the Turners' paradigm of pilgrimage, particularly its liminal aspect, useful for assessing the status
of pilgrims vis-à-vis society as a whole.[105] Julie Ann Smith, for example, remarks that Egeria seems to have intentionally extended her
liminal status as a pilgrim:

> Several times she declared that she intended to begin the journey
> home, which would have marked the beginning of the process
> of reaggregation with her community, only to postpone it in
> order to undertake yet another holy detour. Her final comment
> was that she might die before her sacred journeying was over.
> She chose the permanence of her liminality. She had obviously
> enjoyed travelling and was consciously extending, for as long
> as possible, the liminoid state.[106]

---

[103] See Turner, *The Ritual Process*, 103.

[104] Turner and Turner, *Image and Pilgrimage in Christian Culture*, 9.

[105] See, for example, Robert A. Markus, *The End of Ancient Christianity* (Cambridge: Cambridge University Press, 1990), 154–55. This paradigm has also been
applied to related contexts, such as tourism. Erik Cohen's classification of tourism as recreational, experiential, or existential draws upon a Primary Centre as
a starting point and a particular relation to a liminal "Other" (as opposed to a
Sacred Centre) as part of the tourist's goal. See Erik Cohen, "Pilgrimage and
Tourism: Convergence and Divergence," in *Sacred Journeys: The Anthropology of
Pilgrimage*, ed. Alan Morinis (Westport, CT: Greenwood, 1992), 47–61.

[106] Smith, "Sacred Journeying," 48.

Egeria's open-ended journey is not accounted for by the Turners' focus on pilgrimage as a delimited journey with the presumption at the outset of return and reaggregation; yet "Egeria's voluminous correspondence may have been an endeavour to make up for her failure to return. She attempted to recompense her sisters for her absence by writing in such detail of her pilgrimage experience." There are other aspects of Egeria's journey that do not align well with the Turners' vision of pilgrimage. For example, she does not seem to be focused on a particular sacred site, and this paradigm does not account for her equally intense interest in visiting holy people as holy places. On the other hand, the proliferation of holy places in the general vicinity of the Holy Land, including those in Asia Minor and Egypt, could be seen as a means of prolonging "continuous, active liminoid status" focused on this more dispersed sense of a holy place.[107]

More recent reassessments of the Turners' studies on pilgrimage and others that are heavily reliant upon them have critiqued their largely ahistorical and general approach to pilgrimage as a category of ritual practice, recognizing this as *one* possible view of a certain type of pilgrimage as opposed to an overarching explanatory model for all pilgrimages.[108] These studies are also critiqued for not taking sufficient account of the pilgrimage experiences of women, who according to their own accounts seem to have found unique ways of constructing themselves and their journeys that were not constrained by particular expectations of what a pilgrimage should be.[109] This shift in perspective invites studies of pilgrimage that are less monolithic and unitive and more attentive to the interaction of ideology, ritual, and context in particular manifestations of pilgrimage. Such studies

[107] Ibid., 55.

[108] As a prominent example, see the collection of essays in *Contesting the Sacred: The Anthropology of Christian Pilgrimage*, ed. John Eade and Michael J. Sallnow (London/New York: Routledge, 1991), as well as those in *Pilgrimage Explored*, ed. Stopford.

[109] See, for example, Smith, "Sacred Journeying," 55, based on her studies of women's pilgrimage correspondence in the fourth and eighth centuries. For a similar critique of rites-of-passage theories in general as not reflecting female experience, see Caroline Walker Bynum, "Women's Stories, Women's Symbols: A Critique of Victor Turner's Theory of Liminality," in *Anthropology and the Study of Religion*, ed. Robert L. Moore and Frank Reynolds (Chicago: Center for the Scientific Study of Religion, 1984), 105–25.

"suggest that the continued success of Christian pilgrimage has often been achieved through the combination of a fluid ideology, open to diverse and personalised adaptation, alongside an adherence to supposedly traditional observances and material assemblages."[110]

Even when a more capacious definition of pilgrimage is used that permits late antique travelers who undertook religiously motivated journeys to particular places like the Holy Land to be categorized as pilgrims, Dietz advises caution in applying certain aspects of the Turners' model to them, given the substantial discrepancies between the Turners' understanding of pilgrimage and data on religious travel from late antiquity:

> Pilgrimage was not a uniform, regulated, or codified phenomenon in the Mediterranean basin during late antiquity or the early Middle Ages. It is difficult to see what was considered "the holy" as so neatly inscribed in a specific location or holy place. Often it was the act of visiting holy people, rather than their location, that was important to travelers. Reaching a particular destination was often less important than the journey itself. During late antiquity there was no set form of pilgrim dress, no established routes or rituals that defined a pilgrimage. The Turners' idea of pilgrimage stresses a singularity of motivation and goal, yet many of the figures usually called pilgrims in this period do not meet even this simple criterion. A multiplicity of aims and motives, rather, seems to have shaped religious travel and movement in late antiquity.[111]

In short, if pilgrimage is viewed as it often is in contemporary English, many of its aspects do not coincide well with the actual experience of late antique religious travelers. For example, the modern conception of pilgrimage typically extends beyond a generic religiously motivated journey to encompass more specific presumptions such as a significant degree of organization, a defined holy place as the destination (often with an underlying motive for healing and/or forgiveness of sin associated with one's presence and/or ritual participation at this sacred site), the expectation that the journey is temporary and that pilgrims will return home if possible, the desirability

---

[110] Stopford, "Introduction," in *Pilgrimage Explored*, xii.
[111] Dietz, *Wandering Monks, Virgins, and Pilgrims*, 30.

of acquiring souvenirs or tokens of the journey, and a relatively democratic process in which common people aggregate with like-minded strangers as traveling companions.[112] This sort of conception of pilgrimage, Dietz argues, is largely a medieval creation made possible by the Cluniac reform movement and the establishment of Santiago de Compostela as a relatively more accessible sacred site, promoting a new vision of "goal-centered, long-distance [religious travel] aimed at the laity rather than at monks."[113]

Almost none of these criteria applies well to Egeria's journey. It seems to be highly self-directed and self-organized; she does not seem to operate based on a prearranged itinerary, and her plans are flexible enough that she seems to be able to change them at will and set her own agenda, sometimes based on new information she collects from holy people along the way (for example, 13.1, 17.1).[114] She is not bound for any one particular holy place and in fact seems to be determined to visit as many holy places as possible—in part not to visit the places themselves but the holy *people* she can find at these places. She does not seem to have a singular overriding motivation that informs her entire journey. She makes no mention of any physical illness or ailment for which she seeks healing, and forgiveness of sins does not emerge as a motivating factor for her journey. Unlike some later medieval pilgrimage accounts, there are no stories of miracles experienced either first- or secondhand.[115] Egeria sees one of the most famous relics of the age, "the holy wood of the cross" in Jerusalem (37.1), but while she talks of other people gathering "souvenirs," such as twigs from the sycamore tree said to have healing properties (8.3) or the person who tried to obtain a relic by biting off a piece of the cross (37.2), she never mentions any personal desire to collect holy mementos of her journey to bring home. She gathers experiences and is delighted to obtain a more complete copy of the Abgar correspondence (19.19), but that is all.[116]

---

[112] Ibid., 27.

[113] Ibid., 10.

[114] Ibid., 50.

[115] Smith, "Sacred Journeying," 44.

[116] On Egeria's tendency to accumulate and "archive" immaterial elements and texts through her journey and her written account, see Scott Fitzgerald Johnson, *Literary Territories: Cartographical Thinking in Late Antiquity* (Oxford/New York: Oxford University Press, 2016), 17–28.

With the introduction and conclusion of her manuscript missing, it is unclear if Egeria set out on her journey with the intention of returning home after a predetermined time span; her repeated side trips and prolongations of the journey suggest that this did not remain a high priority for her, if it ever was initially. Aside from the respect she pays to her holy guides, she does not seem particularly interested in traveling companions she might meet along the way as individuals or as a collective; she does not dwell on any sense of *communitas* she might form with those she comes to know. (As mentioned previously, Marthana is the only living individual named in the entire account, although Egeria sometimes remarks about other visitors to the same site or stories about previous visitors to these places.) She seems to take great delight in the experience of traveling and recounting the experience to her sisters. If she did conceive of herself as something of a permanent or perpetual spiritual wanderer, this dimension does not emerge prominently in her writings; however, the overall impression provided is of a woman almost perpetually on the move, with the possible exception of her extended stay in Jerusalem (which likewise involved a substantial amount of movement from one place to another on a more local scale).[117] Although we shall continue to describe the journeyings of Egeria—and others at the time—as pilgrimage, readers should keep qualifications such as these in mind.

3. The Origins of the Christian Practice

Very early in its history Christianity had rejected the concept of sacred places, an attitude based on the principle neatly articulated in St. Paul's speech at the Areopagus in Acts 17:24: "The God who made the world and everything in it, being Lord of heaven and earth, does not dwell in temples made with hands." On the contrary, it was the Christians themselves who were the temples of the living God (2 Cor 6:16), who was to be worshipped neither in Jerusalem nor on Mount Gerizim but "in spirit and truth" (Jn 4:21-23). This view continued to be reflected in Christian writers of the second and third centuries. It was argued that, unlike the Jews who could only worship God in one place, the Temple, Christians worshipped God at all times and in all places.[118] Clement of Alexandria affirmed that "it is not now

---

[117] Dietz, *Wandering Monks, Virgins, and Pilgrims*, 51.
[118] See, for example, Justin Martyr, *Dialogue with Trypho* 41.2; 116.3; 117.

the place, but the assemblage of the elect, that I call the Church," and Origen reiterated the New Testament concept that Christians constituted the true temples of God.[119]

A similar attitude can still be seen in the views of Eusebius (ca. 260–339), church historian and bishop of Caesarea, before the emperor Constantine's enthusiasm for the construction of churches at holy places at the end of the first quarter of the century led Eusebius to modify his position.[120] In spite of the emperor's lead, however, not all church leaders were immediately won over. While Cyril of Jerusalem later in the fourth century not surprisingly embraced the new cult of the sacred sites that had emerged within his jurisdiction,[121] other voices, like that of Gregory of Nyssa, could still be heard opposing pilgrimage to Jerusalem: "The changing of one's place does not bring about any greater nearness to God. No, God will come to you wherever you are, if the abode of your soul is such that the Lord himself comes to dwell within you and walk with you."[122] On the other hand, the fact that he enthusiastically supported the local cult at the shrines of the martyrs in his native Cappadocia suggests that his opposition had more to do with rivalry between places than the rejection of the concept of holy places per se.[123]

Even Jerome, who had chosen to settle in the Holy Land himself and had been enthusiastic about the sacred sites, could still discourage Paulinus of Nola from visiting Jerusalem and argue that it was unsuitable for one wanting to pursue the monastic ideal: "What is praiseworthy is not to have been at Jerusalem but to have lived a

[119] Clement of Alexandria, *Stromata* 7.5 (ET from *Ante-Nicene Fathers* 2, 530); Origen, *Contra Celsum* 8.19–20.

[120] See Robert Wilken, *The Land Called Holy* (New Haven: Yale University Press, 1992), esp. 88–91.

[121] On the contrast between the views of Eusebius and Cyril, see Peter W. L. Walker, *Holy City, Holy Places? Christian Attitudes to Jerusalem and the Holy Land in the Fourth Century* (Oxford: Clarendon/New York: Oxford University Press, 1990). On Cyril in general, see Jan Willem Drijvers, *Cyril of Jerusalem: Bishop and City* (Leiden: Brill, 2004).

[122] Gregory of Nyssa, *Ep.* 2.16; ET from Anna M. Silvas, *Gregory of Nyssa: The Letters* (Leiden: Brill, 2007), 121.

[123] See Brouria Bitton-Ashkelony, *Encountering the Sacred: The Debate on Christian Pilgrimage in Late Antiquity* (Berkeley: University of California Press, 2005), 30–64.

good life while there. . . . But I do not presume to limit God's omnipotence or to restrict to a narrow strip of earth Him whom the heaven cannot contain. Each believer is judged not by his residence in this place or in that but according to the deserts of his faith. . . . Access to the courts of heaven is as easy from Britain as it is from Jerusalem; for 'the kingdom of God is within you.' "[124] As in the case of Gregory of Nyssa, however, the opposition expressed in this letter seems to have been occasioned more by his bitter quarrel with the church in Jerusalem at the time and his preference for Bethlehem, where he lived, than by a permanent change of view about pilgrimage as such.[125]

Notwithstanding such reservations, travel to the Holy Land, even by women, was well established before Egeria made her journey.[126] The pilgrim from Bordeaux, who came to the Holy Land in 333, may possibly have been a woman,[127] and, as we have seen already, we know not only of Helena, the mother of the emperor Constantine, who traveled to the holy places of Palestine in 326–328,[128] but also of Melania the Elder, who arrived in Jerusalem a few years before Egeria's visit, of Poemenia, who was said to have built the church on the Imbomon, the site of Christ's ascension,[129] of Silvia of Aquitaine, who appears to have lodged with Melania before going on to Egypt,[130] and of Paula, the friend and benefactor of Jerome, who together with him and her daughter Eustochium journeyed to the holy places and finally settled in Bethlehem apparently just after Egeria's visit.[131] Even

[124] Jerome, *Ep.* 58.2-3; ET from *NPNF* 2:6, 119–20.

[125] For further discussion of Jerome's apparent ambivalent attitude toward pilgrimage, see Bitton-Ashkelony, *Encountering the Sacred*, 65–105.

[126] Indeed, the considerable attention given to women travelers in recent studies can easily give rise to the mistaken impression that pilgrimage was a disproportionately female phenomenon: see Rebecca Stephens Falcasantos, "Wandering Wombs, Inspired Intellects: Christian Religious Travel in Late Antiquity," *Journal of Early Christian Studies* 25 (2017): 89–117.

[127] See Appendix A, pp. 197–98.

[128] Eusebius, *Vita Constantini* 3.42-45.

[129] John Rufus, *Vita Petri Iberi* 43. See above, p. 24, n. 71. For the Imbomon, see below, p. 67.

[130] Palladius, *Hist. laus.* 55. See E. D. Hunt, "St. Silvia of Aquitaine: The Role of a Theodosian Pilgrim in the Society of East and West," *Journal of Theological Studies* 23 (1972): 351–73.

[131] See Jerome, *Ep.* 46; 108.

Gregory of Nyssa's disapproval of women making the journey is evidence that some were doing just that![132]

Susanna Elm has also drawn attention to a letter of Athanasius preserved in a seventh/eighth-century Syriac manuscript but dating very probably from somewhere around the middle of the fourth century and addressed to a community of female ascetics in Egypt who had recently returned from a pilgrimage to Jerusalem. They had gone first to Bethlehem and the cave of the nativity, and then to Jerusalem, where they visited Golgotha and Christ's tomb. Their return route included Mount Sinai, and while in the Holy Land they had stayed with a community of other female religious and had received guidance from local presbyters.[133]

Although Constantine's building program at the various sacred sites must have provided a huge impetus to the phenomenon of pilgrimage, Eusebius seems to imply that it had already begun somewhat earlier than that. In his *Demonstratio evangelica*, written well before 324 when Constantine became emperor of the eastern provinces of the Roman Empire, he asserted that Bethlehem was so famous that people were coming from the ends of the earth to see it; that a cave was shown there by the locals to those coming from abroad to view it; and that believers from all parts of the world were also congregating on the Mount of Olives.[134]

It has been the subject of some debate among recent scholars, however, as to whether pilgrimage can be said really to have existed even earlier, before the fourth century. As the previous section of this Introduction implied, disagreement turns on the question of what specific activities can be held to constitute "pilgrimage." Thus, it is unanimously agreed that at least some Christians did travel to what

---

[132] "For it is impracticable for a woman to pursue so long a journey unless she has a conductor, for on account of her natural weakness she has to be put on her horse and be lifted down again, and she has to be steadied in rough terrain. . . . Whether she leans on a stranger or on her own servant, she fails to observe the law of modesty" (Gregory of Nyssa, *Ep.* 2.6; ET from Silvas, *Gregory of Nyssa*, 119).

[133] Susanna Elm, "Perceptions of Jerusalem Pilgrimage as Reflected in Two Early Sources on Female Pilgrimage (3rd and 4th centuries A.D.)," *Studia Patristica* 20 (1989): 219–23.

[134] Eusebius, *Demonstratio evangelica* 1.1.2; 3.2.47; 6.18.23; 7.2.14. See E. D. Hunt, "Were There Christian Pilgrims before Constantine?" in *Pilgrimage Explored*, ed. Stopford, 25–40, here at 32–39.

would later be called the Holy Land in the preceding centuries. It is known that Melito of Sardis went to Palestine in the second century in order to verify the authoritative order and contents of the Old Testament canon; that the presbyter Pionius, who was put to death in Smyrna in 250, had been in Palestine and, according to him, had there seen in the parched and barren land the evidence of God's punishment of the sins of its inhabitants; and that in the same century Origen had visited some sites "in search of traces of Jesus, of his disciples, and of the prophets."[135]

Some scholars, however, do not recognize these journeys as the equivalent of the later pilgrimages. Thus, Pierre Maraval concluded that these individuals "went out of a sense of curiosity or in search of theological insight," rather than being "intent on praying in places deemed to be holy."[136] Interestingly, however, he failed to mention the case of Alexander of Cappadocia, d. 251, who was said by Eusebius to have gone to Jerusalem explicitly "for the sake of prayer and knowledge of the places."[137] In her presentation of a detailed argument that there was no evidence that Christians venerated any sites as sacred prior to the fourth century, Joan Taylor did refer to Alexander but denied that his prayer was associated with any "holy places."[138] On the other hand, David Hunt reasoned that because such visitors approached the places of the Bible with a sense of reverence, there was something that could legitimately be termed "pilgrimage" in these early forays.

> Individually and collectively, Christians can be demonstrated visiting places deemed to have a sacred significance for their faith long before the advent of the first Christian emperor. Even if such journeys had not yet acquired some of the associations

[135] Eusebius, *Hist. eccl.* 4.26.13-14; *Passio Pionii* 4.18-20; Origen, *Comm. in Johan.* 6.204; see also idem, *Contra Celsum* 1.51.

[136] Pierre Maraval, "The Earliest Phase of Christian Pilgrimage in the Near East (before the 7th Century)," *Dumbarton Oaks Papers* 56 (2002): 63–74, here at 65. See also Wilken, *The Land Called Holy*, 108.

[137] Eusebius, *Hist. eccl.* 6.11.1-2.

[138] Joan E. Taylor, *Christians and the Holy Places: The Myth of Jewish-Christian Origins* (Oxford/New York: Oxford University Press, 1993), esp. 312. See also Kenneth G. Holum, "Hadrian and St. Helena: Imperial Travel and the Origins of Christian Holy Land Pilgrimage," in *The Blessings of Pilgrimage*, ed. Robert G. Ousterhout (Urbana: University of Illinois Press, 1990), 66–81.

of more fully-developed pilgrimage—there is no evidence that they were undertaken for ascetic, penitential, or therapeutic purposes—none the less it would be unduly pedantic to deny these travellers the label of "pilgrims." In any case we have to go much *later* than Constantine . . . to discover the phenomenon in such a fully-fledged guise.[139]

Nevertheless, where there does seem to be agreement is that pilgrimage to the Holy Land developed out of the early Christian practice of visiting the tombs of the departed—and especially those of martyrs—in cemeteries outside the cities,[140] a practice that had probably been at least equal in ritual significance to the weekly gathering for the eucharistic meal for the earliest generations of believers. The funerary traditions of the ancient world that were apparently continued by Christians involved regular gatherings at the place of burial, and especially on the anniversary of death, with the consumption of a meal there, which became for Christians a celebration of the Eucharist. While in the case of many deceased Christians it would have been family and friends who gathered, in the case of a local martyr the whole Christian community would have turned out. Thus, the third/fourth-century Syrian church order, the *Didascalia Apostolorum*, directed: "In accordance with the Gospel and in accordance with the power of the Holy Spirit, gather in the cemeteries to read the Holy Scriptures and to offer your prayers and your rites to God without observance and offer an acceptable Eucharist . . . both in your congregations and in your cemeteries and on the departure of those who sleep."[141] Cyprian, bishop of Carthage during the Decian persecution in the middle of the third century, likewise spoke of celebrating the

---

[139] E. D. Hunt, "Space and Time Transcended: The Beginnings of Christian Pilgrimage," in *The Sense of the Sacramental*, ed. David Brown and Ann Loades (London: SPCK, 1995), 59–77, here at 53–54. See also Hunt, "Were There Christian Pilgrims before Constantine?"; and *Holy Land Pilgrimage in the Later Roman Empire*, esp. chapters 4 and 5.

[140] See, for example, Robert A. Markus, "How on Earth Could Places Become Holy? Origins of the Christian Idea of Holy Places," *Journal of Early Christian Studies* 2 (1994): 257–71, esp. 262, 268ff.; Maraval, "The Earliest Phase of Christian Pilgrimage," 65–66.

[141] *Didascalia* 6.22; ET from Alistair Stewart-Sykes, *The Didascalia apostolorum* (Turnhout: Brepols, 2009), 255–56. The expression "without observance" means not observing the Jewish prohibition against contact with dead bodies.

anniversaries of the death of martyrs and instructed his clergy to note the dates of those who died in prison during the persecution so that they too could be commemorated along with the martyrs.[142]

Without question, key elements of the later practice of pilgrimage were already present in this phenomenon: travel to a place made holy by the presence of a holy person, ending in participation in a ritual act there. As David Hunt observed:

> Such (primarily local) festivals brought together congregations of the faithful who may not have journeyed far in terms of distance, but who certainly forged a great gap in other ways between themselves and the world which they had, albeit temporarily, left behind them. If pilgrimage is indeed some sort of "movement towards the Center," then their "Center" was transported to the margins of the society in which they lived, amid the burial-grounds which lay at the perimeter, beyond the boundaries of city-based civilization. In attending martyr commemorations, the faithful moved themselves outside their secular world, on a pilgrimage to encounter the glorious forebears who were the formative and identifying influences on their Christian community.[143]

4. Visiting Living Saints

It is noteworthy that these early Christian visits to tombs were not understood simply as trips to places that were sanctified by the bones of the martyrs: they were acts of communion with the holy ones themselves. Indeed, archeological evidence has revealed the existence of tubes built into the tombs for the purpose of pouring a libation of wine inside and thereby sharing in communion with the deceased.[144] This constitutes another parallel with later pilgrimage practice.

---

[142] Cyprian, *Ep.* 33.3; 36.2. See also the *Passio Polycarpi* 18, which speaks of the collecting and burial of the bones of the martyred Polycarp in a place where subsequent anniversaries of his death might be celebrated. Although the martyrdom itself happened ca. 160, the account probably took its present form in the third century: see Candida Moss, "On the Dating of Polycarp: Rethinking the Place of the *Martyrdom of Polycarp* in the History of Christianity," *Early Christianity* 4 (2010): 1–37.

[143] Hunt, "Were There Christian Pilgrims before Constantine?" 28–29.

[144] See Ramsay MacMullen, *The Second Church: Popular Christianity A.D. 200–400* (Atlanta: Society of Biblical Literature, 2009), 24–25, 77.

Fourth-century pilgrims did not merely go to supposed biblical sites but they also visited living holy men and women in these lands. Their desire was to make contact with holy people, whether through meeting them alive or by being in the places that had been made holy by their former presence there. So, for example, when Egeria spoke of having previously made an excursion into the Thebaid in Egypt, the area around Thebes (9.1, 6), it can only have been in order to visit the many holy men and women who were there, as it had no sites associated with the Bible or with famous Christian martyrs; and when she made a journey to the shrine of St. Thecla at Seleucia, she also spent two days visiting all the male and female religious communities there (23.6). In some cases, her further excursions were directly prompted by stories she heard of holy monks in the general vicinity, whom she then took the opportunity to visit (as, for example, in 21.3).

From the late third century onward some Christians had begun to retreat into the deserts of Egypt and Syria in order to pursue an ascetic life of holiness and solitude, and the cessation of the persecution of Christians early in the fourth century led to a large increase in their numbers, not least from those who looked to it as a substitute for the martyrdom they otherwise would have desired but which changed circumstances now denied them. In the course of time informal gatherings of these hermits resulted in the creation of the first monastic communities, although the desert monks that Egeria visited generally still seemed to be living in individual cells rather than sharing a more intentional form of common life that would become characteristic of later monasticism proper. According to Jerome, it was Hilarion, a disciple of Antony in Egypt, who had initiated Palestinian monasticism by founding a community of hermits in the desert of Gaza in the first half of the fourth century.[145]

The middle and later decades of the fourth century witnessed extensive progress both in the development of various forms of monastic life and in the cultivation of holy places in and around the Holy Land, and the two phenomena are interrelated to the extent that monks in Palestine and Egypt seized opportunities to locate and popularize nearby sites with biblical associations—endorsing the greater authenticity of devotion to *their* holy places in cases where

[145] Jerome, *Vita Hilarionis.*

rival claims to the *real* location were an issue.[146] Their visitors included not only lay men and women but also those who were already engaged in the religious life, particularly itinerant monks from the West.[147] Moreover, their provision of hospitality to travelers would also have afforded them a source of revenue.

For Egeria, monks not only mediated the traveler's desire to see holy places by "showing" where they were; the monks of Palestine and Egypt themselves became those who were sought out to *be seen* by Christian travelers. As David Hunt has observed, "the monks and their doings were an extension of the scriptural panorama which [Egeria] beheld all around her: she longed to see, converse with them and learn of their deeds, just as to look upon the places of the Bible."[148] These holy monks help make the scriptural story a present, living reality in the places associated with holy happenings of the past.

Egeria applies the term "holy" (*sanctus, sancta*) very liberally, using it 186 times in relation to places (mountains, churches, relics), to deceased holy people from the Christian Era, but also to personages from the Hebrew Scriptures (such as Moses, Abraham, Melchizedek, and Rebecca) *and* to the holy monks who serve as her guides, hosts, and motivation for thanksgiving—after, of course, her primary gratitude directed toward God who fulfills all her desire. Sometimes the holy ones from various eras overlap, as in 4.8, when the *sancti monachi* who dwell on Mount Sinai show Egeria the place where *sanctus Moyses* spoke with God in the burning bush. Thus Egeria "is not simply visiting empty 'holy places,' but instead places populated with monks, true holy people worthy of the places."[149] While this emphasis on holy people is perhaps most obvious in the first twenty-three chapters, in which monks are encountered mostly as individuals or in small groups, Jerusalem as well is populated with monks and ascetics whose behavior attracts Egeria's attention (as in, for example,

---

[146] See Hagith Sivan, "Pilgrimage, Monasticism, and the Emergence of Christian Palestine in the 4th Century," in *The Blessings of Pilgrimage*, ed. Robert G. Ousterhout, 54–65.

[147] See, for example, Bitton-Ashkelony, *Encountering the Sacred*, 140–83; Daniel F. Caner, *Wandering, Begging Monks: Spiritual Authority and the Promotion of Monasticism in Late Antiquity* (Berkeley: University of California Press, 2002); Dietz, *Wandering Monks, Virgins, and Pilgrims*.

[148] Hunt, "Space and Time Transcended," 73.

[149] Dietz, *Wandering Monks, Virgins, and Pilgrims*, 51.

her description of the monks and virgins arriving at the church to pray before cockcrow in 24.1, the vigil kept by Bethlehem monks at Epiphany in 25.12, and the monks and ascetics from regions near and far who flock to Jerusalem to celebrate the anniversary of the dedication of the Church of the Holy Sepulcher in 49.1). The sanctity of a particular place is connected in part to the sanctity of its inhabitants.

Egeria is one of many travelers who sought out both holy people *and* holy places from the late fourth to the seventh centuries. "That so many pilgrims to the holy places also made visits to holy people suggests that journeying to holy destinations, whether people or places, reflects a coextensive piety."[150] As with seeing the holy places, *seeing* holy people becomes particularly important. The anecdotes of previous travelers, later complemented by more consolidated accounts like *The History of the Monks in Egypt* (composed by a monk from Jerusalem toward the very end of the fourth century) and the *Lausiac History* of Bishop Palladius of Helenopolis (completed around 420), circulated tales of monks in distant places. Some were motivated to take to the road to see the holy monks for themselves, whereas others—like Egeria's "sisters," presumably—soaked up more stories secondhand through the accounts of those who did go. "If the aim is to understand the totality of pilgrims' experiences as represented through their stories, we should regard these [sometimes incredible] tales as meaningful fictions through which pilgrims generated an image of monastics with which their audience could interact."[151] Through selective descriptions of their encounters with monastics in distant places, which typically do not attempt to provide exhaustive accounts of monastic lifestyles in all their rich diversity but rather mold the exotic monks into more familiar categories, people like Egeria drew connections for themselves and for their readers between the world of the Bible and the world inhabited by monks.[152] "Egeria's vivid telling of her journey—in its intertwining of ancient story and present place, holy Moses and holy monks, the literal and the spiritual—becomes a narrative of transformation, inviting the reader to come in."[153]

---

[150] For more on this phenomenon, see Georgia Frank, *The Memory of the Eyes: Pilgrims to Living Saints in Christian Late Antiquity* (Berkeley: University of California Press, 2000); quotation from 7.

[151] Ibid., 5.

[152] Ibid., 29–34.

[153] Hamilton, "Egeria," 181.

Notable among the many others who followed a similar path to
Egeria were Basil of Caesarea, who in a letter written in 375 described
the profound impression made upon him by the monks he had met
in Egypt, Palestine, Syria, and Mesopotamia;[154] Melania the Elder, who
stayed with the desert fathers in Egypt for about six months before
founding her monastery in Jerusalem and who later escorted Silvia
of Aquitaine on a further visit to Egypt;[155] and Paula, who (according
to Jerome) also visited monastic communities in Cyprus and in Egypt
in addition to seeing a multitude of holy places on her travels:

> Was there any cell that she did not enter? Or any man at whose
> feet she did not throw herself? In each of his saints she believed
> that she saw Christ himself; and whatever she bestowed upon
> them she rejoiced to feel that she had bestowed it upon the Lord.
> Her enthusiasm was wonderful and her endurance scarcely
> credible in a woman. Forgetful of her sex and of her weakness
> she even desired to make her abode, together with the girls who
> accompanied her, among these thousands of monks.[156]

Very tellingly, Paulinus of Nola, who never went to the Holy Land,
asserted in a letter written around 409 the superiority of encountering
a living saint over visiting the holy places associated with Christ. He
cited as an example a certain Valgius, whose delivery from shipwreck
was regarded as having been miraculous and so had earned him the
status of just such a person:

> If the manger of his [Christ's] birth, the river of his baptism, the
> garden of his betrayal, the palace of his condemnation, the column
> of his scourging, the thorns of his crowning, the wood of his
> crucifixion, the stone of his burial, the places of his resurrection
> and ascension are as famed as recalling God's former presence,
> and if living proofs in lifeless objects demonstrate the ancient
> truth for today's belief, then with what reverence must this man
> [Valgius] be regarded, with whom God deigned to converse,
> before whom God's face was not concealed, to whom Christ
> revealed now His martyr [St. Felix] and now His own person?[157]

[154] Basil of Caesarea, *Ep.* 223.
[155] Palladius, *Hist.* laus. 46, 54–55.
[156] Jerome, *Ep.* 108.7, 14; ET from *NPNF* 2:6, 202.
[157] Paulinus of Nola, *Ep.* 49.14; ET from P. G. Walsh, *Letters of St. Paulinus of Nola* 2, Ancient Christian Writers 36 (New York: Newman Press, 1967), 273.

5. Reactions to Holy Places

Pilgrims visiting the sites mentioned in the Scriptures were not merely sightseers. Egeria used the expression "for the sake of prayer" to indicate the purpose of her own journeys as well as those of other pilgrims, especially to the graves of saints (13.1-2; 17.1-2; 23.3, 10). It seems that by this phrase she had in mind not merely private devotion at the shrine, but participation in a corporate liturgical rite that included an appropriate reading and psalm as well as prayer or sometimes the celebration of the Eucharist (see the section on worship in the holy places below). The ritual act emphasized and heightened the sanctity of the place.[158]

Although Egeria sometimes speaks of "seeing" various holy places, she more often uses the verb *ostendo*, "show," either in the passive ("were shown us") or in the active form ("they showed us"), or very rarely the verb *monstro*, which we have translated as "pointed out" (3.8; 5.1, 3). Apart from occasionally expressing a brief note of pleasure at being able to visit these sites (for example, 12.4), however, she reveals nothing about the spiritual benefits she might have gained from the experience. Only twice does she break into a slightly more excited response to something—the encounter with the deaconess Marthana (23.3) and the adornment of the churches at Epiphany (25.8-9)—and each time she quickly recognizes that this is a digression from her primary purpose and immediately says, "but to return to the point" (23.4; 25.10). According to Mary Campbell, this "deep reserve" is because her composition was "a merging of two genres, perhaps the first such merger," the travel narratives of the Roman world, comprised of lists of cities, staging posts, places of interest, and the distances between them, of which the diary of the pilgrim from Bordeaux was really only a modest expansion,[159] and the literary letter.

---

[158] Compare the more extreme view of Jonathan Z. Smith, *To Take Place: Toward Theory in Ritual* (Chicago: University of Chicago Press, 1987), 105, that ritual is "not an expression of or a response to 'the Sacred'; rather, something or someone is made sacred by ritual."

[159] See Appendix A, pp. 197–204, for a comparison between that diary and Egeria's writing.

In the inevitable zigzagging between the sacred map and the distortion it suffers through her temporal experience of it, her allegiance is chiefly with the map. This is clear in her suppression of almost all personal details of the journey: the names of the people she meets, the nature of the gifts she receives, the identities of her fellow travelers, the feelings evoked by what she sees. . . . Places not appearing in the Scriptures are, to her, empty. . . .[160]

Catherine Sider Hamilton similarly observes that Scripture was the primary motivating factor influencing Egeria's descriptions of these sites:

Scripture shapes her journey so thoroughly as to transform the fourth-century landscape: current events, local customs, politics on the edges of a weakening Roman Empire, the daily life of a busy city like Jerusalem—none of this interests her. Mount Sinai is the place where Moses talked to God; the plain in front of it is the place where the Israelites sojourned . . . Scripture thus renders the world: what Egeria sees is the story of Moses and the Israelites, of Melchizedek and the vine-filled valley, of Jesus and the cross and empty tomb—not the contemporary exotica of a foreign land. Further, the land thus mapped by Scripture is a land transformed: all the people are holy, and all the valleys are "very beautiful."[161]

Others were more effusive about expressing their reaction to what they saw. Cyril of Jerusalem, addressing candidates for baptism who were literally surrounded by the sacred sites, asserted that the very sight of the physical signs of what they had read about in the Scriptures confirmed the truth of those biblical narratives and so were to be included among the many testimonies or witnesses to the veracity of the Christian claims: "Others only hear, but we see and handle. . . . The Lord was crucified; you have received the testimonies. You see this spot of Golgotha! . . . even the stone which was then rolled away

---

[160] Campbell, *The Witness and the Other World*, 27–29. Smith, "Sacred Journeying," 48, also comments that "she was not emotional and sought no mystical union with the episodes related."

[161] Hamilton, "Egeria," 180.

itself bears witness to the resurrection, lying there to this day. . . . You have therefore many witnesses; you have this very place of the resurrection; you have also the place of the ascension towards the east."[162]

Jerome went further still. We have already seen earlier how, when describing the visits made by Paula to the cells of monks, he said that "in each of his saints she believed that she saw Christ himself." He reports that her experience was even more intense when she went to the sites of Christ's birth and of his death and resurrection, though we cannot be certain, of course, how faithfully he represents her own feelings as opposed to his.[163] At Bethlehem,

> when she looked upon the inn made sacred by the virgin and the stall where the ox knew his owner and the ass his master's crib . . . when she looked upon these things I say, she protested in my hearing that she could behold with the eyes of faith the infant Lord wrapped in swaddling clothes and crying in the manger, the wise men worshipping Him, the star shining overhead, the virgin mother, the attentive foster-father, the shepherds coming by night to see "the word that was come to pass" and thus even then to consecrate those opening phrases of the evangelist John "In the beginning was the word" and "the word was made flesh." She declared that she could see the slaughtered innocents, the raging Herod, Joseph and Mary fleeing into Egypt.[164]

According to him, her response at the Church of the Holy Sepulcher in Jerusalem had been equally profound:

> In visiting the holy places so great was the passion and enthusiasm she exhibited for each, that she could never have torn herself away from one had she not been eager to visit the rest. Before the Cross she threw herself down in adoration as though she beheld the Lord hanging upon it: and when she entered the tomb

---

[162] Cyril of Jerusalem, *Baptismal Catecheses* 13.22, 23; 14.22, 23; ET from *NPNF* 2:7, 88, 100. See also ibid. 10.19. Eusebius too, *Vita Constantini* 3.28, described Christ's tomb as "testifying by facts louder than any voice to the resurrection of the Saviour" (ET from Cameron and Hall, *Eusebius: Life of Constantine*, 133).

[163] See the quotation from Elm, 'Virgins of God,' 382, above, p. 16, n. 51.

[164] Jerome, *Ep.* 108.10; ET from *NPNF* 2:6, 199.

which was the scene of the Resurrection she kissed the stone which the angel had rolled away from the door of the sepulchre. Indeed so ardent was her faith that she even licked with her mouth the very spot on which the Lord's body had lain, like one athirst for the river which he has longed for. What tears she shed there, what groans she uttered, and what grief she poured forth, all Jerusalem knows; the Lord also to whom she prayed knows.[165]

In another of his letters Jerome speaks in similar terms of his own experience when visiting the place of Christ's burial: "As often as we enter it we see the Saviour in His grave clothes, and if we linger we see again the angel sitting at His feet, and the napkin folded at His head."[166]

In a recent study of this language of "seeing" at the holy places, Juliette Day argues that it obviously cannot have meant physical sight but equally should not be thought of simply as imagining. She concludes that Jerome believed that Paula's holiness, resulting from a life of ascetic discipline that controlled her passions, enabled her to perceive with "spiritual eyes" not just the past biblical event associated with the place but the very presence of Christ himself.[167]

6. Egeria and Worship in the Holy Places

Egeria participated in a range of liturgical events during her travels and chronicled many of them for her intended audience—from the great annual commemorations of Holy Week to regular Sunday eucharistic celebrations to daily gatherings for prayer with ascetics, clergy, and laypeople to more private acts of worship with her traveling companions. She gives the clear impression that when she visited sacred sites on her various journeys outside Jerusalem, she played a part in shaping the act of worship in which she and her companions

---

[165] Ibid. 108.9; ET from *NPNF* 2:6, 198–99.

[166] Ibid. 46.5; ET from *NPNF* 2:6, 62.

[167] Juliette Day, "Seeing Christ at the Holy Places," in *Spaces in Late Antiquity: Cultural, Theological and Archaeological Perspectives*, ed. Juliette Day, Raimo Hakola, Maijastina Kahlos, and Ulla Tervahauta (Abingdon/New York: Routledge, 2016), 69–88. See also Frank, *The Memory of the Eyes*, and her essay, "'Taste and See': The Eucharist and the Eyes of Faith in the Fourth Century," *Church History* 70 (2001): 619–43.

participated, in particular in the choice of reading: "I had always desired very greatly for us that, wherever we came, the [relevant] passage from the book should always be read" (4.3). She also asserts that such acts of worship had a standard pattern: "It was always our custom that whenever we were about to visit places we desired, first prayer was made there, then the reading was read from the codex, also one psalm relevant to the matter was recited and prayer was made there again" (10.7). She explicitly records this same pattern being used on some other occasions (14.1; 20.3; 21.1), and so it is reasonable to assume that when she gives a more abbreviated outline, omitting mention of the psalm and/or the final prayer (4.4, 8; 11.1, 3; 12.3; 15.4; 19.2; 23.5) or giving no details besides simply "prayer" (21.3; 23.6), the full pattern was still followed. This would also account for her use of the plural "prayers" at 19.2. Moreover, when she speaks of "giving thanks to God there according to custom" (16.2; see also 16.4), having just seen the cave of Elijah, it seems probable that by thanksgiving here and elsewhere in her narrative she was referring to the use of this form of worship too.

Was this pattern one that was entirely created by Egeria? That seems unlikely when she was accompanied on her journeys by monks and presbyters, who would surely have wanted to adopt forms with which they were already familiar. Indeed, in at least one case this act of prayer took place in a church in the presence of the presbyter and monks who were stationed there (14.1) and in another two instances in the presence of the local bishop, who gave a blessing at the end and in the second case is explicitly said to have led the prayer (20.3; 21.1). Surely, these men would have followed a form of worship that accorded with their own custom? In most of the occasions that Egeria describes, the leader of this prayer is unspecified, which neither proves nor precludes the possibility that women sometimes may have served in this role.

Furthermore, the pattern that is described for these pilgrim devotions bears a strong resemblance to certain of the acts of worship that formed part of the Jerusalem liturgy. Thus, during the procession from the Mount of Olives to the city in the early hours of Good Friday, short services were held in the places where Jesus was said to have prayed and where he was arrested, and these consisted of an appropriate prayer, an appropriate psalm, the gospel reading about the event, and at least in the first case a further prayer (36.1, 3). A similar act of worship occurred on the Saturday before Holy Week in a church marking the spot where Mary, the sister of Lazarus, was believed to have met Jesus (Jn 11:29-30): "One hymn is recited and one antiphon and that passage from the gospel is read where the sister of Lazarus meets the Lord. And then when prayer has been made and all have been blessed . . ." (29.4). Although in all these instances the order of the psalm and reading is the reverse of the worship at the holy places outside the milieu of the Jerusalem church (conceivably because these were gospel readings rather than the Old Testament lections used elsewhere?), it does tend to confirm that in those latter places Egeria was experiencing a standard pattern rather than something devised by her at the time. Her own contribution perhaps may have been simply to request that prayer be made on those occasions and sometimes to suggest which Bible passage should then be read.

On one occasion she appears to have participated in a regular Sunday Eucharist with presbyters and monks (3.6), but on other occasions her party seems to have asked that the Eucharist should be celebrated specially for them—as when they celebrated the Eucharist in another church later that same day (4.3). Although that too may have been a regularly scheduled Sunday service and Egeria does not say that they received Communion again, she explicitly states that the following morning they did ask the presbyters to offer the Eucharist at the place where they had spent the night (4.8). They did the same on another occasion when they had visited the tomb of Job (16.7). There seems to have been some limitation, however, as to when their request could be granted: they had been unable to have yet a further Eucharist on the first Sunday, quite possibly because of the late hour of the day (4.8). On another occasion Egeria records them having prayed and received Communion, but does not mention an actual celebration of the Eucharist (23.6). Was that omission simply accidental, or was there really not a Eucharist, perhaps because no presbyter was present, and Communion was instead received from bread (and possibly wine) consecrated on a previous Sunday and preserved by the monks and nuns living there for their daily Communion?

Egeria's accounts of the various eucharistic celebrations also raise the question as to whether they always included several prearranged readings. For the first Sunday Eucharist that she mentions, she states that there was an appropriate reading "from the book of Moses" and the "oblation" (her standard expression for the eucharistic action) was made (3.6); for the second that day, "we made both the oblation there and most earnest prayer, and that passage from the book of the Kingdoms was read" (4.3; she went on to imply that she selected the reading); and for the other two occasions she simply says that the oblation was made. Of course, it is possible that each celebration was indeed preceded by a full liturgy of the word and that Egeria only chose to mention the reading from Exodus on the first occasion and refer to the reading from 1 Kings at the end of the second because those readings were concerned with the specific places in which the service was being held. It is also possible, however, that as yet every Eucharist did not automatically include readings. As we will see later in this Introduction when we examine the eucharistic liturgy at Jerusalem, Egeria regularly uses the Latin verb *procedo* there to indicate a eucharistic liturgy of the word and seems to limit "the oblation" to the eucharistic action proper.[168] Thus it may be significant that she omits *procedo* in relation to the second Eucharist on Holy Thursday, when there apparently was no liturgy of the word attached to it, and also in relation to the Saturday morning Eucharists in Lent, which seem to have followed directly on from the overnight vigil of readings and psalmody.

At least one further question remains unanswered. Why does she request a celebration of the Eucharist at some of the holy places that she visits but not at others, where instead there is a service of prayers, reading, and psalm? We have noted that the lateness of the hour may have precluded a Eucharist in one instance (4.8), but that does not appear to have been the case in others. Sometimes it is possible that there may not have been a presbyter present to lead the worship, but that was not always so. Thus, after celebrating the Eucharist for a second time on a Sunday, another place is shown to her "by presbyters and monks," but prayer and not a Eucharist is held there (4.4); and when she visits the plain near Livias, she is accompanied by a presbyter and deacons, but the Eucharist is not celebrated (10.3, 7). The answer may appear to be that there was no church building there in these two instances, but this does not seem to have been the reason for there being no Eucharist when she visited the church on the summit of Mount Nebo, as the presence of presbyters and monks is mentioned (12.1-3), nor when she went to Sedima, where the presbyter of that place and other clergy take her to the church (14.1). Indeed,

---

[168] See below, pp. 82–83.

when she was at Carrhae, there was both a church building and a bishop (20.3); the same was true later when she visited the well where Jacob was said to have watered Rachel's sheep (21.1); and yet in neither case did she mention requesting that a Eucharist be celebrated. Could it be that on at least some of those occasions she did ask but her request was refused for some reason? Otherwise, this variation in her piety must remain a mystery.

Jerusalem and Its Ecclesiastical Buildings

Prior to the fourth century Jerusalem had been a small and insignificant city. After the Jewish revolt in the year 70, it had been partially destroyed, and following the end of the Bar Kochba rebellion in 135, the Jewish population had been expelled and the city then refounded by Roman Emperor Hadrian as the pagan Aelia Capitolina—Aelia after the emperor's second name and Capitolina in reference to the three Roman "capitoline" gods, Jupiter, Juno, and Minerva. It was built according to the standard plan of a Roman city, which had a gate in the middle of each of its four sides and two principal streets connecting them, one running north to south, the *cardo maximus*, and the other east to west, the *decumanus maximus*. Roman engineers tried to build their roads as straight and level as possible but here they had to contend with Jerusalem's hilly terrain and in particular with the Temple Mount on the east side, as well as a military camp on the south side. Hence, in this case a second pair of main roads was added, as can be seen in Figure 2. The main *cardo* was wide, flanked by rows of columns and shops, and, following usual Roman practice, the main Forum was located at its junction with the main *decumanus*. Adjacent to the Forum, at the junction of the same *cardo* with the other *decumanus*, the emperor Hadrian erected a large temple to Venus, which later became the site of the Church of the Holy Sepulcher. Other temples and shrines were built throughout the city, but the vast Temple Mount was left in ruins except for a temple to Jupiter, demolished in the fourth century, and two statues.[169]

---

[169] The pilgrim from Bordeaux described them as being two statues of the Emperor Hadrian (see Appendix A, p. 201), but Wilkinson, 30, n. 4, suggested that the second may have been of Antoninus, his heir and successor. Jerome, *Comm. in Isaiam* 1.2.9, spoke of a statue of Hadrian and an idol of Jupiter.

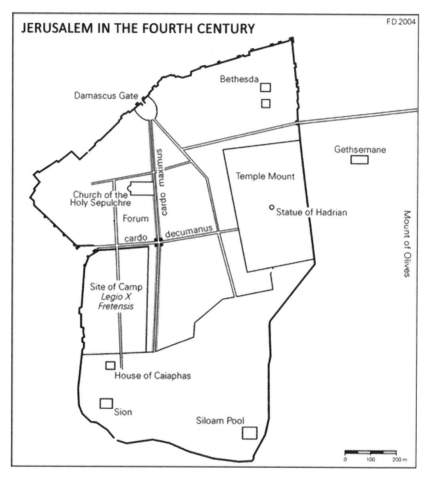

Figure 2

Eusebius recorded a list of each of the successive bishops of the minority Christian community in Jerusalem from earliest times down to the beginning of the third century; whether historically accurate or not, the list's compilation suggests a growing sense of self-importance by that church and a desire to demonstrate its apostolic roots.[170] It is

---

[170] Eusebius, *Hist. eccl.* 4.5; 5.12; 6.10. On the Christian community in Jerusalem before Constantine, see Oded Irshai, "From Oblivion to Fame: The History of the Palestinian Church (135–303 CE)," in *Christians and Christianity in the Holy Land*, ed. Ora Limor and Guy G. Stroumsa (Turnhout: Brepols, 2006), 91–139.

possible that the Christian inhabitants had already begun to cultivate the biblical sites that would come to be regarded as sacred and as places of pilgrimage in the fourth century even before the emperor Constantine embarked on his program to build the Church of the Holy Sepulcher on the supposed site of the crucifixion and burial of Jesus and another church on the Mount of Olives as well as the Church of the Nativity in Bethlehem.[171] But this development, coupled with the cessation of the persecution of Christians, naturally boosted the numbers of those visiting the city, leading to an increase in its economic prosperity, the size of its resident population, and its importance in the secular world as well as in Christian circles. [172] More churches and hospices for pilgrims were built, as were monasteries for the several male and female religious communities that were attracted to settle there. Nevertheless, even by the end of the fourth century it still cannot properly be described as a Christian city: pagan temples, festivals, and other suchlike practices continued to exist and were no doubt supported by a sizable number of its inhabitants.

1. Sion

The earliest Christian community in Jerusalem seems to have been centered in the area of Sion, located southwest of the city, outside the original walls of Aelia Capitolina and set on a hill. According to Epiphanius, bishop of Salamis in Cyprus from 367 onward, when the emperor Hadrian visited the city in 130, he found the city in ruins,

> except for a few houses and for the small church of God, which stood where the Disciples, who returned after the Saviour ascended from the Mount of Olives, went up to the upper chamber. For there it was built, that is in the part of "Zion" that escaped devastation; and [there were] parts of houses around "Zion"

---

[171] For the disputed question as to whether Jerusalem was already a place of pilgrimage before this, see above, pp. 42–44. For Constantine's influence on Jerusalem, see E. D. Hunt, "Constantine and Jerusalem," *Journal of Ecclesiastical History* 48 (1997): 405–24.

[172] For a postcolonial perspective on these developments, see Andrew S. Jacobs, *Remains of the Jews: The Holy Land and Christian Empire in Late Antiquity* (Stanford: Stanford University Press, 2004).

itself and seven synagogues, which stood alone in "Zion" merely
as huts, of which one survived to the time of Maximonas the
Bishop and the Emperor Constantine "as a cottage in a vineyard"
according to the Scripture.[173]

By the time of Egeria's visit the main focus had shifted to the new
buildings over the sacred sites erected by Constantine, but some liturgies for the Jerusalem Christian community were still held on Sion
(25.11; 27.5; 39.2, 5; 40.2; 43.3), which suggests that a larger church
had been built there during the fourth century. Such a church is not
mentioned by Eusebius as among those that Constantine erected, nor
explicitly by the pilgrim from Bordeaux, who only noted the existence
of the one remaining synagogue there, but it was described in the
middle of the fourth century by Cyril of Jerusalem as "the upper
church of the Apostles," where the Holy Spirit descended on them
at Pentecost,[174] the description of it as "upper" seemingly referring
to its location in a higher part of the city.

In addition to other services there, Egeria records that the Jerusalem Christians assembled in the church on the evening of Easter
Day and again one week later (39.5; 40.2) to commemorate the ap-
pearances of the risen Christ to the disciples "when the doors were
shut" (Jn 20:19-29) and also in the morning of the feast of Pentecost
(43.3) to commemorate the descent of the Spirit (Acts 2:1-41), in both
cases when and where those events were believed to have happened.
She does not refer to any association of Sion with the place of the Last
Supper—the evening Eucharist on Holy Thursday was not offered
there but "behind the Cross," the only day in the year when this was
done (35.2)—although later tradition certainly made that connection.[175] Many Christians also went to Sion on the morning of Good
Friday to pray at the pillar where Christ was scourged (37.1).

---

[173] ET from Renan Baker, "Epiphanius, *On Weights and Measures* 14: Hadrian's
Journey to the East and the Rebuilding of Jerusalem," *Zeitschrift für Papyrologie
und Epigraphik* 182 (2012): 157–67, here at 158. For a critical view of the existence
of a church building there at this time, see Taylor, *Christians and the Holy Places*,
207–19.

[174] Cyril of Jerusalem, *Baptismal Catecheses* 16.4 (ET from *NPNF* 2:7, 116).

[175] See p. 94.

2. The Rotunda of the Resurrection (Anastasis)

According to Eusebius, when Constantine ordered the temple of Venus to be cleared from its site, Christ's tomb was discovered there, and the cave, as it was known, was then excavated from the rock that had previously surrounded it, so that it stood clear above ground, after which the emperor adorned it with columns.[176] As neither Eusebius, nor the pilgrim from Bordeaux, nor Cyril of Jerusalem in his *Baptismal Catecheses* mentions anything enclosing the cave, it seems highly likely that the large rotunda over it, measuring approximately 120 feet in diameter, must have been added somewhat later, as Egeria certainly speaks of the existence of a building with doors (24.1, 9; 25.2; 47.2), which she calls the Anastasis ("Resurrection") and where the daily hours of prayer were observed.[177] She also mentions an enclosure (*cancelli*) at the mouth of the cave itself (24.2; 47.1), which appears to have been a waist-high pierced stone balustrade,[178] and the existence of a lamp constantly burning within (24.4), something often noted by later pilgrims. She speaks of worshippers "coming down" to the Anastasis (24.1, 3, 4, 9): John Baldovin thought that this meant that the Anastasis was on a lower level than the rest of the church complex, while Maraval argued instead that there were rooms on an upper floor where pilgrims and ascetics might rest and where the clergy resided.[179] Although not mentioned by Egeria, both Cyril of Jerusalem and Jerome speak of the presence of the stone that had originally sealed the mouth of the tomb.[180]

3. The Martyrium or Major Church

Again according to Eusebius, after the tomb was excavated, Constantine then ordered the construction of a very large and grand

---

[176] Eusebius, *Vita Constantini* 3.25-28, 33-34.

[177] On the shape of the building, see Edward J. Yarnold, *Cyril of Jerusalem* (London/New York: Routledge, 2000), 18–20.

[178] See Wilkinson, 173–74.

[179] John F. Baldovin, *The Urban Character of Christian Worship: The Origins, Development and Meaning of Stational Liturgy*, Orientalia Christiana Analecta 228 (Rome: Pontifical Oriental Institute, 1987), 47; Maraval, 234, n. 3.

[180] Cyril, *Baptismal Catecheses* 14.22; Jerome, *Ep.* 108.9.

basilica to its east, with a courtyard between the two that had colonnades on three sides.[181] This basilica seems to have been generally
known as the Martyrium—in Greek, *martyrion*. In the New Testament,
this term means testimony or witness (see, for example, Mt 8:4; 10.18;
24.14; Acts 4:33; 1 Cor 1:6), but it had come to be used by later Christians, together with its plural *martyria*, to denote the tombs or shrines
of martyrs and so, by extension, this building too. Cyril of Jerusalem
refers to it by this name, offering the rather fanciful explanation that
it may have been foreseen in Zephaniah 3:8;[182] but Egeria gives the
more likely reason that it was because it was on the site of Christ's
passion (30.1). She also calls it "the major church," either because of
its actual size—it measured approximately 190 feet by 130 feet—or
to indicate that it was the principal church of the city, in effect its
cathedral, though that term would be anachronistic.

Dedicated in 335, timed to coincide with the celebration of thirty
years of Constantine's reign, its primary use was for the regular celebration of the Eucharist,[183] presumably as much because its size enabled it to accommodate a large congregation as for its association
with the death of Christ. The orientation of the church toward the
west rather than the traditional east was dictated by Jerusalem's
topography and city plan. Eusebius described the building as follows,
moving from west to east:

> On the side opposite the cave, which looked towards the rising
> sun, was connected the royal temple, an extraordinary structure
> raised to an immense height and very extensive in length and
> breadth. Its interior was covered with slabs of varied marble,
> and the external aspect of the walls, gleaming with hewn stone
> fitted closely together at each joint, produced a supreme object
> of beauty by no means inferior to marble. Right up at the top the
> material which encased the outside of the roof was lead, a sure
> protection against stormy rain; while the interior of the structure
> was fitted with carved coffers and like a vast sea spread out by

[181] Eusebius, *Vita Constantini* 3.35. For the suggestion that in reality Constantine
intended to build this basilica first, and only began to excavate the tomb afterward, see Taylor, *Christians and the Holy Places*, 138–42; but cf. Martin Biddle,
The Tomb of Christ (Stroud: Sutton Publishing, 1999), 70.

[182] Cyril of Jerusalem, *Baptismal Catecheses* 14.6.

[183] For occasions when the Eucharist was celebrated elsewhere in and around
Jerusalem, see the section on Eucharist below, pp. 79–83.

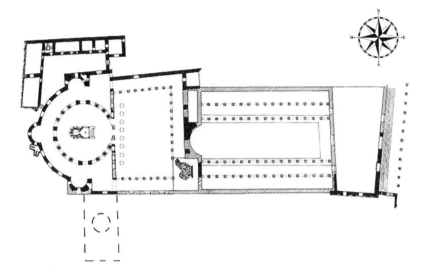

Figure 3: Plan of the Church of the Holy Sepulcher
                in the Fourth Century

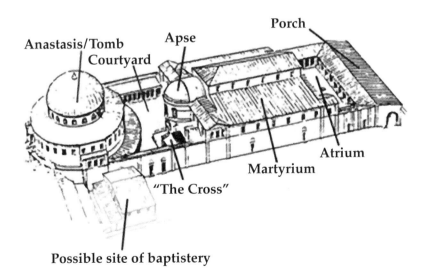

Figure 4: Artist's Impression of the Church Buildings

a series of joints binding to each other through the whole royal house, and being beautified throughout with brilliant gold made the whole shrine glitter with beams of light. Round each of the sides extended twin ranges of double colonnades, in upper and lower storeys, their tops also decorated with gold. Those at the front of the house rested upon huge pillars, while those inside the front were raised under blocks plentifully decorated all round their surfaces. Three doors well placed to face the sunrise received the crowds flowing in. Facing these as the chief point of the whole was the hemisphere attached to the highest part of the royal house, ringed with twelve columns to match the number of the Apostles of the Saviour, their tops decorated with great bowls made of silver, which the emperor himself had presented to his God as a superb offering.

For those going on from there to the entrances situated at the front of the shrine, another open space awaited them. Arcades stood there on either hand, a first court and colonnade beyond, and finally the gates of the court. Beyond these, right in the middle of the open square, the porticoes forming the entrance to the whole, beautifully wrought, offered to those passing outside a striking view of what was to be seen within.

This then was the shrine which the emperor raised as a manifest testimony of the Saviour's resurrection, embellishing the whole with rich imperial decoration. He adorned it with untold beauties in innumerable dedications of gold and silver and precious stones, set in various materials. In view of their size, number and variety, to describe in detail the skilled craftsmanship which went into their manufacture would be beyond the scope of the present work.[184]

Eusebius makes no mention of the site of Christ's crucifixion, nor does he allude here to the discovery of the supposed wood of the cross that was claimed to be responsible for the identification of the tomb as being that of Jesus,[185] although he seems to do so in an earlier

---

[184] Eusebius, *Vita Constantini* 3.36-40; ET from Cameron and Hall, *Eusebius: Life of Constantine*, 136–37. On the disputed nature of the "hemisphere," see Yarnold, *Cyril of Jerusalem*, 18.

[185] For the various theories that have been advanced to explain his silence, see Louis van Tongeren, *Exaltation of the Cross: Toward the Origins of the Feast of the Cross and the Meaning of the Cross in Early Medieval Liturgy*, Liturgia Condenda 11 (Leuven: Peeters, 2000), 24–26.

speech in praise of Constantine delivered in 336 that refers to the appearance of "the saving sign," as also does the emperor himself in a letter to Macarius, bishop of Jerusalem from 312 to 335, quoted by Eusebius that mentions the "token" and "proof" of Christ's passion that had been hidden in the earth for so many years.[186] Both Cyril[187] and Egeria (37.1-3; 48.1) were certainly aware of the existence of the wood of the cross, but neither of them specifically identified the rocky outcrop that had been incorporated into the corner of Constantine's basilica as having been the site of Christ's crucifixion. It is true that the pilgrim from Bordeaux spoke of "the little hill of Golgotha" as the place where Christ had been crucified, but as both Cyril and Egeria regularly apply the name Golgotha to the whole area of the complex of ecclesiastical buildings rather than to that particular place within it, the pilgrim may not have had the rocky protuberance in mind as being the "little hill."[188]

Nevertheless, the rock featured prominently in the devotional life of the Jerusalem church. Egeria referred to it as "the Cross," an expression that has led some scholars to believe that it was not simply the rocky outcrop but that a jeweled replica or some other representation of the cross itself had been set up there,[189] a view encouraged by a particular phrase in the manuscript referring to Good Friday, "which is now standing" (see the commentary on 37.1). She spoke of the Christian congregation going "before the Cross" and "behind the Cross." The former meant assembling in the courtyard facing the

---

[186] Eusebius, *De laudibus Constantini* 9; *Vita Constantini* 3.30. On the interpretation of both references, see Yarnold, *Cyril of Jerusalem*, 12–14; Vered Shalev-Hurvitz, *Holy Sites Encircled: The Early Byzantine Concentric Churches of Jerusalem* (Oxford: Oxford University Press, 2015), 49, n. 32.

[187] In a letter written to the Emperor Constantius in 351, Cyril stated that it was found in the time of Constantine (see Yarnold, *Cyril of Jerusalem*, 69), and in his *Baptismal Catecheses* 10.19 (ET from *NPNF* 2:7, 63), he says that it is "seen among us to this day, and from this place now almost filling the whole world, by means of those who in faith take portions from it," an allusion to the many fragments of the wood that had been acquired by Christians in other places, as he also indicates in ibid. 4.10; 13.4.

[188] For the pilgrim from Bordeaux's remark, see Appendix A, p. 202; for Cyril, see, e.g., *Baptismal Catecheses* 1.1; and for Egeria, see, e.g., 25.1.

[189] See, for example, Taylor, *Christians and the Holy Places*, 122–23, 141; Yarnold, *Cyril of Jerusalem*, 21; and for a critique of the theory, Christine Milner, " 'Lignum Vitae' or 'Crux Gemmata'? The Cross of Golgotha in the Early Byzantine Period," *Byzantine and Modern Greek Studies* 20 (1996): 77–99.

rock; the latter seemingly involved gathering in and around the space on the opposite side of it, but a space so small that it is difficult to envisage many people being accommodated there or why they should want to do so, which has led some to suggest that by "behind the Cross" Egeria did not mean that space but the Martyrium itself,[190] although that seems unlikely.

Every day immediately after evening prayer the bishop led an act of devotion before the Cross, which he then immediately repeated behind the Cross (24.7). The reason for this repetition is not apparent, because on other occasions worship took place only in one of the two settings. Thus, on Sunday mornings the vigil of the resurrection ended with an act of worship before the Cross (24.11); on the octave of the Epiphany the Eucharist was celebrated there (25.11); on Holy Thursday it was offered behind the Cross (35.2); on the morning of Good Friday there was an act of worship before the Cross (36.4), the veneration of the wood of the cross took place behind the Cross (37.1), and then the principal liturgy of the day took place before the Cross (37.5); and on the Saturday of Easter Week the Eucharist was celebrated before the Cross (39.2).

The Golgotha complex must also have included a baptistery in the fourth century, as it is mentioned by the pilgrim from Bordeaux and presumably used for the Easter baptisms referred to by Egeria (38.1). Its precise location has not been identified. Most scholars place it on the south side of the buildings, but Juliette Day has followed some others in arguing for a site to the north.[191]

4. Eleona

Construction of this church on the west side of the Mount of Olives (Eleona from the Greek meaning "olive grove") was attributed by Eusebius to both Constantine and his mother Helena, the site being chosen because it was over a cave in which it was believed that Jesus

[190] See Shimon Gibson and Joan E. Taylor, *Beneath the Church of the Holy Sepulchre, Jerusalem* (London: Palestine Exploration Fund, 1994), 78–79; Shalev-Hurvitz, *Holy Sites Encircled*, 34–35.

[191] Juliette Day, *Baptism in Early Byzantine Palestine 325–451*, JLS 43 (Cambridge: Grove Books, 1999), 18–27.

used to teach when he and his disciples visited the Mount of Olives.[192] Although such a cave is not mentioned in the New Testament, the tradition known to Eusebius is corroborated by Egeria (30.3). Described as "very beautiful" by Egeria (25.11), the church was used for worship chiefly in Holy Week and Easter Week and again on the afternoon of Pentecost, when the Jerusalem church celebrated Christ's ascension, as it was also close to the hillock from which Jesus was thought to have ascended into heaven, the Imbomon (meaning "on the hillock").[193] Hence the visits to this church very often also included a further service at the Imbomon (see, for example, 31.1). Although a church was eventually built at the Imbomon as well through the patronage of the noblewoman Poemenia —it was mentioned by Jerome in 392—this seemingly had not yet happened when Egeria was there. As John Wilkinson rightly observed, she called it simply a "place" and not a church, and she did not speak of it as specially decorated at the great festivals like other churches, or as a place in which the Eucharist was celebrated.[194]

5. Other Churches

Egeria mentions three other churches in the area around Jerusalem that were not part of Constantine's building program. On the way down from the Mount of Olives to Gethsemane was what Egeria calls "a fine church" (36.1) at the place where Jesus was believed to have

---

[192] Eusebius, *Vita Constantini* 3.43: "The emperor's mother erected on the Mount of Olives the monument to the journey into heaven of the Saviour of the Universe in lofty buildings; up by the ridges at the peak of the whole mountain she raised the sacred house of the church, and constructed just there a shrine for prayer to the Saviour who chose to spend his time on that spot, since just there a true report maintains that in that cave the Saviour of the Universe initiated the members of his guild in ineffable mysteries. There also the Emperor bestowed all kinds of offerings and ornaments on the great King"; ET from Cameron and Hall, *Eusebius: Life of Constantine*, 137–38. See also Eusebius's earlier works, *Demonstratio evangelica* 6.18; *De laudibus Constantini* 9.16–17. For the tradition among many Gnostic groups of Christ handing on secret mysteries on the Mount of Olives, see Taylor, *Christians and the Holy Places*, 149.

[193] Although the pilgrim from Bordeaux understood it to be the mount of the transfiguration: see Appendix A, p. 202.

[194] Jerome, *Comm. in Zeph.* 1.15ff.; Wilkinson, 15, 171. See below, p. 82.

prayed on the night he was betrayed, and hence it formed a location for prayer and a reading of the relevant passage from Mark 14 on the night of Holy Thursday. There was also a church at Bethany about two miles east of Jerusalem in the place where it was thought that Jesus met Mary, the sister of Lazarus, whom he raised from the dead (Jn 11:29-30); this was about five hundred paces from the tomb of Lazarus itself, which was known as the Lazarium (29.4). Although both Eusebius and the pilgrim from Bordeaux refer only to Lazarus's tomb and not to another church at the Lazarium, it seems evident that a church had been built at the site by the time of Egeria's visit because she includes the Lazarium among the churches that were richly decorated at the paschal season (39.1) and speaks of it as constituting one of the places where the Eucharist was celebrated in the octave of the Epiphany (25.11). Jerome confirms the existence of the church in about 390.[195]

Although not in Jerusalem itself but over five miles south of the city, we may include here the Church of the Nativity at Bethlehem, both because it was one of the churches built by Constantine[196] and also because it played a part in the liturgical observances of the Jerusalem Christians. The belief that Jesus had been born in a cave was already well established before the fourth century, and Constantine erected an octagonal sanctuary over the supposed cave with a nave extending westward from it.[197] Unfortunately, the part of Egeria's manuscript that described the nocturnal celebration of the nativity/Epiphany at Bethlehem is missing, but from what remains (25.6) it is clear that the Christians from Jerusalem had gone there for that event and then returned to Jerusalem to keep the eight days of the festival, while the Christians of Bethlehem continued the celebrations there. Egeria also records a further visit to Bethlehem on the fortieth day after Easter, which we shall consider in the section on the liturgical year.

The Liturgies of Jerusalem

Egeria's documentation of liturgical life in late fourth-century Jerusalem is extensive but not exactly systematic. She addresses some

---

[195] Jerome, *Onomasticon, Bethania*; cf. Maraval, 268, n. 2, who believed that there was as yet no church as such there in Egeria's day.
[196] Eusebius, *Vita Constantini* 3.41-43.
[197] See Taylor, *Christians and the Holy Places*, 99–112.

topics in multiple places, and an offhand comment in one chapter frequently complements information provided elsewhere in her writings. Piecing material from various parts of the manuscript together results in a more coherent vision of the whole, but also leaves readers and scholars with questions and inconsistencies to ponder when comparing the data she reveals with that from other roughly contemporary sources. Some inevitable gaps remain where Egeria simply skips over facts we greatly desire to know in the interest of not repeating what she presumes her readers *already* know.

Perhaps one of the most remarkable things about Egeria's description of public worship in Jerusalem is the way she nearly always mentions the *missa*, the ritual dismissal at the end of every service, which apparently involved the blessing by the bishop of the catechumens, if present, and then of the faithful, after which individuals "come to his hand" (see, for example, 24.2, 6-7), a phrase probably meaning that they received a personal laying on of hands in blessing from him, rather than that they each kissed his hand.[198] This concluding rite must have taken quite some time on each occasion, which probably explains the attention Egeria gives to it. However, she sometimes uses the word *missa* in a way that seems to imply she is thinking of the complete liturgical rite rather than just this final part at points where she does not mention any other elements of the rite taking place (see, for example, 39.1; 41). Furthermore, in those two particular instances she uses the word in conjunction with the phrase "in its order," which seems for her to denote a celebration of the Eucharist (see the commentary on 3.6). Nevertheless, for the sake of consistency, we have translated it as "dismissal" every time it occurs. A similar tendency to use the word to denote a complete rite can also be seen in other Western sources: John Cassian describes the monastic night office as a *missa*,[199] and the sixth-century monastic rules of Caesarius of Arles and his successor Aurelian regularly refer to a variable number of *missae*, each made up of three readings, three prayers, and three psalms, to be repeated during the night. The word had not yet acquired the narrower sense it would have later, however, of referring exclusively to the Eucharist.

---

[198] *Pace* John F. Baldovin, *Liturgy in Ancient Jerusalem*, JLS 9 (Bramcote: Grove Books, 1989), 31, n. 4; Gingras, 89–92; Maraval, 237, n. 2. For the meaning of the terms "the catechumens" and "the faithful," see below, p. 84.

[199] John Cassian, *De inst. coen.* 3.6.

A significant feature of liturgy at Jerusalem was that it was often what is called "stational," that is, it was not always held in one place but the same service might be held each day in a different predetermined place (the Latin word *statio* meaning "standing place")—or alternatively the worshipping community itself might move from one place to another on the same occasion, performing a liturgical rite in each place as it went. These rites were often, though not always, brief commemorations of a biblical event associated with the place and centered around the reading of a relevant Scripture passage, very similar to the worship offered in the other holy places visited by Egeria elsewhere on her travels.[200] The journey from place to place would be made in procession, always with the presence of the bishop and usually accompanied by the singing of psalms or hymns, thus rivaling the public processions of the surrounding pagan culture.[201] For example, after evening prayer each day "the bishop is led from the Anastasis to the Cross with hymns," where there was prayer and blessing, but no Bible reading (24.7). Stational liturgy was not a phenomenon unique to Jerusalem at the time, as Christians in cities throughout the Roman Empire laid claim to public space after the cessation of persecution, but the abundance of holy sites in and around Jerusalem gave this trend even greater scope than in those other places.[202]

1. Daily Worship

The daily services of Jerusalem were distinctive in two principal ways. First, as *the* great center of Christian pilgrimage, Jerusalem had more people with leisure and inclination to attend them than would have been the case in other cities in the ancient Christian world; and second, the many male and female monastics who lived there regu-

---

[200] See above, pp. 53–55. The term *Verkündigungsgottesdienst* (proclamation service) was applied to such rites by Rolf Zerfass, *Die Schriftlesung im Kathedraloffizium Jerusalems*, Liturgiewissenschaftliche Quellen und Forschungen 48 (Münster: Aschendorff, 1968), 5.

[201] See, for example, Fritz Graf, *Roman Festivals in the Greek East* (Cambridge: Cambridge University Press, 2015).

[202] The definitive study of this feature of early Christian liturgy is Baldovin, *Urban Character*.

larly joined in those services with the bishop, clergy, and people, rather than observing their hours of prayer in their own communities, as seems generally to have been the case elsewhere. It is not surprising that what Egeria describes, therefore, has the appearance of a combination of what have been designated by modern scholars as "monastic" and "cathedral" patterns of daily prayer. The appellation "monastic" does not merely denote the main participants but also the particular kind of prayer, primarily meditation on Scripture, or more often specifically on the canonical psalms, usually recited in their biblical order and characterized by the alternation of psalms and silent prayer, and done by individuals alone as well as in groups. "Cathedral" prayer, on the other hand, was essentially corporate in character—the local Christian community at prayer—presided over by its ordained ministers and engaged in praise of God on behalf of all creation and intercession for the needs of the world. "Urban monastic" communities, such as those in Jerusalem, tended to have a hybrid pattern of daily worship, fusing aspects of "monastic" prayer with elements from "cathedral" liturgy.[203]

The best attested pattern of regular prayer recommended to early Christians was three times each day and once again during the night. By the middle of the third century, at least in North Africa, this counsel had increased to five times a day—morning, third, sixth, and ninth hours, and evening—as well as in the night, [204] and that expanded regimen continued to be encouraged by preachers everywhere in the fourth century.[205] In reality, however, only morning and evening were generally celebrated publicly in the churches at this period, and the observance of the other hours was usually limited to exceptionally pious individuals and to monastic groups. Although these morning and evening services were now beginning to be regarded as the spiritual fulfillment of the twice-daily sacrifices prescribed in the Old

---

[203] For more on the distinction between these fourth-century forms of daily prayer, see Paul F. Bradshaw, *Daily Prayer in the Early Church*, Alcuin Club Collections 63 (London: SPCK, 1981/New York: Oxford University Press, 1982; reprinted Eugene, OR: Wipf & Stock, 2008); idem, *Reconstructing Early Christian Worship* (London: SPCK, 2009/Collegeville, MN: Liturgical Press, 2010), 101–16; Robert F. Taft, *The Liturgy of the Hours in East and West* (Collegeville, MN: Liturgical Press, 1986, 2d ed., 1993).

[204] See Tertullian, *De or.* 24–25; Cyprian, *De Dom. orat.* 34–36.

[205] See John Chrysostom, *De Anna sermo* 4.5; *Expos. in Ps.* 133; *Hom. in Act.* 26.

Testament,[206] there is really no sign that their form at Jerusalem or elsewhere at this time was at all influenced by what had been the actual practices of the temple several centuries earlier, in spite of the valiant attempt by Wilkinson to see parallels between the Christian and Jewish evening liturgies.[207]

From Egeria's extended description of the daily services at Jerusalem in chapters 24 and 25 together with scattered references elsewhere in her writing, we have attempted to represent that pattern in tabular form in Figure 5. Interestingly, Egeria notes that some lay people, probably for the most part pious pilgrims, would be present at the "monastic" night office (24.1), celebrated each day at cockcrow (by which is meant about three hours before sunrise), as well as at the combined "cathedral" and "monastic" services during the day. The presence of pilgrims may also have been responsible for encouraging the retention of the sixth hour within the regular "cathedral" pattern throughout the year (rather than morning and evening prayer alone), as well as the addition of the ninth hour to this pattern, except for Sundays[208] and during the Easter season (which thus continued to reflect the more ancient Christian tradition of prayer just three times a day). While public prayer at the third hour was added to the weekday cycle at Jerusalem only during Lent (27.4), it is highly probable that the hour was still observed during the rest of the year by the monastic communities there, either in their own houses or individually wherever they were working.

Because the bishop generally only arrived well after each service had begun, some have concluded that he only attended the part of it for which he was required to act—the leading of the intercessions.[209] But that was not true of evening prayer, where he came and sat for further "hymns and antiphons" (24.4) before those prayers, nor of the Sunday vigil, where he was present from the beginning (24.9). This suggests the possibility that his arrival actually marked the end of the "monastic" part and the beginning of the true "cathedral" portion of each service, and that, apart from evening prayer, the other daily "cathedral" services in Jerusalem consisted only of prayer and

---

[206] See in particular Chrysostom, *Expos. in Ps.* 140.3.
[207] Wilkinson, 68–70.
[208] For details of this, see 24.8–25.4 and the accompanying commentary.
[209] See, for example, Taft, *Liturgy of the Hours*, 53.

THE CYCLE OF DAILY SERVICES AT JERUSALEM IN THE LATE FOURTH CENTURY

M = "monastic" service; C = "cathedral" service

	Sunday	Monday	Tuesday	Wednesday	Thursday	Friday	Saturday
Pre-cockcrow	M						
Cockcrow	Vigil	M	M	M	M	M	M
Morning	Eucharist	M + C	M + C	M + C	M + C	M + C	M + C or Eucharist?
Third hour		(Lent only)	(Lent only)	(Lent only)	(Lent only)	(Lent only)	(Lent only)
Sixth hour	C	M + C	M + C	M + C	M + C	M + C	M + C
Ninth hour		M + C	M + C	Word or Eucharist	M + C	Word or Eucharist	M + C
Evening	M + C	M + C	M + C	M + C	M + C	M + C	M + C

Figure 5

not of selected psalms and hymns as well as prayer, and thus had retained a more primitive character than elsewhere. For example, at Antioch, "cathedral" morning prayer as well as evening prayer already included both selected psalms and intercessions.[210]

Egeria apparently uses the terms "antiphons," "hymns," and "psalms" interchangeably, and she does not seem to intend any specific differences between them (cf. Eph 5:19; Col 3:16). Other writers at the time similarly often use the word "hymns" when speaking of the canonical psalms.[211] The use of the word "antiphons" suggests that at least some of the psalms were performed responsorially, that is, with the verses sung by a soloist and the congregation responding to each one with a repeated refrain or antiphon, and indeed Egeria confirms that this was the method employed at the Sunday vigil service (24.9). She uses the Latin verb *dico*, literally "say," to describe the performance of the hymns and psalms, which we have consistently rendered as "recite" in this context in our translation, but that certainly does not mean that these texts were not chanted.[212] She also remarks, apparently with some surprise, that the psalms chosen for all the regular daily services were always "appropriate" to the occasion (25.5). If she is to be believed, this seems to imply that the community from which she came tended instead to recite psalms in their biblical sequence in their worship—regardless of the hour, day, or season. This would be quite typical of a more monastic milieu. In Jerusalem, however, not only did "cathedral" services use the psalms very selectively, as was also the case elsewhere, but even "monastic" services did the same, including—very unusually—the night office too. She gives no indication at all, however, what any of these "appropriate" psalms and hymns might have been.

None of the regular daily services as Egeria describes them included any Scripture readings, but she reveals that on Wednesdays and Fridays in Lent the services at the ninth hour on other days were replaced

---

[210] See *Apostolic Constitutions* 2.59; John Chrysostom, *Expos. in Ps.* 140.1; *Hom. in Matt.* 11.9.

[211] See, for example, Augustine, *Retract.* 2.11; Epiphanius, *Adv. haer.* 3.23; Eusebius, *Comm. in Ps.* 60.1.

[212] See Taft, *Liturgy of the Hours*, 50; Peter Jeffery, "The Earliest Christian Chant Repertory Recovered: The Georgian Witnesses to Jerusalem Chant," *Journal of the American Musicological Society* 47 (1994): 1–39.

by a service of the word that included preaching by the bishop and presbyters (27.5). She adds that the same service also continued in the other weeks of the year, but she is not clear whether it then included the Eucharist or not (see the section on the Eucharist below). Because this particular service was held in a different location from the other services in the rest of the week—on Sion, the ancient center of the Jerusalem church, rather than in the much more recent Anastasis—it may well have represented an older tradition than the public celebration of the daily hours of prayer. Indeed, Tertullian in North Africa at the beginning of the third century already implied the existence of a similar service at the ninth hour, coinciding with the time of the conclusion of the fast on those two regular days of fasting in early Christianity.[213] That the service known to Egeria was also connected to the practice of fasting seems to be supported by the fact that it apparently did not take place if the feast day of a martyr fell on it, when presumably fasting was also suspended (except during Lent). Furthermore, during the Easter season, when there was no fasting, it was transferred to the morning (27.5; 41). According to Epiphanius, this was the practice everywhere in the fourth century.[214]

On occasion, one of the usual hours of prayer could be replaced by another service. This was particularly true of the ninth hour, which was superseded not only by the service of the word on Wednesdays and Fridays throughout the year, but also by a special service each weekday in Holy Week (32.1; 33.1; 34; 35.1; 37.8).

2. Vigils

A vigil is essentially an extended period of watching and waiting before a major liturgical event, which early Christians filled with the recitation of psalms and/or the reading of Scripture together with prayer, each such unit being repeated a varying number of times as needed. Egeria mentions several all-night vigils in the course of the liturgical year in Jerusalem, as well as some shorter ones, distinct from the regular "monastic" night office. The most frequent of this latter group was held in the early hours of every Sunday morning, and was clearly intended to be a weekly commemoration of Christ's

---

[213] Tertullian, *De ieiun.* 10.
[214] Epiphanius, *De fide* 22.

resurrection on the very day of the week and in the very place—
around the tomb—where it had happened, because it culminated in
a reading of one of the gospel narratives of Christ's passion and
resurrection (24.9-11). This reading was preceded by a group of three
psalms sung responsorially, with prayer after each psalm—one of
the most typical units of ancient vigil services, and indeed of monastic
prayer generally, in ancient Christianity. The prayer usually consisted
of a short period of silence followed by a brief collect, for which the
worshippers knelt.[215] Egeria gives no details of this practice, but it
was probably also done this way in Jerusalem. Nor does she state
which psalms were used for the vigil: normal "monastic" practice
was to use them in consecutive order from the Psalter, but as she says
that the psalms were always appropriate (25.5), that may not have
been so here.

Egeria gives no hint that the unit of three psalms was repeated at
this Sunday vigil, and so it must have been a relatively short liturgy.
But the daily "monastic" night office at Jerusalem appears to follow
an extended version of this pattern, almost certainly with multiple
groups of three psalms, each psalm being followed by prayer, which
accounts for the constant presence of deacons to pronounce the
bidding to pray and presbyters to recite each collect (24.1). Because
in other monastic communities their own members normally recited
the prayers, this provides yet another indication—like the public
celebration of prayer at the third, sixth, and ninth hours—of some
"cathedral" influence here on what had otherwise been essentially
"monastic" practice.

The weekly all-night vigil in Lent, beginning with the evening office
on Friday evening and ending on Saturday morning, had a different
structure, with alternated psalms and biblical readings (27.7-8; 29.1-
2). John Cassian mentions identical vigils being held throughout the
year in Palestinian monasticism, which implies that, as with prayer
at the third hour, the Jerusalem custom was simply a Lenten extension to the whole local church of something done year-round by its
monastic communities on their own. He provides a more detailed
description of these vigils than Egeria, with each unit consisting of

[215] See, for example, *Ps.*-Athanasius, *De virginitate* 20; Cassian, *De inst. coen.*
2.7–8.

two groups of three psalms, followed by a group of three readings. He says that the monks there divide the vigils

> into an office in three parts, that by this variety the effort may be distributed and the exhaustion of the body relieved by some agreeable relaxation. For when standing they have sung three psalms antiphonally, after this, sitting on the ground or in very low stalls, one of them repeats three psalms, while the rest respond, each psalm being assigned to one of the brethren, who succeed each other in turn; and to these they add three lessons while still sitting quietly. And so, by lessening their bodily exertion, they manage to observe their vigils with greater attention of mind.[216]

Although neither Egeria nor Cassian here explicitly mentions prayer after each psalm, it is most likely that it was done. Nor do they say how many times this unit was repeated in the course of the night, perhaps because that might vary in order to fill the period completely.

The main services added in Holy Week seemingly adopted the same vigil structure, even though they were held during the day rather than at night.[217] On the preceding Saturday, there was an afternoon gathering at the Lazarium at which "hymns and antiphons appropriate to the day and place are recited, similarly also readings all appropriate to the day are read" (29.5). Likewise, on Palm Sunday there was a gathering on Eleona from the seventh to the ninth hour at which "hymns and antiphons appropriate to that day and place are recited, similarly also readings," and at the ninth hour they moved on to the Imbomon, where until the eleventh hour "hymns and antiphons appropriate to the place and day are also recited there; similarly also readings and prayers are interspersed" (31.1). From Monday to Wednesday there were similar gatherings at the Martyrium also lasting four hours, from the ninth hour of the day until the first hour of the night (32.1), as well as a service of the same kind at the ninth hour on Good Friday (37.8). Egeria listed exactly the same elements for the longer vigil during the night from Holy Thursday to Good

---

[216] Cassian, *De inst. coen.* 3.8; ET from *NPNF* 2:11, 217.
[217] For a tabular display of these vigil services, see Figure 6, p. 93.

Friday both on Eleona and at the Imbomon (35.3-4), as well as for a
shorter daytime vigil service again on Eleona on the feast of Pentecost
(43.5). The later Armenian Lectionary places the Holy Thursday vigil
on Eleona alone and not at the Imbomon; by this time it consisted
only of psalms and not readings as well, the psalms being arranged
in five units of three psalms each, with a prayer "said with kneeling"
after each group of three psalms.[218] The only reading here was John
13:16–18:1, at midnight following the vigil.

A third vigil structure occurred at the major festivals of Epiphany
and Easter. Although the portion of Egeria's manuscript referring to
the former is missing and she supplies no details at all of the latter,
the Armenian Lectionary once more helps to fill these gaps by reveal-
ing that these vigils focused primarily on Old Testament readings
rather than on psalmody. Those at Epiphany were: Genesis 1:29–3:20;
Isaiah 7:10-18; Exodus 14:24–15:21; Micah 5:2-7; Proverbs 1:1-9; Isaiah
9:5b-7; Isaiah 11:1-9; Isaiah 35:4-8; Isaiah 40:10-17; Isaiah 42:1-8a; followed by Daniel 3:1-90, divided into three parts with nonbiblical
antiphons between each part. The Epiphany vigil seems to have been
modeled on the Easter vigil, as the first, third, and final readings are
found substantially (and more appropriately) there as the first, fifth
and final one, including the same division of that final one into three
parts with the same antiphons. Clemens Leonhard has suggested
that the motive behind the adoption of two of these Easter readings
at Epiphany may have been as much musical as theological, because
Daniel 3 is a canticle and Exodus 14 ends with one in Exodus 15.[219]
The Easter vigil readings were twelve in number, rather than the
eleven of Epiphany: Genesis 1:1–3:24; Genesis 22:1-18; Exodus 12:1-
24; Jonah 1:1–4:11; Exodus 14:24–15:21; Isaiah 60:1-13; Job 38:1-28; 2
Kings 2:1-22; Jeremiah 31:31-34; Joshua 1:1-9; Ezekiel 37:1-14; Daniel
3:1-90. While the oldest manuscripts make no reference to psalmody
at the Epiphany vigil, it appears that parts of Psalm 118 may have
been used before each of the readings at the paschal vigil. The rubrics

[218] For the Armenian Lectionary, see below, p. 87. See also Athanase Renoux,
"Liturgie de Jérusalem et lectionaries arméniens. Vigiles et année liturgique," in
La Prière des Heures, ed. Msgr. Cassien and Bernard Botte, Lex Orandi 35 (Paris:
Cerf, 1963), 167–99, here at 187–90.
[219] Clemens Leonhard, *The Jewish Pesach and the Origins of the Christian Easter*
(Berlin/New York: de Gruyter, 2006), 302, 310, n. 515.

for the latter make clear that each reading was followed by prayer with kneeling. There was also a vigil on the eve of the celebration held in Bethlehem on the fortieth day of the Easter season, whatever that festival may have been (42), but Egeria supplies no details of it.

Finally, the principal service of the day that began at noon on Good Friday for three hours has a similar form to these vigils, but this time including readings from the New Testament as well. Egeria says that the readings all concern Christ's passion, from the Psalms (evidently treated as messianic prophecy), from the Epistles and Acts, and from the gospels (37.5). She adds that hymns and prayers were also interspersed (37.6). The Armenian Lectionary, on the other hand, has a pattern of eight psalms, eight readings from the prophets, and eight readings from the New Testament, arranged in the traditional groups of three, so that each psalm is followed first by a prophetic reading and then by a New Testament reading, with a prayer said kneeling concluding the group. The last four groups also have a reading of the passion narrative from each of the four gospels in turn added to them. The late third-/early fourth-century Syrian church order, the *Didascalia Apostolorum*, describes an Easter vigil that consisted of "reading the prophets and the Gospel and the psalms" (5.19.1) and thus suggests the possibility that this pattern of vigil may have been more widely known in the region.

3. Eucharist

Egeria reveals very little about the contents or frequency of the Eucharist at Jerusalem. She describes the main Sunday morning service each week as taking place in the Martyrium rather than in the Anastasis where all the other regular daily services were held. She says that "everything is done according to the custom by which it is also done everywhere on the Lord's Day" (25.1), but of course she does not tell us what that custom was. She does not even state explicitly that it was a Eucharist, but it obviously was so, and in her later description of Pentecost she does note that the Eucharist was celebrated every Sunday morning throughout the year (43.2). Apparently, the only element in the Eucharist that was unfamiliar to her was the Jerusalem custom of the preaching of multiple sermons on a single occasion by the bishop and presbyters, as she does not comment on anything else. She also mentions later that the bishop normally sat to preach (46.4). For more detailed information about the Eucharist in Jerusalem one must rely on other sources, and especially the *Mystagogical Catecheses* usually attributed to Cyril of Jerusalem, though they may have been edited by—or even be the work of—his immediate successor, John.[220] Yet, even the *Mystagogical Catecheses* reveal nothing about the first part of the rite, the liturgy of the word.

Egeria makes no reference to a service of morning prayer preceding the Sunday Eucharist. Did the earlier resurrection vigil or the Eucharist itself substitute for it, or was it one of the things done everywhere and so did not merit a comment? The fact that she does not mention morning prayer on the feast of the Epiphany, but only the Eucharist followed by midday prayer (25.10), or morning prayer on Saturday mornings in Lent when the Eucharist was celebrated (27.8), may perhaps confirm that it was also omitted on Sundays. Moreover, because the regular daily prayer services were held in the Anastasis, if there had been a distinct morning prayer on Sundays, we might have expected it to have been there and not in the Martyrium.

Was the Eucharist also celebrated on days other than Sundays? In her description of the service of the word at the ninth hour on Wednesdays and Fridays in Lent, Egeria says that they do "everything that it is the custom to do at the ninth hour, except for the oblation" (27.6). This certainly could mean that outside Lent the service did include the Eucharist, but it is also possible that Egeria could be saying that a Eucharist at the ninth hour on these days was customary in the region from which she came, but not at all in Jerusalem. On the other hand, the celebration of the Eucharist at the conclusion of the fast on those days throughout the year would have been quite appropriate, and its suspension in Jerusalem during Lent, when people were encouraged to fast all week (28), would have been understandable, as fasting would have included fasting from the reception of Communion. During the Easter season, when there was no fasting,

[220] See Maxwell E. Johnson, *Lectures on the Christian Sacraments, Saint Cyril of Jerusalem: Greek Original and English Translation*, Popular Patristics Series (Crestwood: St Vladimir's Seminary Press, 2017). On the question of authorship, see also Alexis Doval, *Cyril of Jerusalem, Mystagogue: The Authorship of the Mystagogic Catecheses*, Patristic Monograph Series 17 (Washington, DC: Catholic University of America Press, 2001); and Juliette Day, *The Baptismal Liturgy of Jerusalem: Fourth- and Fifth-Century Evidence from Palestine, Syria and Egypt* (Aldershot/Burlington, VT: Ashgate, 2007), 11–25, 138–40.

this service was transferred to the morning (41). Whether the use of the expression "in its order" in connection with it might imply that it was eucharistic, at least in that season, see the commentary on this phrase at 3.6 (pp. 107–8). Practice outside Jerusalem appears to have been mixed. Canon 49 of the Council of Laodicea (380) directed that "during Lent bread must not be offered except on Saturday and Sunday alone," seemingly implying, like Egeria, that outside Lent it *was* offered on other days. *Apostolic Constitutions*, however, makes no reference anywhere to the Eucharist on days other than Saturday and Sunday, and certainly at Alexandria the services on Wednesday and Friday remained as services of the word throughout the year.[221]

There is similar uncertainty about the celebration of the Eucharist on Saturday mornings. Egeria states that during Lent the Eucharist was held in the Anastasis at the end of the all-night vigil there (rather than in the Martyrium) "earlier" in the morning, before sunrise, for the sake of those who had been fasting all week, who could now break their fast (27.7-9). Does that mean that during the rest of the year there was also a Eucharist on Saturday mornings, but at a somewhat later hour? The use of the comparative word "earlier" (*maturius*) seems to imply that, but Egeria was not always precise in her use of comparatives and superlatives. It is possible that it was a purely Lenten phenomenon to mark the conclusion of the week's fast, which would not have been the case in the rest of the year, especially if there had already been a Eucharist on the preceding Friday afternoon to mark the end of that day's fast. She certainly did not mention a Saturday Eucharist in her description of the regular weekly cycle of services, but neither did she mention there the existence of the Wednesday and Friday services. On the other hand, there is evidence for the regular celebration of the Eucharist on Saturdays throughout the year in other centers of Christianity at this period, which may support the supposition that it was also held on every Saturday in Jerusalem.[222]

Finally, it seems that the Eucharist was celebrated daily during the Easter octave, as Egeria says that the community assembled in the

[221] Socrates, *Hist. eccl.* 5.22.

[222] Ibid., "Although almost all the churches throughout the world celebrate the sacred mysteries on the sabbath of every week, yet the Christians of Alexandria and Rome, on account of some ancient tradition, refuse to do this"; ET from *NPNF* 2:2, 132. See also *Apostolic Constitutions* 5.20.19.

Martyrium not only on Easter Day itself and the following Sunday, but also on the Monday and Tuesday, while on Wednesday they assembled on Eleona, Thursday in the Anastasis, Friday on Sion, and Saturday "before the Cross" (39.2). As the gatherings in the Martyrium were quite obviously eucharistic, or they presumably would have been held in the Anastasis like other daily services, there is no reason to suppose that any of the others were not eucharistic too. The same appears to be the case for the octave of the Epiphany (25.10-11) and for the octave of the anniversary of the dedication of the Martyrium (49.3). It is no clearer, however, whether or not the Eucharist was preceded by morning prayer on these days than it was on Sundays.

As for where the Eucharist was celebrated, the Sunday service was always in the Martyrium, and indeed the Eucharist seems to have been celebrated elsewhere in and around Jerusalem rather than in the Martyrium for only one of three reasons: first, when it immediately followed another liturgical rite that had occurred in another place, as for example on Saturday mornings in Lent in the Anastasis at the end of an all-night vigil (27.8); second, during the octaves of the three major festivals in the year, Epiphany, Easter, and the Encaenia, when on some days it was held in a different church in the vicinity each time (25.10-11; 39.2; 49.3); and third, when in the course of the liturgical year another place was directly associated with the particular biblical event being observed on that day, as, for example, on the day of Pentecost, when it was celebrated on Sion, believed to have been the place where the Holy Spirit had descended on the disciples (43.3). Egeria states that this was the only time in the whole year when a Sunday Eucharist was celebrated somewhere other than in the Martyrium (25.6), but even then the Eucharist was also held there earlier in the morning before the second celebration on Sion (43.2).

Regarding the structure of the eucharistic rite, it has been suggested that Egeria regularly used the Latin verb *procedo* (which we have consistently translated as "assemble" in this context) as a quasi-technical term for assembling for a eucharistic-type liturgy of the word,[223] and that certainly seems to be the case, as it is used only of the services on Sundays and festivals in the Martyrium (25.1, 6; 27.3;

---

[223] See A. A. R. Bastiaensen, *Observations sur le vocabulaire liturgique dans l'Itinéraire d'Égerie*, Latinitas Christianorum primaeva 17 (Nijmegen: Dekker & Van de Vegt, 1962), 26–39; Christine Mohrmann, "Missa," *Vigiliae Christianae* 12 (1958): 67–92, here at 76ff.; Wilkinson, 179.

30.1; 39.2; 41; 43.2; 49.3), of festal Eucharists held elsewhere (25.6, 11; 26; 39.2; 49.3), and of the Wednesday and Friday services of the word on Sion, whether followed by the Eucharist or not (27.5-6; 41). It is never used for the daily prayer services in the Anastasis, nor for any of the various special services held in either the Martyrium or other locations during the year, nor even in relation to the Lenten Saturday morning Eucharist in the Anastasis, which probably did not have its own liturgy of the word but followed directly on the vigil readings. On the other hand, the verb is not entirely exclusive to that context: Egeria uses it twice of the sun rising (27.8; 37.1).

Egeria's standard term for the Eucharist, *oblatio*, "oblation," with its cognate verb, *offerre*, "offer," seems to relate to the eucharistic action proper rather than to the whole rite that included the liturgy of the word. Thus, in some instances the expression follows a reference to a preceding Old Testament reading (3.6; 4.3-4), a reading from Acts (43.3), the resurrection gospel (38.2), a full service of the word (27.6), or a longer vigil of readings (27.7-8; 29.1, 3). In other cases, what preceded is described in more vague terms: "they do what is to be done" (35.1), "they do there what is also customary with us" (38.2), and "everything also is done that is customary to do" (43.2), which seems to imply some form of liturgy of the word. It is also possible, however, that in at least some instances where there is no mention of anything preceding the "oblation" (4.8; 16.7), there might not have been a liturgy of the word at all. This seems even more likely where the reference is to the second celebration of the Eucharist following immediately after the first on Holy Thursday (35.2). Moreover, on those occasions listed above where only one reading is mentioned, we should not automatically assume that there were always other readings as well: there is no reason to suppose that as yet the Eucharist could not possibly take place unless at least an epistle and a gospel were included.

4. Christian Initiation

Egeria supplies more information about the process of preparation for baptism than she does about the Eucharist, even if she is similarly brief about the baptismal rite itself —in this case not surprisingly, as she would not have been able to witness personally what took place in the baptistery. In common with the rest of the ancient Christian world after the Council of Nicaea in 325, Easter had become the normative occasion for the celebration of the baptism of new converts, and the season of Lent was devoted to their preparation. Egeria makes no mention of baptisms taking place at any other point in the year. Those preparing for baptism were known as catechumens, from the Greek for "those being instructed," while baptized Christians were described as "the faithful." In Jerusalem catechumens submitted their names on the day before Lent began, and on Monday, the first day of Lent, there was an examination of their prior conduct (45.1-3). Only those whose sponsors vouched for their virtuous behavior then had their names formally inscribed by the bishop and were permitted to proceed. Thereafter, each weekday during Lent the candidates underwent exorcism in order to drive out any remaining traces of evil, and they also received three hours of teaching by the bishop between morning prayer and prayer at the third hour.

Egeria states that the bishop's teaching for the first five weeks covered the Scriptures, beginning with Genesis, and in the sixth and seventh weeks he expounded the Creed to them (46.2-3). A similar program is outlined in *Apostolic Constitutions* 7.39, and the book of Genesis featured prominently in the Lenten readings at Antioch.[224] Ambrose of Milan also drew moral lessons in his preaching to his baptismal candidates from the patriarchal narratives read to them in Lent.[225] There is, however, an apparent discrepancy between Egeria's testimony and Cyril of Jerusalem's *Baptismal Catecheses* from the mid-fourth century, which are only eighteen in number and focus almost exclusively (nos. 4–18) on the contents of the Creed, without a clear indication that another series of lectures on the Scriptures had preceded them. Nor would they have been sufficient to fill three hours of teaching each day. Moreover, the listing of the biblical readings used in baptismal instruction in the later Armenian Lectionary correlates very closely with those mentioned by Cyril. Various theories have been put forward to account for these disparities, including the possibility that the teaching was not really given on every single day of the week, or that Egeria was simply mistaken about what it covered, or that the additional time would have been needed to translate Cyril's words into Syriac (see 47.3-4).[226] Maxwell Johnson, however, has argued that Cyril's lectures reflect an older tradition when the final period of baptismal preparation was only three weeks in length and con-

---

[224] See Zerfass, *Die Schriftlesung im Kathedraloffizium Jerusalems*, 132–37.
[225] Ambrose, *De mysteriis* 1.1.
[226] See, for example, Baldovin, *Liturgy in Ancient Jerusalem*, 12–14.

centrated on the Creed alone.[227] Moral teaching based on the Old Testament would at that period have belonged to a prior stage of the catechumenate. Given the extent of liturgical developments in the fourth century more generally, it is certainly possible that some changes in the catechumenal process were introduced in the decades separating Cyril's *Baptismal Catecheses* and Egeria's Jerusalem journey.

At the end of those seven weeks each of the candidates was required to repeat back to the bishop the Creed they had learned (46.5-6), and they were baptized at the Easter vigil. Egeria provides no detail of this rite. As in the case of the Eucharist, one needs to turn to the *Mystagogical Catecheses* attributed to Cyril of Jerusalem for that.[228] She says simply that "the paschal vigil is done in the same way as with us," with one exception: after the newly baptized had been clothed and left the baptistery, they were led with the bishop to the Anastasis, where the bishop went inside Christ's tomb, and after one hymn had been sung, he said a prayer for them and then returned with them to the Martyrium, where the people were keeping the vigil (38.1-2). This unique postbaptismal ceremony was presumably intended to relate their initiation to the resurrection of Christ.[229]

---

[227] See Maxwell E. Johnson, "Reconciling Cyril and Egeria on the Catechetical Process in Fourth-Century Jerusalem," in *Essays in Early Eastern Initiation*, ed. Paul F. Bradshaw, JLS 8 (Bramcote: Grove Books, 1988), 18–30; Johnson, "From Three Weeks to Forty Days: Baptismal Preparation and the Origins of Lent," *Studia Liturgica* 20 (1990): 185–200 = *Living Water, Sealing Spirit: Readings on Christian Initiation*, ed. Maxwell E. Johnson (Collegeville, MN: Liturgical Press, 1995), 118–30. See also Nicholas V. Russo, "The Distribution of Cyril's *Baptismal Catecheses* and the Shape of the Catechumenate in Mid-Fourth-Century Jerusalem," in *A Living Tradition: On the Intersection of Liturgical History and Pastoral Practice*, ed. David Pitt, Stefanos Alexopoulos, and Christian McConnell (Collegeville, MN: Liturgical Press, 2012), 75–100.

[228] See n. 220 above; also Maxwell E. Johnson, "Baptismal Liturgy in Fourth-Century Jerusalem in the Light of Recent Scholarship," in *Inquiries into Eastern Christian Worship*, ed. Bert Groen, Steven Hawkes-Teeples, and Stefanos Alexopoulos, Eastern Christian Studies 12 (Leuven: Peeters, 2012), 81–98; Juliette Day, "The Catechetical Lectures of Cyril of Jerusalem: A Source for the Baptismal Liturgy of Mid-Fourth Century Jerusalem," in Paul F. Bradshaw and Juliette Day, *Further Essays in Early Eastern Initiation*, JLS 78 (Norwich: SCM-Canterbury Press, 2014), 24–56.

[229] For a critical review of Egeria's evidence concerning these postbaptismal actions, see Day, *The Baptismal Liturgy of Jerusalem*, 121–22.

During the eight days from Easter Day to the following Sunday, Egeria reports that the newly baptized continued to assemble in the mornings for an explanation of the rites in which they had just participated, but in the Anastasis rather than the Martyrium as before Easter (47.1).[230] The Christian tradition of concealing its central teachings from the uninitiated had caused catechumens who were not yet going to be baptized to be excluded from the Lenten instruction sessions.[231] Similarly, baptismal candidates were not told anything about the rites of baptism and Eucharist before they had undergone them, hence the emergence of this postbaptismal mystagogy, as it is called. The intention behind this latter development, which had also been adopted in some other places, such as Milan, but not in Antioch, was apparently to heighten the sensory and dramatic impact of the rites because they were a surprise to the candidates and so to produce a profound psychological effect on those experiencing them. Perhaps this was done in part to make up for the frequent lack of a genuine prebaptismal conversion experience as the number of Christians increased in the post-Constantinian era.[232]

The Liturgical Year in Jerusalem

Many of what later became standard elements in the liturgical year elsewhere had their roots in fourth-century Jerusalem. As in other places in the surrounding area that were associated with the biblical narratives, so too in Jerusalem growing numbers of pilgrims wanted to visit the sacred sites linked to the life and death of Jesus and, if possible, to be in those places on the very days of the year when he was said to have been there. It was inevitable, therefore, that the local

---

[230] Cyril, *Baptismal Catecheses* 18.13, confirms the Anastasis as the place of assembly for this teaching. Egeria's statement should probably not be taken literally to mean every single morning, as the preceding Eucharist on at least two days of that week, Wednesday and Friday, was at such a distance (on Eleona and Sion, respectively: see 39.2) as to make an immediate return to the Anastasis quite difficult. Moreover, there are only a total of five *Mystagogical Catecheses* for this week.

[231] 46.2; see also Cyril, *Procatechesis* 12.

[232] See Paul F. Bradshaw, "The Fourth Century: A Golden Age for Liturgy?" in *Liturgie und Ritual in der Alten Kirche*, ed. Wolfram Kinzig, Ulrich Volp, and Jochen Schmidt (Leuven: Peeters, 2011), 99–115, here at 108–12.

church would arrange liturgical commemorations in those holy places for those occasions, and thus expand the liturgical year. The visitors would then carry back to their home churches some of the ceremonies that had impressed them on their visit and attempt to reproduce them there to some extent.[233] But the traffic may not have been all one way: the pilgrims would naturally also bring with them local practices of their own, which they would expect to find in Jerusalem too, and the host church there would probably have been willing to oblige and adopt them.

While Egeria only occasionally notes the specific biblical readings that were read on the various festivals and holy days of the year, we are fortunate in having the Armenian Lectionary (hereafter AL) to assist in filling in the blanks.[234] While this early fifth-century work does not list any readings for the ordinary Sundays or weekdays in the year, it not only reproduces the readings for the festivals and commemorations of the liturgical year that were observed in Jerusalem at the time of its compilation but also notes the locations in which the various liturgies were celebrated and a number of other ritual directives. Some changes and elaboration had obviously taken place in the intervening period, but much of what it contains can reasonably be assumed to reflect the practice at the time of Egeria's visit, and consequently reference to its provisions will be made where appropriate in this Introduction and in our commentary.

Although there were some variations in the patterns of readings through the year, and particular forms for vigils and stations, in AL

[233] See, for example, Paul F. Bradshaw, "The Influence of Jerusalem on Christian Liturgy," in *Jerusalem: Its Sanctity and Centrality to Judaism, Christianity, and Islam*, ed. Lee I. Levine (New York: Continuum, 1999), 251–59. On the unique possibilities for convergence of text, time, and topography in fourth-century Jerusalem see chapter 4 of Smith, *To Take Place*, especially 88–95. On the movement of rites more generally, see Anne McGowan, "Eastern Christian Insights and Western Liturgical Reforms: Travelers, Texts, and Liturgical Luggage," in *Liturgy in Migration: From the Upper Room to Cyberspace*, ed. Teresa Berger (Collegeville, MN: Liturgical Press, 2012), 179–208.

[234] Introduction, text, and French translation in Athanase (Charles) Renoux, *Le Codex Arménien Jérusalem 121*, Patrologia Orientalis 35.1, 36.2 (Turnhout: Brepols, 1969–71); ET in Wilkinson, 175–94. For the later liturgies of Jerusalem, see Stig Simeon Frøyshov, "The Georgian Witness to the Jerusalem Liturgy: New Sources and Studies," in *Inquiries into Eastern Christian Worship*, 227–67.

regular services of the word usually comprised two or three Old
Testament readings followed by a psalm with an antiphon formed
from one of its verses. Eucharistic liturgies normally had a psalm, an
epistle, a psalm verse for the Alleluia chant, and a gospel. We have
generally included the psalms when we have listed the readings and
consequently used the ecclesiastical expression "propers" to designate the whole group, but have not added the antiphon or Alleluia
verse. Readers interested in knowing those details should consult an
edition of the whole lectionary.

1. Epiphany

The year began with Epiphany, celebrated on the night of the
equivalent of January 5–6 and focused exclusively at Jerusalem on
Christ's nativity and not, as at Alexandria and elsewhere in the Christian East, on his baptism.[235] Hence the whole Jerusalem church went
to Bethlehem to celebrate it. Unfortunately, as noted earlier in this
Introduction, the part of Egeria's diary describing that celebration is
missing, but the notes in AL indicate that there was first on January
5 a brief stational liturgy at the "place of the shepherds," with Luke
2:8-19, the angelic visit to the shepherds, being read there. Then
Matthew 1:18-25, the account of the birth of Jesus, was read in the
cave of the nativity, followed by a nocturnal vigil and Eucharist in
the Bethlehem church itself, for which the propers were Psalm 2, Titus
2:11-15, and Matthew 2:1-12, the visit of the Magi. The bishop and
the Jerusalem Christians then returned to their city to celebrate Epiphany there on January 6 and throughout its octave, with stations at
various places in and around Jerusalem (see the section below on
octaves), while the Bethlehem church kept the octave where they
were (25.7-12).

2. Lent

Early Christians everywhere called Lent "the forty" or "the fortieth," in Latin *Quadragesima*, the term Egeria uses. Modern scholars

[235] For the origins and early history of Epiphany, see Paul F. Bradshaw and
Maxwell E. Johnson, *The Origins of Feasts, Fasts and Seasons in Early Christianity*,
Alcuin Club Collections 86 (London: SPCK/Collegeville, MN: Liturgical Press,
2011), 131–51.

mostly concur with locating the origin of Lent in a forty-day season of fasting observed by the church in Egypt in imitation of Jesus's forty days in the wilderness that was not connected in any way to Easter but may have followed the commemoration of his baptism on January 6. Because this season apparently culminated in the baptism of new converts, who had been fasting with the faithful, it was adopted by other churches in the fourth century, but moved to a position such that it ended on the Thursday immediately prior to the established fast days of the Friday and Saturday before Easter, as that festival was already the preferred occasion for baptism at Rome and in North Africa.[236] Some Eastern churches, however, had already extended the pre-Easter two-day fast to six days beginning on Monday, which would later evolve into Holy Week as we know it. In an attempt to preserve that week's distinctive identity, they tended to move the forty-day Lenten season proper back one week, ending it on the Friday immediately before that final week began and thus beginning it on the Monday six weeks earlier, thus making the whole period seven rather than six weeks long.[237]

AL prescribed just such a pattern for Jerusalem in the early fifth century. Egeria claimed, however, that Jerusalem already knew a total of *eight weeks* in her day—a seven-week Lent and the six-day fast of Holy Week. Since in the East actual fasting occurred only on Monday through Friday each week and never on Saturday or Sunday, except for Holy Saturday, this would have brought the number of actual days fasted to forty-one (27.1; 46.5). Her statement has been dismissed as misinformation,[238] or as "an experiment that did not last,"[239] or as reflecting the practice of an ascetic community in Jerusalem that

---

[236] For a full account, see Nicholas V. Russo, "The Origins of Lent" (Ph.D. dissertation, University of Notre Dame, 2010); and for some recent challenges to the theory, Harald Buchinger, "On the Early History of Quadragesima: A New Look at an Old Problem and Some Proposed Solutions," in *Liturgies in East and West: Ecumenical Relevance of Early Liturgical Development*, ed. Hans Jürgen Feulner (Zurich: LIT Verlag, 2013), 99–117; and Maged S. A. Mikhail, "The Evolution of Lent in Alexandria and the Alleged Reforms of Patriarch Demetrius," in *Copts in Context: Negotiating Identity, Tradition, and Modernity*, ed. Nelly van Doorn-Harder (Columbia, SC: University of South Carolina Press, 2017), 169–180.

[237] So, for example, *Apostolic Constitutions* 5.13.

[238] A. A. Stephenson, "The Lenten Catechetical Syllabus in Fourth Century Jerusalem," *Theological Studies* 15 (1954): 103–16, here at 116.

[239] Baldovin, *Urban Character*, 92, n. 37.

began the Lenten fast one or two weeks before others did,[240] but some supporting evidence has been provided by Frans van de Paverd, who has argued that fourth-century Antioch also knew a similar eight-week Lenten pattern.[241]

In addition to the daily baptismal catechesis mentioned earlier in this Introduction, liturgical practice at Jerusalem in Lent primarily involved the addition of a public celebration of the third hour each weekday, parallel to those at the sixth and ninth hours (27.4), and an all-night vigil every Friday (27.7-8; 29.1-2), which we have discussed above in the section on vigils. Although AL does not list any readings for the Saturday or Sunday eucharistic services for the Lenten season, it does provide a complete six-week set of readings for the Wednesday and Friday afternoon services of the word on Sion (now at the tenth hour rather than the ninth hour of Egeria's day). Just two readings are normally specified for each Wednesday and three for each Friday, all from the Old Testament. The Wednesday readings are taken from Exodus and Joel, and the Friday readings from Deuteronomy, Job, and Isaiah, all in a semicontinuous fashion.[242] Why there should be this difference in the number of readings between Wednesday and Friday is not obvious. Perhaps it was to help extend the Friday service so that it really did form a continuous whole with the evening office and the all-night vigil. A psalm is also prescribed for each service, again in a semicontinuous series from Psalm 51 to Psalm 88, with one slight dislocation on the first Friday.[243]

Oddly, however, during the second week three readings each day for Monday, Tuesday, and Thursday are inserted, from the early

---

[240] Thomas J. Talley, *The Origins of the Liturgical Year* (New York: Pueblo, 1986), 172–74.

[241] Frans van de Paverd, *St. John Chrysostom, The Homilies on the Statues*, Orientalia Christiana Analecta 239 (Rome: Pontifical Oriental Institute, 1991), XXIII, 210–16, 250–54, 358, 361.

[242] Exodus was read from 1:1 to 5:3; Joel from 1:14 to the end, but omitting 2:12-20 and adding Zech 9:9-16a to fill the final week; Deuteronomy from 6:4 to 11:25, but omitting 8:2-10, 9:25-29, and 10:16–11:9; Job from 6:2 to 21:34, but omitting 7:14–9:1, 10:2b–11:20, 13:7–16:1, 18:1–19:1, and 20:1-29; and Isaiah from 40:1 to 47:4, but omitting 40:18–41:29, 42:8b–43:21, 44:9-28, and 45:14–46:2.

[243] See further M. F. Lages, "Étapes de l'évolution du Carême à Jérusalem avant le Ve siècle. Essai d'analyse structurale," *Revue des études arméniennes* 6 (1969): 67–102, here at 81–84.

chapters of 1 Samuel, Proverbs, and Jeremiah, respectively, as though beginning a whole other series for the season. These are said to be in the Anastasis rather than on Sion, and a reading of Micah 4:1-7 is also added to the Wednesday service, so that all five days have three readings. Although it has been suggested that these services may once have belonged to the first week of Lent and simply remained there when the beginning of the season was moved back one week, that would still not explain why they do not continue in the other weeks, nor why Egeria did not know of their existence. Charles Renoux proposed that they were part of a far older pattern of Lenten readings that had fallen into disuse by the time of Egeria and resurfaced only much later, but his theory has been challenged by Harald Buchinger, who sees these readings as the beginning of a later extension of the weekday services in Lent.[244]

3. Great Week

A substantial portion of Egeria's narrative is devoted to a description of the services of Holy Week, or Great Week as she called it. These observances were preceded by an afternoon visit to Bethany on the Saturday before, ending at the Lazarium, the tomb of Lazarus, whom Jesus had raised from the dead (29.3-6). Although Thomas Talley thought that this commemoration was not native to Jerusalem but had been imported and was centered around a dramatic reenactment of the raising of Lazarus (Jn 11:1-46),[245] Nicholas Russo has more recently argued that it did originate in Jerusalem after all but by the time of Egeria's visit the focus had shifted to the subsequent visit of Jesus to Bethany, when Mary anointed his feet, which was said to have taken place six days before the Passover (Jn 12:1).[246] AL prescribes John 11:55–12:11 as the gospel reading at the Lazarium.

Foundational to this week seems to be an assembly every day patterned after a vigil (see above, pp. 77–78), in most cases held in the Martyrium beginning at the ninth hour and lasting for four hours, as shown in Figure 6, where all assemblies having a vigil structure are marked by shading. It looks as though this was the oldest way

---

[244] Buchinger, "On the Early History of Quadragesima," 105–6.
[245] Talley, *Origins of the Liturgical Year*, 181–82.
[246] Russo, "Origins of Lent," 230–54.

in which the Christian community here had prepared for the Pascha at the end of the week, with adjustments to the time and place of some of the vigil services having gradually been made, as stations at places associated with the biblical events of that week were added. Even Lazarus Saturday had acquired a vigil service of this type in the afternoon (29.5). The ninth hour was probably chosen for the vigil to begin because it was the normal end of the working day and also marked the usual conclusion of a day's fasting in the rest of the year. Was the institution of this lengthy daily vigil associated with the original extension of fasting to the full week before Pascha?

On Palm Sunday the vigil began earlier, at the seventh hour on Eleona, then moved after two hours to the Imbomon for another two hours before the triumphal entry into Jerusalem was reenacted from there in a procession with palm or olive branches from the Mount of Olives to the city (31). On Monday through Wednesday the vigil was kept in the Martyrium and again lasted four hours, from the ninth hour to the first hour of the night, ending with the regular daily evening service, but held there rather than in the Anastasis and followed by a brief station in the Anastasis instead of the usual evening devotions at the Cross (32). On Thursday the vigil was moved to Eleona and the Imbomon again, but beginning later into the evening and increased in length in order to lead into a procession from there back to the city marking the significant moments of that night (35.3-4). On Good Friday the afternoon vigil remained in its normal place and time, in spite of the introduction of a passion vigil in the three hours preceding it (37.8). On Saturday there was, unusually, no service at the ninth hour, but Egeria tells us that preparations were made for the paschal vigil (38.1).

On Holy Thursday the Eucharist was celebrated twice, first in the Martyrium at the eighth hour, and then immediately again behind the Cross, at which Egeria makes the point that all received Communion and that it was the only occasion in the year when it was celebrated there (35.1-2), so there must have been some special significance attached to it. The fact that the archdeacon makes an announcement about the evening at the end of the first celebration rather than the second implies either that the latter had been added to the original pattern or that most of the congregation at the first celebration did not remain for the second, but the reason for this double celebration has been debated.

HOLY WEEK SERVICES

Vigils of psalms, readings, and prayers are marked by shading

HOUR	SATURDAY	SUNDAY	MONDAY	TUESDAY	WEDNESDAY	THURSDAY	FRIDAY	SATURDAY
6th		Usual service in Anastasis	6th hour in Anastasis	6th hour in Anastasis	6th hour in Anastasis	6th hour in Anastasis		3rd hour only; 6th hour in Anastasis
7th	Vigil at Lazarium	Vigil on Eleona					Passion vigil before the Cross	*Lucernarium?* Paschal vigil in Martyrium
8th	Vigil at Lazarium	Vigil at Imbomon				Eucharist in Martyrium		
9th		Vigil at Imbomon	Vigil in Martyrium	Vigil in Martyrium	Vigil in Martyrium			
10th	*Lucernarium* in Anastasis		Vigil in Martyrium	Vigil in Martyrium	Vigil in Martyrium	2nd Eucharist behind Cross + usual prayer, but in Anastasis	Vigil in Martyrium	
11th		Palm procession						
12th		*Lucernarium* in Anastasis						
1st		+ usual prayer at Cross	*Lucernarium* in Martyrium +usual prayer, but in Anastasis	*Lucernarium* in Martyrium + usual prayer, but in Anastasis; then station on Eleona	*Lucernarium* in Martyrium + station in Anastasis	Vigil on Eleona until 5th hour; vigil on Imbomon, 6th hour to cockcrow; Procession to city with stations	Station in Anastasis; Voluntary vigil in Anastasis	

—All morning services as usual—

Figure 6

Was it simply to accommodate an overflow congregation from the first? But the limited space behind the Cross would not easily have provided room for many people, and there must surely have been a particular reason why that specific location, never otherwise used for the Eucharist, was chosen. Talley suggested that the two may have been intended for quite different pilgrim communities that were following different chronologies of Holy Week,[247] but there is no other evidence for that. Pierre Jounel made the more promising suggestion that the first celebration had originally marked the end of the Lenten fast and the second commemorated the Last Supper.[248] Augustine certainly knew of the existence in some places of two celebrations on this day, but in his case one in the morning and the other in the evening, and he thought the reason for this was so that those who wished to bathe on that day might break their fast earlier in the day by receiving Communion.[249] AL implies that the two celebrations followed just a single liturgy of the word with propers that focused on the Last Supper (Ps 23; 1 Cor 11:23-32; Mt 26:17-30), but it moved the second celebration to before the Cross (perhaps because the courtyard there would have afforded more space than behind the Cross) and it added a third celebration on Sion with similar propers (Ps 23; 1 Cor 11:23-32; Mk 14:1-26), no doubt because that location had become associated with the Last Supper by the fifth century.

The eucharistic celebrations over, after a brief station at the Anastasis the worshippers returned home for a meal, thus breaking their fast, and then went to the cave on the Mount of Olives, where they kept the vigil from the first to the fifth hour of the night, during which Egeria says Jesus's discourse given in that very spot was read (35.2-3). AL identifies this as John 13:16–18:1, which that gospel associates with the Supper, not the Mount of Olives. At midnight they went to the Imobomon to continue the vigil, and at cockcrow they moved on to a church believed to be the site where Jesus prayed during that night (35.4–36.1). Afterward they continued on to Gethsemane for a gospel reading about the Lord's arrest, identified by AL as Matthew 26:31-56, and on into the city as dawn was breaking, ending before

[247] Talley, *Origins of the Liturgical Year*, 44–45.
[248] Pierre Jounel, "The Year," in *The Church at Prayer*, vol. 4, ed. A.-G. Martimort et al. (Collegeville, MN: Liturgical Press, 1986), 31–150, here at 48.
[249] Augustine, *Ep.* 54.4-7.

the Cross, where the account of Jesus before Pilate was read, again identified by AL as John 18:28–19:16. The bishop then sent them home with words of encouragement for a short rest before the Good Friday observances began, though Egeria records that the people made an additional station on Sion to pray at the column where the Lord was scourged (36:2–37:1).

Although this long stational vigil was obviously intended to commemorate significant moments in the passion narrative in the very places in which they were believed to have happened, it is to be noted that no attempt was made to replicate every detail of the story. The procession through the city did not seek to imitate exactly the route taken by Jesus, with a detour to the house of Caiaphas or Pilate as happened in the later AL, and there was no dramatic reenactment of the events leading up to the crucifixion. It did not even adhere closely to the timescale of the gospel events: at cockcrow the procession was only just beginning its descent from the Imbomon (36.1), whereas by that time Jesus had already been arrested and been denied by Peter.

The activity conforms, therefore, more to a liturgical style that Kenneth Stevenson many years ago labeled as "rememorative," in which biblical events were celebrated but not directly reenacted.[250] The visits to places and the readings helped to remind worshippers of the story and to bring it alive for them, but this procession did not try to reproduce every detail in the manner in which later medieval passion plays would do or even the later observance of Palm Sunday, when a live donkey or a wooden replica of one would be brought into the scene. The primary element governing the choice of what to include and what to leave out on this route seems to have been not so much their mention in the gospel accounts as the prior existence on the pilgrim trail of specific places that were already associated with those particular events. In other words, it was geography, rather than history, that shaped the initial development of this procession and indeed many of the other Holy Week rites.

On Good Friday the regular daily services appear to have been entirely suspended. In the morning there was no liturgy as such but an opportunity for people to view and venerate the wood of the cross and other relics in the space behind the Cross (37.1-3). The main

---

[250] See Kenneth Stevenson, *Jerusalem Revisited. The Liturgical Meaning of Holy Week* (Washington, DC: Pastoral Press, 1988), 9–10.

liturgy of the day was held before the Cross and lasted from the sixth to the ninth hour, taking the form of a vigil of psalms, readings, and prayers (37.4-7), culminating in the reading of the account of the death of Christ from John's Gospel. When that was over, there was a similar vigil service in the Martyrium as had been held there on Monday through Wednesday, ending with a brief liturgy in the Anastasis commemorating the burial of Jesus (37.8). A formal all-night vigil like those on the other Friday nights in Lent was not held, but Egeria reports that many people did in fact keep vigil in the Anastasis for some or all of the night, as they were able (37.9).

4. The Easter Season

Easter, known as "Pascha" by all early Christians—the same Greek word being used to designate the Jewish Passover as to denote the premier Christian festival—centered around a vigil held during some part of the night between Holy Saturday and Easter Day. Egeria provides no details of this vigil, because it was, she said, the same as at home, beyond her reference to the visit to the Anastasis by the newly baptized. After the Eucharist had been celebrated in the Martyrium at the conclusion of the vigil, however, there was a second celebration of it in the Anastasis that included the reading of one of the gospel accounts of the resurrection (38). At the end of the day after the usual evening service there was a gathering on Sion (39.4-5) to commemorate Christ's appearance to the disciples "on . . . the first day of the week" (Jn 20:19-25). The following Sunday evening the appearance eight days later (see Jn 20:26-29) was similarly commemorated (40.2).

By the end of the second century Christians had begun to extend the celebration of Easter into a season lasting for a total of fifty days, every day of which was treated like a Sunday with no fasting or kneeling for prayer,[251] and this continued to be the case in Jerusalem. In the fourth century, however, we encounter in some places a tendency to give special emphasis to the first week, from Easter Day to the following Sunday, thus creating an octave of celebration. At Jerusalem the Eucharist was celebrated each day of the octave at various places in and around the city (39.1-2; see the section below on oc-

---

[251] See further Bradshaw and Johnson, *The Origins of Feasts, Fasts, and Seasons*, 69–74.

taves). In addition to this and to the delivery each day of addresses to the newly baptized during Easter Week (see above, p. 86), there was also a daily assembly of those members of the Christian community who were willing on Eleona and at the Imbomon for psalmody and prayer before returning to the Anastasis for the usual evening service (39.3-4). For the rest of the fifty-day season, there was neither fasting nor a service at the ninth hour any day, those on Wednesdays and Fridays being relocated to the morning.

Egeria describes a special liturgy on the fortieth day, which, not surprisingly, some commentators have thought must be a commemoration of Christ's ascension, even though it took place in Bethlehem (42).[252] However, because she refers to two distinct liturgical acts on the fiftieth day as celebrating the bestowal of the Holy Spirit and Christ's ascension, respectively (see below), scholars today are generally agreed that the rite on the fortieth day was definitely not in honor of the ascension, even though they are puzzled about what it might have been. The commemoration of the slaughter of the Innocents occurs on May 18 in one manuscript of AL, which would have been the fortieth day after Easter in the year 383. Did Egeria assume that it happened on that fortieth day every year? [253]

On the fiftieth day, there were the normal Sunday services in the morning, but they finished much earlier than usual so that the people could get to Sion at the third hour to commemorate the descent of the Holy Spirit at the time and in the place where it was thought to have happened, concluding with another celebration of the Eucharist (43.1-3). Then after returning home to eat, they went up to the Imbomon to commemorate the ascension. The normal evening service was held afterward in the nearby church on Eleona, presumably because there was not time to return to the Anastasis for it, as was customary (43.4-6). That, however, was not the end of the day: they went all the way back to the Martyrium for a further liturgical rite, followed by another in the Anastasis, another at the Cross, and then back up to Sion for a final observance, ending around midnight (43.7-9). Although celebrating the ascension on the same day as the descent of the Spirit at Pentecost may seem strange to modern eyes, especially as the Acts of the Apostles states clearly that it took place after forty

---

[252] For example, Wilkinson, 78–79.
[253] Baldovin, *Urban Character*, 88–90; Talley, *Origins of the Liturgical Year*, 64.

days (Acts 1:3), it was not unknown elsewhere in fourth-century Christianity.[254]

5. Octaves

Egeria provides one of the earliest descriptions of a liturgical phenomenon that would become universal in later centuries—the prolongation of a major festival throughout the week that followed it, resulting in a total of eight days of celebration. This custom seems to have begun with Easter, possibly inspired by the duration of the Feast of Unleavened Bread that followed the Passover in Jewish practice. At Jerusalem not only Easter but two other annual festivals were augmented in this way—Epiphany and the anniversary of the dedication of the Church of the Holy Sepulcher—and in each case the daily Eucharist was stational, held in different places on some of their eight days. Unfortunately, because Egeria's manuscript breaks off before she had finished describing the arrangements for the octave of the anniversary of the dedication, and because the octave does not exist in AL, we cannot compare its locations with either of the other two octaves, beyond noting that the first two days were at the Martyrium and the third on Eleona (49.3).

EPIPHANY (25.11)		EASTER (39.2)	
Day 2	Martyrium	Monday	Martyrium
Day 3	Martyrium	Tuesday	Martyrium
Day 4	Eleona	Wednesday	Eleona
Day 5	Lazarium	Thursday	Anastasis
Day 6	Sion	Friday	Sion
Day 7	Anastasis	Saturday	Before the Cross
Day 8	Before the Cross	Sunday	Martyrium

Just as we have seen that the Epiphany vigil appears to have been modeled on the Easter vigil,[255] so too does its octave seem to be derived from that of Easter. John Baldovin has noted that it was tra-

---

[254] See Robert Cabié, *La Pentecôte: L'evolution de la Cinquantaine pascale au cours des cinq premiers siécles* (Paris: Desclée, 1965), 117–38.

[255] See above, p. 78.

ditional to go to Sion on Wednesdays and Fridays, which would account for Sion as the choice for the Friday station in the Easter octave,[256] and Eleona provides a similarly distant station for Wednesday, one that was close to the site of the ascension on the Imbomon, which would have been particularly appropriate for the Easter octave. But for some of the other days the Epiphany vigil appears to have preserved an older arrangement of the Easter stations. Thus, Baldovin suggested that the Lazarium was probably considered too far away to use during the Easter octave because of the need to return immediately to the Anastasis for the postbaptismal mystagogical catechesis,[257] and so we may surmise that once that catechesis had become established, the station was changed to the Anastasis instead and the open-air location before the Cross introduced for the Saturday station even though the Eucharist was normally held in the Anastasis on a Saturday morning, at least during Lent if not year-round. That would also explain why, according to Egeria, the Lazarium was decorated for Easter (39.1), even though it was not actually used for a service. Sunday in the Easter octave would naturally involve a return to the Martyrium, as the Sunday Eucharist was always held there, which was not necessarily so at Epiphany as the eighth day there did not always fall on a Sunday. Further minor changes in the locations were also made in AL, including the introduction of the use on the second day of both octaves of the martyrium of St. Stephen, built by Melania the Younger in 439.[258]

6. *Other Festivals*

Apart from a very brief reference to fasting on a Wednesday or Friday being suspended if a martyr's day happened to fall on one of them, except if it were during Lent (27.5), Egeria makes no other mention of the existence of saints' days in the annual Jerusalem calendar, so we do not know how many such days there were. AL,

---

[256] Baldovin, *Urban Character*, 94.

[257] Ibid., 94–95.

[258] For a detailed study of the development of this day in honor of Stephen and its relation to the feast of Stephen on December 27, see Hugo Méndez, "Stephen the Martyr (Acts VI–VIII) in the Early Jerusalem Lectionary System," *Journal of Ecclesiastical History* 68 (2017): 22–39.

however, lists a large number of saints' days and other festivals, including the commemoration of some major Old Testament figures: Peter Abshelama, martyr (Jan 11); Antony, hermit (Jan 17); the Emperor Theodosius (Jan 19); the forty martyrs of Sebaste (Mar 9); Cyril, bishop of Jerusalem (Mar 18); John, bishop of Jerusalem (Mar 29); Jeremiah (May 1); Apparition of the Holy Cross (May 7); Holy Innocents (May 9 or 18); the Emperor Constantine (May 22); the prophet Zechariah (June 10); the prophet Elisha (June 14); the Ark of the Covenant (July 2); the prophet Isaiah (July 6); the Maccabees (Aug 1); the Virgin Mary (Aug 15); the apostle Thomas (Aug 23); John the Baptist (Aug 29); dedication of the holy places at Jerusalem (Sep 13); the apostle Philip (Nov 15); the apostle Andrew (Nov 30); Jacob and King David (Dec 25); Stephen, protomartyr (Dec 27); the apostles Paul and Peter (Dec 28); the apostles James and John (Dec 29).[259]

Clearly, at least several of these must have been added after Egeria's time, as their deaths had not occurred by then (Theodosius, Cyril, and John of Jerusalem), and it is likely that some others were also later additions. Although, therefore, many of the other days must have been celebrated at Jerusalem in the late fourth century, the only one of which we have absolute certainty is the anniversary of the dedication of what AL calls "the holy places at Jerusalem," the Martyrium and the Anastasis, on September 13, known as the Encaenia ("Dedication"). Both the word and the concept were apparently taken over from the feast of the dedication of the Jerusalem Temple (see 1 Kgs 8; 2 Chr 7). According to Michael Fraser, the feast was designed as a Christian interpretation of the Jewish Feast of Tabernacles,[260] in conjunction with which the original dedication of the temple had taken place. It has been suggested that Constantine chose September 13 for the dedication because it was the date of the dedication of the temple of Jupiter on the Capitoline hill in Rome,[261] and the Martyrium

[259] See further Harald Buchinger, "Das Jerusalemer Sanctorale: Zu Stand und Aufgaben der Forschung," in *A Cloud of Witnesses: The Cult of Saints in Past and Present*, ed. Marcel Barnard, Paul Post, and Els Rose, Liturgia Condenda 18 (Leuven: Peeters, 2005), 97–128.

[260] Michael Fraser, "The Feast of the Encaenia in the Fourth Century and in the Ancient Liturgical Sources of Jerusalem" (Ph.D. dissertation, Durham University, 1995); accessible at www.encaenia.org.

[261] Anton Baumstark, *Comparative Liturgy* (London: Mowbray, 1958), 183.

was built over a shrine to Jupiter. Egeria reported that it was also the anniversary of the day on which the cross of Christ had been found, and it was obviously accorded equal status with Epiphany and Easter, with an octave of celebration and huge crowds gathering there from other provinces for it (48–49).

TRANSLATION AND COMMENTARY

1 ¹ . . . were shown according to the Scriptures. Meanwhile, as we journeyed, we arrived at a certain place where the mountains through which we were going opened up and made an immense valley, huge, very flat, and quite beautiful, and across the valley appeared the holy mountain of God, Sinai. This place where the mountains opened up is next to that place in which are the "Graves of Lust." ²When we came into that place, those holy guides who

1 1. In its present incomplete state, the manuscript begins partway through a sentence. For what might have preceded this, see the Introduction, pp. 15–19. The valley that Egeria entered was the Wadi el Rahah, "Valley of Rest," and what she would have seen would have been Jebel Sufsafa, its peak about 7,100 feet above sea level, which would have obscured the view of Jebel Musa, literally "Mount Moses," behind it, rising to about 7,500 feet, which had become identified with the biblical Sinai during the fourth century. What are called the "Graves of Lust" were being identified with *Kibroth Hattaavah* of Num 11:34, where the Israelites were buried who had lusted after the fleshpots of Egypt and consequently died of a plague. These large stones were possibly ancient tombs, although probably not of the wandering Israelites. Gingras, 162, n. 5, identified this as an example of the transposition by guides to the neighborhood of Sinai of a site that should have been far away, either an innocent mistake or a calculated effort to boost the local tourist/pilgrim economy. On rival claims to holy sites, see the Introduction, p. 47, n. 146. And for more on the topography and history of the Sinai peninsula in general and Christian appropriation and development of sites within it, see the introduction in Daniel F. Caner, *History and Hagiography from the Late Antique Sinai*, Translated Texts for Historians 53 (Liverpool: Liverpool University Press, 2010), especially 17–39.
2. The "holy guides" would have been monks and possibly some clergy as well (see 7.2; 11.3), a not unusual arrangement, especially for female religious:

were with us reminded us, saying, "The custom is that prayer should be made here by those who come when the mountain of God is first seen from this place"; as we also did. From that place to the mountain of God was about four miles altogether across that huge valley that I mentioned.

2 ¹The valley is very huge, lying under the side of the mountain of God, and was, as far as we could estimate by looking or they said, about sixteen miles in length and they claimed was four miles in width. So we had to cross this valley in order that we could reach the mountain. ²This is the huge and very flat valley in which the children of Israel stayed on those days when holy Moses ascended the mountain of God and was there forty days and forty nights. This is the valley in which the calf was made, the place of which is shown to this day; for a great stone stands fixed there in that place. So this is the same valley at the head of which is that place where, when holy Moses was feeding his father-in-law's flocks, God spoke to him again from the burning bush.

³And because our route was that we should first ascend the mountain of God, because the ascent was better from the direction

---

see the Introduction, p. 29, n. 88. A Roman mile measured 5,000 feet (1,000 paces of five feet each), i.e., a little shorter than a U.K./U.S. mile. On worship in the holy places, see the Introduction, pp. 53–57.

2 1. Sixteen miles exaggerates the length greatly, and could only come near to being the case if the lengths of other valleys to which it was conjoined were added. Wilkinson, 107, n. 6, suggested that this may be something Egeria had heard her guides say; Caner, *History and Hagiography*, 218, n. 43, similarly proposes that Egeria may have estimated the valley's length herself based on information she was given about its width. The Wadi el Rahah proper is only about half a mile at its widest point, but she may be including in its width the Wadi el Deir, which extends from that valley at a right angle and is nearly four miles from end to end.

2. The references are to Ex 19:2; 24:18; 32:1-6; 3:1–4:18. When Egeria says that God spoke "again" from the burning bush, she is reproducing that word from the LXX of Ex 3:15 and 4:6, or more probably from the Old Latin translation of it.

3. In the sixth century the monastery of St. Catherine was built near the site of the burning bush. "Desire" is a concept Egeria invokes frequently, often, as here, in reference to seeing certain places or following a particular route; sometimes it is specifically identified as one fulfilled by God: see, e.g., 3.2; 16.4; 23.5. This is one of only a few occasions on which she explicitly refers

we were coming, and then from there descend to the head of the valley, that is, where the bush was, because the descent from the mountain of God was better from there, thus this was agreed, that having seen everything we desired, descending from the mountain of God, we should come to where the bush is, and return from there to the route right through the middle of that valley, where it extends in length, with the men of God who were showing us each of the places that are in Scripture throughout that valley; as was also done.

⁴So, as we went from that place where, on coming from Pharan, we had made our prayer, our route was that we should cross through the middle of the head of that valley and so turn to the mountain of God. ⁵The mountain itself appears from around to be singular, but when you reach it, there are more, but the whole is called the mountain of God, but that particular one on the summit of which the glory of God descended, as it is written, is in the middle of them all. ⁶And whereas all these that are around are so very high as I think I never saw, yet that middle one, on which the glory of God descended, is so much taller than all those that, when we had gone up it, absolutely all those mountains that we had perceived as very high were so far below us as if they were very little hills. ⁷This certainly is quite marvelous and without

to "men" or "men of God" rather than just to "holy ones" in the masculine plural: see also 4.6; 5.11. In other contexts "man of God" seems to have had a particular meaning for her, over and above "holy one," as indicating someone of extraordinary renown or with a special reputation for holiness: see 9.1; 20.2, 6.

4. Pharan, or Paran, the modern Feiran, was a town built at an oasis in the Wadi Feiran about thirty-one miles from Mount Sinai.

5. Egeria explains that, when approaching, there appears to be only one mountain, but actually it is a range made up of several peaks. The biblical references to the descent of God's glory on Sinai are Ex 19:18-20; 24:16.

6. In fact, Egeria's impression here and at 3.8 was mistaken, as it was not actually the highest peak in the mountain range: Jebel Katharina was over 1,100 feet higher. Maraval, 127, n. 1, suggested that its relative isolation could create the illusion to a climber that it was higher.

7. The Latin phrase *de contra* is translated literally here as "from the other side," but is rendered as "at a distance" by Gingras, 166, n. 20, and as "facing you" by Wilkinson, 108, n. 6. Although "brothers" can be used simply to

God's grace I think it would not be, that, whereas the middle one, which is properly called Sinai, that is, on which the glory of the Lord descended, is taller than them all, yet it cannot be seen unless you come to the very foot of it, but before you go up it; for afterward, having fulfilled your desire, you come down from there and see it from the other side, which it is not possible to do before you go up. Before we arrived at the mountain of God, I had already known this from what the brothers reported, and after I arrived there, I knew that it was definitely so.

3 ¹So we reached the mountain late on the Sabbath, and arriving at some monastic cells, the monks who lived there received us there very kindly, affording us every kindness; for there is also a church there with a presbyter. So we stayed there that night, and from there early on the Lord's Day we began to ascend each of the mountains with that presbyter and the monks who lived there. The mountains are ascended with immense labor, because you cannot go up them very slowly by going round, in a spiral as we say, but you go completely straight up as if by a wall and it is necessary to descend straight down each of those mountains until you arrive at the very foot of that middle one, which is properly Sinai.

²So, by the will of Christ our God and helped by the prayers of the holy ones who were accompanying [us], and with great labor,

---

refer to fellow Christians, as apparently in 47.4, here it probably means the monks guiding her, one of the earliest examples of its use in that sense. She has to clarify that she does mean monk when she uses it in 10.3; 15.3; 16.2.

3 1. "Sabbath" is the standard early Christian name for Saturday, the seventh day of the week: see Gen 2:2-3. The Latin terms rendered here as "kindly" and "kindness" had become specialized among Christians to describe the hospitality shown to travelers: see also 5.10; 11.1; and Gingras, 167, n. 24. Egeria and her companions probably stayed in some sort of guest house attached to the monastic community. This is the first of four churches with presbyters in the vicinity of Sinai that she mentions (see 3.4; 4.1, 6), the main purpose of which must have been to minister to the monks living in their cells nearby, as most monks at this time would not have been ordained clergy. The word "spiral" here is the Latin word for a snail, with this secondary meaning no doubt arising from its shape.

2. The reference to the necessity to go on foot indicates that Egeria generally rode during her journeys, presumably on a donkey or mule, or possibly on a camel across desert regions; see also 7.7; 11.4; 14.1. For "the fourth hour," see the Preface, p. vii, on the Roman divisions of the day. "When the mountain smoked" is a reference to Ex 19:18.

it was necessary for me to ascend on foot because it was not possible to ascend in the saddle (however, the labor itself was not felt, but the labor was partly not felt because I saw the desire that I had being fulfilled by God's will), at the fourth hour then we arrived at the summit of the holy mountain of God, Sinai, where the Law was given, that is, at the place where the glory of the Lord descended on that day when the mountain smoked. ³So in that place there is now a church, not large because the place itself, that is, the summit of the mountain, is not very large, but the church has great grace.

⁴So, when by God's will we had reached that summit and arrived at the door of that church, behold, a presbyter who was assigned to that church, coming from his monastic cell, met [us], a healthy old person and a monk from his early life and, as they say here, an ascetic and—what more [shall I say]?—one who was worthy to be in that place. Other presbyters also met [us], as well as all the monks who lived there near that mountain, that is, those who were not hindered either by age or by infirmity. ⁵Indeed, no one lives on the summit of that middle mountain, for nothing is there other than the church alone and the cave where holy Moses was.

⁶When everything from the book of Moses had been read in that place and the oblation had been made in its order with us

---

3. This church, the second at Sinai that Egeria mentions (see 3.1), had been built by the monk Julian Saba (d. 367), according to Theodoret, *Hist. eccl.* 2.13.
4. Egeria uses this local term "ascetic" six times to describe a particular category of monk: see also 10.9; 16.5; 20.5, 11, 13. In 20.5 it is applied to those "who live in solitude," but her other uses indicate that cannot have been the defining characteristic of an ascetic as far as she was concerned. That more than one presbyter was present here, in contrast to the other churches that she visited in the area, seems to imply that they had gathered from the churches around to celebrate the regular Sunday liturgy together at this sacred site on the summit of Sinai (see 3.6).
5. For the cave, see Ex 33:22. It was also mentioned by Theodoret, *Hist. eccl.* 2.13. On the custom forbidding overnight stays on the summit of Mount Sinai, see Caner, *History and Hagiography*, 20–21, 63–66.
6. By "everything from the book of Moses," Egeria means all of the passages in Exodus relevant to that place. The "oblation" is her standard term for the Eucharist: see the Introduction, p. 83. She uses the phrase "in its order" seven times altogether: see also 26; 39.1 ("in their order"); 41; 42; and 43.3 (twice). In every case it is clearly in connection with a celebration of the Eucharist, except for 41 where there might have been a liturgy of the word alone; but

receiving Communion at it, as we were leaving the church the presbyters gave us *eulogiae* from that place, that is, of fruits that grow on that mountain. For although the holy mountain of Sinai itself is completely rocky so that it has no bushes, yet, down near the foot of those mountains, that is, either around the one that is in the middle or around those that are in the vicinity, there is a small area of land; the holy monks in their diligence plant little trees and set up orchards and vegetable plots, and next to their monastic cells; they may seem as if they are gathering some fruits from the soil of the mountain itself, but they have produced them with their own hands.

⁷Thus, after we had received Communion here and those holy ones had given us *eulogiae* and we had come outside the door of the church, then I began to ask them to show us various places. Then straightaway those holy ones were gracious enough to show us various places. For they showed us that cave where holy Moses was when he had ascended the mountain of God a second time that he might receive the tablets again, after he had broken the earlier ones when the people sinned; and they were gracious enough to show us the other places that we desired or that they themselves knew better.

⁸But I want you to know, ladies, revered sisters, that from that place where we were standing, that is, around the walls of the

---

does the application of this phrase there suggest that it was actually a Eucharist? *Eulogiae*, literally "blessings," is a Greek term commonly used for food items that have been offered and blessed at the Eucharist, but could also be used to denote gifts, souvenirs, or tokens received by pilgrims: see also 11.1; 15.6; 21.3; and Daniel F. Caner, "Towards a Miraculous Economy: Christian Gifts and Material Blessings in Late Antiquity," *Journal of Early Christian Studies* 14 (2006): 329–77.

7. The biblical references are to Ex 33:22; 34:1-28; and 32:19.

8. "Ladies, revered sisters" is one of several forms that Egeria uses to address the recipients of her writing: see 12.7; 19.19; 20.5; 23.10; 46.1, 4; and also 5.8 for an expression in the third person. The term "sisters" does not necessarily mean they were members of a religious order: like "brothers" (see the commentary on 2.7), it was also commonly used to denote fellow Christians as well as blood relatives. On the relative heights of the mountains, see the commentary on 2.6. Maraval, 136, n. 1, plausibly suggested that her judgment can be explained by her enthusiasm for the sanctity of the place and the fact

church, that is, from the summit of the middle mountain itself, those mountains that at first we could hardly ascend seemed so far below us next to the middle one on which we were standing, as if they were little hills, when, however, they were so immense that I thought I had not seen any higher, except that this middle one exceeded them by far. From there we saw Egypt and Palestine and the Red Sea and the Parthenian Sea, which leads to Alexandria, as well as the immense territory of the Saracens, so far below us that it could hardly be believed; but those holy ones pointed out each of them to us.

4 ¹So, having fulfilled every desire for which we had hastened to ascend, we began also to descend from the summit of the mountain of God to which we had ascended, to another mountain that adjoined it; the place is called "on Horeb," for a church is there. ²For this place is Horeb, where the holy prophet Elijah was when he fled from the face of King Ahab, where God spoke to him, saying, "What [are] you [doing] here, Elijah?" as it is written in the books of the Kingdoms. For the cave where holy Elijah lay hidden is also shown there today in front of the door of the church that is there; a stone altar that holy Elijah set up to make an offering to God is also shown there, as also the holy ones were gracious enough to show us each place.

---

that she had never made such an ascent before. The Parthenian Sea referred to part of the eastern Mediterranean Sea, although it would not really have been visible from there, and perhaps her reference at the end to her guides having pointed out those distant sights is an indication that she could not actually see them herself. The Saracens were nomads in the Syro-Arabian desert; see Caner, *History and Hagiography*, 39–51, for a sophisticated assessment of their presence on Rome's eastern frontier.

4 1. "On Horeb" is a literal rendering of the LXX of Ex 17:6. Wilkinson, 111, n. 2, suggested that this and similar expressions were used to denote the name of churches: see also 13.4.

2. The quotation is from 1 Kings 19:9. The books of Samuel and Kings are known as "the books of the Kingdoms" in the LXX and in some Old Latin versions, no doubt including one with which Egeria was familiar. The abbreviated form that Egeria quotes is a literal rendering of the LXX text, and presumably also of the Latin version that she knew. The cave is mentioned in 1 Kings 19:9, 13. No altar is mentioned there, though a stone altar does feature in 1 Kings 18:32.

[3]So we made both the oblation there and most earnest prayer, and that passage from the book of the Kingdoms was read; for I had always desired very greatly for us that, wherever we came, the [relevant] passage from the book should always be read. [4]So, when the oblation had been made there, we then traveled to another place not far from there shown us by the presbyters and monks, that is, to that place where Aaron had stayed with seventy elders when holy Moses had been receiving from the Lord the Law for the children of Israel. So in that place, although it is not roofed, yet there is a huge round rock that has a flat surface on top of it, on which those holy ones are said to have stood; for there in the middle there is, as it were, an altar made of stones. So, that passage from the book of Moses was read there and one psalm appropriate to the place was recited; and then having made prayer, we descended from there.

[5]Behold, it began to be about the eighth hour and three miles still remained to us before we could leave those mountains that we had entered late on the previous day; but we did not have to go out on the same side as we had entered, as I said above, because it was necessary for us to journey past all the holy places and see whatever monastic cells were there and so go out at the head of that valley, which I mentioned above, that is, of this valley that

---

3. Note that Egeria understands the Eucharist to be offered by the whole congregation and not by the ordained minister alone. This was a second celebration in which she participated on the same day, although in a different church, and she does not say that she received Communion again. The "book" to which she refers was of course the Bible. As she appears to have controlled the choice of reading, it is possible that this was a special celebration of the Eucharist in response to the request of the visitors and not a regularly scheduled one that they happened to attend, or alternatively that a formal eucharistic lectionary had not yet developed and so there was still flexibility in the choice of readings: see also the Introduction, p. 56.
4. The reference is to Ex 24:9–14. Gingras, 173, n. 54, followed some others in accepting an emendation of the Latin word translated here as "roofed" (*tectum*) and rendered it as *lectum*, "read." He then translated it as "mentioned in Scripture," but the original makes perfect sense: a building had not yet been erected on the site. The altar made of stones may perhaps be an allusion to Ex 24:4. On worship in the holy places, see the Introduction, pp. 53–57.
5. The route back would have been via the Wadi el Deir.

lies beneath the mountain of God. ⁶It was necessary for us to come out at the head of the valley for this reason: because there were there very many cells of holy men and a church in that place where the bush is; the bush is alive down to today and produces shoots.

⁷Thus, having descended the mountain of God, we arrived at the bush at about the tenth hour. This [is] the bush that I mentioned above, from which the Lord spoke to Moses in the fire, which is in that place where there are very many monastic cells and a church at the head of the valley. In front of that church is a very pleasant garden having excellent water in abundance, and in this garden is the bush. ⁸The place is also shown near there where holy Moses stood when God said to him, "Loosen the fastening of your shoe," and the rest. And when we had arrived in that place, it was already the tenth hour, and for that reason, because it was already late, we were not able to make the oblation. But prayer was made in the church as well as in the garden at the bush; that passage from the book of Moses was also read according to the custom; and so, because it was late, we ate at a place in the garden in front of the bush with the holy ones; and so we made our stay there. And the next day, waking early, we asked the presbyters that the oblation also be made there; as was also done.

6. This is the fourth church mentioned by Egeria in the vicinity of Sinai: see the commentary on 3.1. This is another of the few occasions where Egeria explicitly refers to "men" or "men of God" rather than just to "holy ones" in the masculine plural: see also 2.3; 5.11; 20.6.

7. This spring of water and its garden were later enclosed within the sixth-century fortified monastery of St. Catherine.

8. The biblical reference is to Ex 3:5, which reads, "Put off your shoes from your feet." Egeria may be quoting from a form of the Old Latin of this verse or of Acts 7:33, or she may be confusing it with references to Jesus's footwear in Mk 1:17, Lk 3:16, or Jn 1:27. Something must have prevented a celebration of the Eucharist late in the day—perhaps because no presbyter was able or willing to preside, perhaps because it was after evening prayer—but that it was possible to have a Eucharist on the next day confirms that it was not restricted to Sundays in these places, but might happen when requested by visitors, as is also the case in 16.7. On worship in the holy places, see the Introduction, pp. 53–57. The Latin word we have rendered literally as "at a place" (*locum*) has been variously translated by others, Maraval, 142, n. 2, opting for "immediately."

5 ¹And because our route was such that we should go through the middle of that valley where it extends in length (that is, the valley that I mentioned above, where the children of Israel had stayed while Moses ascended the mountain of God and descended), therefore the holy ones constantly pointed out to us various places when we came through the whole valley. ²For at the very head of the valley where we had stayed and saw that bush from which God spoke to holy Moses in the fire, we also saw that place where holy Moses stood before the bush when God said to him, "Loosen the fastening of your shoe; for the place where you are standing is holy ground."

³And thus, when we set out from the bush, they began constantly to show us the rest of the places. For they also pointed out the place where the camps of the children of Israel were on those days when Moses was on the mountain. They also pointed out the place where that calf was made; for in that place a great stone is fixed down to this day. ⁴Also as we went, we saw from the other side the summit of the mountain that looks over the whole valley; from that place holy Moses saw the children of Israel dancing in those days when they had made the calf. They also showed a huge rock in that place where holy Moses descended with Joshua, son of Nun; on this rock in anger he broke the tablets that he was carrying. ⁵They also showed how throughout the valley each of them had their dwellings, the foundations of which are still visible down to this day, and how they were a stone circle. They also showed the place where holy Moses, having returned from the mountain, ordered the children of Israel to run "from gate to gate."

5 1. The reference to "above" is to 2.2.
2. For this quotation from Ex 3:5, see the commentary on 4.8.
3. The biblical references are to Ex 19:2; 32:1-4. Probably the "great stone" was understood to have been the altar that Aaron built before the calf (Ex 32:5).
4. For "from the other side," see the commentary on 2.7. The biblical reference is to Ex 32:17-19, but it does not mention a rock, nor does the reference to the incident in Deut 9:15-17. No doubt the desire of pilgrims to see tangible remains of biblical events encouraged the identification of physical features with those events.
5. The quotation is from Ex 32:27.

⁶Then they showed us the place where the calf that Aaron had made for them was burned at the bidding of holy Moses. Then they showed that stream from which holy Moses made the children of Israel drink, as it is written in Exodus. ⁷They also showed that place where the seventy men received of Moses's spirit. Then they showed the place where the children of Israel had lust for food. For they also showed us that place which is called "The Burning," because part of the camp was burned, then when holy Moses prayed, the fire ceased. ⁸They also showed that place where it rained manna and quails on them. Thus all the things that are written in the holy books of Moses as having been done in that place, that is, in that valley that I said lay below the mountain of God, that is, holy Sinai, were shown to us. It has been enough to write all these things one by one because so many could not be retained; but when your affection reads the holy books of Moses, you will perceive more accurately everything that was done there.

⁹This is the valley where the Passover was celebrated when a year had been completed after the departure of the children of Israel from the land of Egypt, because in that valley [the children of] Israel stayed for some time, that is, while holy Moses ascended the mountain of God and descended the first time and again; and then they stayed there for a time while the tabernacle and everything that had been shown on the mountain of God was made. For that place was also shown to us in which the tabernacle was first set up [by] Moses and all things completed that God on the

---

6. The biblical reference is probably to Ex 32:20, where water (but not a stream) is mentioned, or possibly to Ex 17:6, where Moses struck the rock at Rephidim, the mention of the "rock at Horeb" in that verse perhaps contributing to the transposition of location.

7. The biblical references are to Num 11:24-25; 11:1-4. These events occurred long after the Israelites had left Sinai: another example of transposition; see the commentary on 1.1.

8. The biblical reference appears to be to the same chapter, Num 11:9, 31, or possibly to Ex 16:13-15. The "books of Moses" are the first five books of the Old Testament, traditionally believed to have been written by him. "Your affection" is a term Egeria used repeatedly for her addressees (7.3; 17.2; 20.13; 23.10, twice; 24.1); see also the commentary on 3.8 for other forms of familiar address.

9. The biblical references are to Num 9:1-5; Ex 40:1-33.

mountain had ordered Moses that they be made. [10]We also saw at the end of that valley the "Graves of Lust" in that place in which we then returned to our route, this is, where leaving that large valley, we reentered the road by which we had come between those mountains which I spoke about above. For also on that day we came to the rest of those very holy monks who, through age or infirmity, were not able to meet on the mountain of God to make the oblation, but who were gracious enough to receive us very kindly when we arrived at their monastic cells.

[11]Thus, having seen all the holy places that we desired as well as all the places that the children of Israel had reached in going to and from the mountain of God, having also seen the holy men who lived there, in the name of God we returned to Pharan. [12]And although I ought always to give thanks to God for all things— I am not speaking of the many such things that he has been gracious enough to bestow on me, unworthy and undeserving, that I should journey through all the places that I did not deserve—yet I cannot sufficiently give thanks for all those holy ones who were gracious enough to receive my unimportance in their monastic cells with a willing mind or to lead me surely through all the places that I was always searching for according to the holy Scriptures. Very many of those holy ones who lived on the mountain of God or around that mountain, those, however, who were stronger in body, were gracious enough to lead us as far as Pharan.

6 [1]Thus, when we had arrived at Pharan, which is thirty-five miles from the mountain of God, it was necessary for us to stay there to rest for two days. On the third day, hastening from there, we

10. For the "Graves of Lust," see 1.1, which is where Egeria "spoke about" coming between the mountains. For "kindly," see the commentary on 3.1.
11. Egeria frequently inserts "in the name of God" or "in the name of Christ our God" into her narrative (9.7; 12.11; 17.1; 18.1, 2, 3; 19.2; 21.5; 23.5, 6, 10; 46.6). This is another of the few occasions on which she explicitly refers to "men" or "men of God" rather than just "holy ones" in the masculine plural: see also 2.3; 4.6; 20.6. For Pharan, see 2.4.
12. Similar expressions of unworthiness and gratitude to that here can be found in, e.g., 16.4 and 23.8-10, and may be inspired by literary convention as much as by personal sentiment. Egeria now returns to Pharan by the same route by which she had come.
6 1. For Pharan, see 2.4 above. Gingras, 178, n. 83, translated "hastening from there" as "after an early morning departure." Staging posts were set a day's

then came to a staging post, that is, in the desert of Pharan, where we had also stayed when going, as I also said above. Then on the next day, taking on water and going from there a little farther through the mountains, we arrived at a staging post that was beside the sea, that is, in that place where one comes out from between the mountains and then begins to travel entirely beside the sea, but beside the sea in such a way that at times the waves strike the feet of the animals, at other times one travels through the desert a hundred or two hundred paces or sometimes even more than five hundred paces from the sea; for a road does not exist there at all, but it is entirely desert sands. [2]The Pharanites, who are accustomed to travel there with their camels, put markers for themselves from place to place, and they head for these markers and so travel by day. But at night the camels turn toward the markers. And what more [shall I say]? The Pharanites travel more securely and safely in that place by night from familiarity than other people can travel in places where there is a clear road.

[3]So, on returning, we came out from between the mountains in the same place at which we had entered into the mountains when going, and thus then turned toward the sea. The children of Israel returning from the mountain of God, Sinai, also returned to this place by the way that they had gone, that is, to the place where we came out from between the mountains and then joined ourselves to the Red Sea; and from there we retraced our route by which we had come, but from the same place the children of Israel traveled on their route, as it is written in the books of holy Moses. [4]We returned to Clysma by the same route and the same staging

---

journey apart and commonly provided overnight accommodations for travelers. When Egeria speaks of having "said above" about the staging post, that must have been in the missing part of the manuscript.
2. Pliny the Elder, *Hist. nat.* 6.167, reported that one of the routes connecting the Mediterranean to the Red Sea from Pelusium across the sands was only marked by reeds fixed in the earth, as the wind effaced all traces of footsteps.
3. The reference to the Israelites' journey is to Num 10:12–12:16, where it is said that they went from Sinai to the desert of Pharan. Gingras, 179, n. 87, observed that this biblical "desert of Pharan" referred to the northern half of the Sinai peninsula and not to this area where Egeria was.
4. Clysma, a little to the north of modern Suez, was—according to the tradition at the time—the place where the Israelites had crossed the Red Sea.

posts by which we had gone. When we came to Clysma, it was then necessary for us then to rest there also, because we had made a very sandy journey through the desert.

7 ¹Although I had indeed already known the land of Goshen, that is, when I was first in Egypt, yet so that I might look at all the places that the children of Israel had reached on their way when leaving Rameses until they arrived at the Red Sea, at the place that is called Clysma from the fort that is there, so it was my desire that we should go from Clysma to the land of Goshen, that is, to the city that is called Arabia, which is in the land of Goshen; for from that the territory itself is so called, that is, "the land of Arabia, the land of Goshen," although it is part of the land of Egypt, but is much better than all Egypt. ²There are from Clysma, that is,

7 1. Egeria probably documented what she did when she "was first in Egypt" in the lost opening section of the manuscript: see the Introduction, pp. 16–17. The land of Goshen is mentioned in Gen 45:10; 46:28-29, 34; 47:1, 4, 6, 27; 50.8; Ex 8:22; 9:26; Josh 10:41; 11:16; 15:51; and Rameses in Gen 47:11; Ex 1:11; 12:37; Num 33:3, 5. The expression "the land of Arabia, the land of Goshen" is a paraphrase of the LXX of Gen 46:34. The reference to it being better than the rest of Egypt is an allusion to Gen 47:6; see 7.9. Maraval, 152–53, n. 3, noted that on the basis of Gen 46:34 Egeria identifies the *nome* (administrative district) known as Arabia with the land of Goshen, when in reality Arabia was a smaller area than Goshen; and she also appears to think that the area got its name from that of its capital city, Arabia, whereas it was probably the other way round.

2. The word "monasteries" (*manasteria* in the manuscript, presumably meant to be *monasteria*) linked with soldiers and officers looks like some sort of scribal error, but Maraval, 154, n. 1, discussed the possibility that the word might have been in use as a popular variant to denote a military post in the desert. Egeria's ability to obtain a military escort in this obviously dangerous environment has been thought by some to be an indicator that she must have had considerable social standing (see the Introduction, p. 12), but it could have been a common service provided to travelers more generally: see the phrase "according to the custom" in 7.4. She indicates clearly here that her guides were not monks alone, but some clergy too. Although she generally uses the word "clergy" in a way that seems to suggest that the term was meant to be inclusive of all ministers except bishops—that is, presbyters, deacons, and minor orders (subdeacons and readers)—as appears to be the case here, she also uses it on occasion to denote those ministers other than presbyters (14.1; 25.12; 45.2), and once possibly to mean the minor orders alone (24.9).

from the Red Sea, as far as the city of Arabia four staging posts in the desert, but in the desert such that at the staging posts there are monasteries with soldiers and officers, who always led us from fort to fort. So, on that journey the holy ones who were with us, that is, clergy and monks, showed us all the places that I was always searching for according to the Scriptures; for some were on the left, others on the right of our route, some also far from the road, others near. ³For I wish your affection to believe me that as far as I was able to see, the children of Israel so journeyed that as far as they went to the right, so far did they return to the left, as far as then they went forward, so far then did they return back; and so they made their way until they arrived at the Red Sea.

⁴For Epauleum was shown to us, but from the other side, and we were at Migdol. For there is a fort there now having an officer with soldiers, who now maintains the authority of Rome there. For according to the custom they led us from there as far as another fort, and Baal-zephon was shown to us, indeed we were in that place. For it is a plain above the Red Sea next to the side of the mountain that I mentioned above, where the children of Israel cried out when they had seen the Egyptians coming after them. ⁵Etham, which is "next to desert" places, as it is written, was also shown to us, as well as Succoth. Succoth is a gentle rise in the middle of a valley, and next to this little hill the children of Israel established a camp; for this is the place where the law of the Passover was received. ⁶The city of Pithom, which the children of Israel

3. For "your affection," see the commentary on 5.8. From the locations of the various sites, Egeria concludes that the children of Israel must have followed a tortuous zigzag route, though she apparently recognizes that this sounds scarcely credible and asks her readers to believe her (and, by extension, the guides who showed her these sites).
4. For the places named here, see Ex 14:2; Num 33:7. Epauleum occurs in the LXX of Ex 14:2, 9 for Pi-hahiroth; both terms simply mean "encampment" in Greek and Hebrew, respectively. For "from the other side," see the commentary on 2.7. The Israelites "cried out" in Ex 14.10.
5. The biblical references are to Ex 13:20 and 12:37; the quotation that Etham is "next to desert" is from Num 33:5-6; and for "the law of the Passover," see Ex 12:43-49.
6. Pithom is said in Ex 1:11 to have been a store-city that the Hebrew slaves built for Pharaoh.

had built, was also shown to us on that journey, but in that place where we already entered the territory of Egypt, leaving the lands of the Saracens; for that same Pithom is now a fort.

⁷Heroopolis, which existed at that time, that is, where Joseph met his father Jacob as he came, as it is written in the book of Genesis, is now a *kōmē*, but a large one, what we call a village. For that village has a church and martyria and very many cells of holy monks; in order to see each of them it was necessary for us to dismount there according to the custom that we kept. ⁸For the village is now called Hero, and it is sixteen miles from the land of Goshen, for it is within the borders of Egypt. The place is very pleasant, for some part of the River Nile also flows there. ⁹So, going from Hero, we arrived at the city that is called Arabia, which is a city in the land of Goshen, of which it is written that Pharaoh said to Joseph, "In the better land of Egypt settle your father and brothers in the land of Goshen, in the land of Arabia."

8 ¹From the city of Arabia it is four miles to Rameses. So that we might come to the staging post in Arabia, we crossed through the middle of Rameses. The city of Rameses is now leveled, so that it does not have a single dwelling. It is certainly evident that it was both huge in extent and had many buildings, for the ruins of it, though fallen, appear immense today. ²But now there is nothing

7. The biblical reference is to Gen 46:28-29, where in the LXX the name Heroopolis occurs. The word κώμη denotes a Greek administrative district and is normally translated as "village." For "martyria," see the Introduction, p. 62. The reference to dismounting confirms that Egeria usually rode rather than walked: see the commentary on 3.2

8. The change of name reflected the fact that it was no longer a "polis," a city. What Egeria calls "part of the River Nile" was actually a canal linking the Nile to the Red Sea.

9. The biblical reference is to Gen 47:6; see also 7.1 above.

8 1. Rameses is mentioned in Ex 1:11 along with Pithom (see 7.6) as a store-city built by the Hebrew slaves for Pharaoh, and also in Ex 12:37 and Num 33:3 as the point of departure for the Exodus.

2. What is called here Theban stone is red granite. The statues would actually have been of Pharaohs or Egyptian gods: Maraval, 160, n. 1, and Wilkinson, 117, n. 4, suggested that it was a king beside a god, something that was common in Egypt. Note Egeria's seeming caution in accepting what she heard about the statues ("they say," twice), as well as the story about the planting

else there except for just one great Theban stone, on which are two huge carved statues, which they say are of holy men, that is, of Moses and Aaron; for they say that the children of Israel erected them in their honor. ³And there is there besides a sycamore tree, which is said to have been planted by the patriarchs; for it is very old and so very small, although it still bears fruit. For those who have any ailment go there and pick off twigs, and it benefits them.

⁴We knew this, being informed by the holy bishop of Arabia, for he told us the name of that tree, what they call it in Greek, that is, *dendros alethiae*, as we say, "Tree of Truth." This holy bishop was gracious enough to meet us at Rameses; for he is already an old man, truly very pious, a former monk and affable, receiving strangers very well; for he is also very learned in God's Scriptures. ⁵So, when he had been gracious enough to be disturbed and to meet us there, he showed us everything there and informed us about those statues that I mentioned, as well as about that sycamore tree. For the holy bishop also informed us that Pharaoh, when he saw that the children of Israel had escaped him, then before he took off after them, had gone with all his army into Rameses and had burned it all, which was very immense, and from there had pursued the children of Israel.

9 ¹By chance it turned out very gratifyingly for us that the day when we came to the staging post in Arabia was the day before the most

---

of the tree in the next verse ("said to have been"), compared to her apparent readiness elsewhere to receive at face value what her guides told her; for other examples of her caution, see 12.7; 15.2; 17.2; 37.2.

3. For the existence of a cult of the sycamore, pagan and Christianized, see Gingras, 185, n. 115.

4. The bishop would have been bishop of the city of Arabia rather than of the province. As in 9.2; 14.2; and 20.9, those bishops and presbyters whom Egeria describes as learned in the Scriptures are invariably those who were monks. For the translation of *peregrinos* as "strangers," see the Introduction, pp. 33–34.

5. There is no scriptural testimony to Pharaoh burning the city: Gingras, 186, n. 118, suggested it might have been "a local Christian legend to explain the barrenness of the plain."

9 1. The day of the arrival would have been January 5, the eve of Epiphany. For Epiphany, see the Introduction, p. 88. Egeria reports in 25.12 that the monks at Bethlehem also kept a vigil the night before Epiphany. For "man

blessed day of the Epiphany; for on that same day a vigil was to
be held in the church. Thus, the holy bishop, a holy and true man
of God, well known to me already from the time I had been in the
Thebaid, kept us there some two days. ²This holy bishop is a
former monk, for he was brought up from childhood in a monastery, and so is as learned in the Scriptures as he is faultless in his
whole life, as I also said above.

³From there we sent back the soldiers who in the name of
Roman authority had afforded us assistance while we journeyed
through dangerous places; but now because there was a public
highway through Egypt that passed through the city of Arabia,
that is, that goes from the Thebaid to Pelusium, there was no
necessity to trouble the soldiers further. ⁴So, setting out from there,
we made our way entirely through the land of Goshen, constantly
among vineyards that produce wine and vineyards that produce
balsam and among orchards and cultivated fields and fine gar-
dens; we had our route entirely along the bank of the River Nile
among very fertile estates that had once been the farms of the
children of Israel and—what more [shall I say]?—I think I had
never seen a more beautiful country than the land of Goshen.

⁵Thus, making our way from the city of Arabia for two days
entirely through the land of Goshen, we arrived at Tathnis, the

---

of God," see the commentary on 2.3. The Thebaid was a region of Upper
Egypt, named from its proximity to the ancient Egyptian capital Thebes
(=Luxor), and no doubt Egeria's visit there was recounted in the lost opening
part of the manuscript.
2. That Egeria had previously met the bishop in the Thebaid strongly suggests the possibility that he may have had his monastic upbringing there,
especially as it was a major center of desert monasticism. She seems to be
implying that his proficiency in the Scriptures arose from his monastic training rather than from his ordination, as also in 8.4; 14.2; 20.9.
3. The final part of this highway to Pelusium ran near the Pelusiac branch
of the Nile, to which Egeria refers in the next verse.
4. Balsam obtains its name from the balm of Gilead, a rare perfume from the
sap of a particular tree, used medicinally, and grown in Egypt as well as
Palestine. Presumably these "farms of the children of Israel" would have
been understood to have been from the pre-Exodus days, when Pharaoh
allowed the sons of Jacob to settle in the land of Goshen: see Gen 45:10–47:6.
5. Most commentators understand Tathnis to be Tanis (= Zoan), although
some judge it to have been Taphnis/Daphnae (= Tahpanhes), sixteen miles
southwest of Pelusium. There is no scriptural testimony that Moses was born

city where holy Moses was born. This is the city of Tathnis, which was once the capital city of Pharaoh. ⁶And although I had already known those places, as I said above, that is, when I had been in Alexandria and the Thebaid, yet because I wished to learn fully about the places where the children of Israel journeyed when setting out from Rameses as far as the mountain of God, holy Sinai, it was necessary also then to return to the land of Goshen and from there to Tathnis. So, setting out from Tathnis, journeying by the route I already knew, I arrived at Pelusium. ⁷And then, setting out from there, making my way through each of the staging posts of Egypt through which we had been before, I arrived at the border of Palestine. And from there in the name of Christ our God, stopping then at several staging posts across Palestine, I returned to Aelia, that is, to Jerusalem.

10 ¹Then having spent some time there, it was next my wish, God willing, to travel as far as Arabia, that is, to Mount Nebo, to the place where God commanded Moses to ascend, saying to him, "Go up into the mountain Arabot, Mount Nebo, which is in the land of Moab over against Jericho, and see the land of Canaan, which I am giving to the children of Israel for a possession, and die on that mountain which you will have gone up." ²Therefore, our God Jesus, who will not abandon those hoping in him, also

---

in Zoan, the only reference to his connection with it being in Ps 78:12, 43, where he is said to have done wonders there. However, as Gingras, 187, n. 124, pointed out, it had once been the capital city of the Pharaohs and Moses had been pulled from the river by the Pharaoh's daughter; hence it would have been a natural assumption that he had been born there.

6. The reference to what she said above is to 9.1, but she then repeats what she had said in 7.1.

7. For "in the name of Christ our God," see the commentary on 5.11. For Aelia as the official name of Jerusalem at this time, see the Introduction, p. 57.

10 1. By "Arabia," Egeria here means the Roman province of that name, not the Arabian peninsula. The quotation is from Deut 32:49-50, but "Arabot" ("plains") is a mistake for "Abarim" in that text, either already existing in the copy of the Scripture known to Egeria or made by her or by a later copyist. See also Deut 34:8 and the commentary on 10.4.

2. One of four occasions on which Egeria refers to Jesus as God as part of the language of piety (see 17.1; 19.19; 23.9). She more often speaks of "Christ our God": see the commentary on 5.11.

was gracious enough to give effect to this my wish. ³So, setting out from Jerusalem and making my way with holy ones, that is, a presbyter and deacons from Jerusalem and some brothers, that is, monks, we arrived at the place on the Jordan where the children of Israel had crossed when holy Joshua, son of Nun, had led them across the Jordan, as it is written in the book of Joshua, son of Nun. For that place was also shown to us, a little higher up, where the children of Reuben and of Gad and the half tribe of Manasseh had made an altar, on that side of the river where Jericho is.

⁴So, crossing the river, we arrived at the city that is called Livias, which is in that plain where the children of Israel had then set up camp. For the foundations from the camp of the children of Israel and from their dwellings where they stayed are also evident in that place to this day. For the plain itself is immense, below the mountains of Arabia and above the Jordan. For this is the place of which it is written, "And the children of Israel wept for Moses in the Arabot of Moab on the Jordan over against Jericho for forty days." ⁵This is also the place where, after the death of Moses, immediately "Joshua, son of Nun, was filled with the spirit of

3. The biblical references are to Josh 3–4; 22:10. This is the only occasion, apart from her description of the Jerusalem liturgy, when Egeria specifically mentions deacons, although they may well have been included within the "clergy" she met elsewhere. She also apparently needs to clarify that by "brothers" she means monks in this instance: see the commentary on 2.7. Maraval, 166, n. 1, noted that she here provides the earliest witness to a specific place where the Israelites were said to have crossed the Jordan; Jerome, *Ep.* 108.12, repeats the claim, but she alone refers to a place where the altar was built. Maraval also remarked that she says nothing at all about any holy sites in and around Jericho, perhaps because she had visited there on a previous occasion and described it in the missing part of her diary, nor even about the place of Christ's baptism in the Jordan, which others at the time situated where the Israelites crossed. Only when she visits Aenon does she mention John the Baptist (15.1-4).

4. There are several biblical references to the Israelites setting up camp in the plains of Moab (Num 22:1; 31:12; 33:47-49), but the biblical quotation here is from Deut 34:8. "Arabot," written by mistake in 10.1, is the Hebrew word for "plains." It is possible that "mountains of Arabia" could also be a mistake for "mountains of Abarim" (Num 33:47); "forty" is an error for "thirty" in Deut 34:8.

5. The quotation is from Deut 34:9.

wisdom: for Moses had laid his hands on him," as it is written. [6]For it is the place where Moses wrote the book of Deuteronomy. This is also the place where "Moses spoke in the ears of all the congregation of Israel the words of this canticle until its end" that is written in the book of Deuteronomy. This is the place where holy "Moses, the man of God, blessed the children of Israel" one by one in order before his death.

[7]So, when we had come into that plain, we traveled to that place, and prayer was made there, also some part of Deuteronomy was read in that place, not only his [Moses's] canticle but also the blessings that he had said over the children of Israel. And after the reading, prayer was again made, and giving thanks to God, we moved on from there. For it was always our custom that whenever we were about to visit places we desired, first prayer was made there, then the reading was read from the codex, also one psalm relevant to the matter was recited and prayer was made there again. So, by God's will we have always kept this custom whenever we have been able to arrive at places we desired.

[8]Thus, in order that the work we had begun should be finished, we began to hurry to arrive at Mount Nebo. As we went, a presbyter of that place, that is, of Livias, advised us. At our request we had brought him with us from the staging post because he had known the places very well. So the presbyter said to us, "If you wish to see the water that flows from the rock, that is, that Moses gave to the children of Israel when they were thirsty, you can see it if you wish to take on yourselves the labor of turning

6. The biblical references are to Deut 31:24, 30; 32:1-43; 33:1, although the concept of "in order" must come from somewhere else, perhaps Jacob's blessing of his sons in Gen 49:28.
7. The reading was Deut 33. On worship in the holy places, see the Introduction, pp. 53–57. "Codex" is the word regularly used to denote a copy of the Scriptures: see also 33.2.
8. Moses twice struck water from a rock (Ex 17:1-7; Num 20:1-13), but neither time was in the plains of Moab: another example of the transposition of events; see also the commentary on 1.1 and 5.7. Maraval, 170, n. 2, observed that it was not the sixth milestone from Livias but the sixth one on the way from Heshbon to Livias, near Khirbet el Mahatta.

out of your way at about the sixth milestone." ⁹When he had said this, we very eagerly longed to go, and immediately turning aside from the road, we followed the presbyter who was leading us. In that place there is a little church below the mountain, not Nebo but another further in; but it is not far from Nebo. Very many truly holy monks, whom they call here ascetics, live there.

11 ¹So these holy monks were gracious enough to receive us very kindly, for they allowed us to go in to greet them. When we had gone in to them and prayer had been made with them, they were gracious enough to give us *eulogiae*, as they have the custom to give to those whom they receive kindly. ²So, there in the middle between the church and the monastic cells flows from a rock abundant water, very beautiful and clear, with excellent taste. Then we also asked those holy monks who lived there what was this water with such a taste. Then they said, "This is the water that holy Moses gave to the children of Israel in this desert." ³So, prayer was made there according to custom and the reading from the books of Moses was read, one psalm was also recited; and so together with all those holy clergy and monks who had come with us we went out to the mountain. Many of those holy monks also who lived there next to the water, those who were able to take on the labor, were gracious enough to ascend Mount Nebo with us. ⁴Thus, setting out from that place, we arrived at the foot of Mount Nebo, which was very high, but such that the greatest part of it could be ascended sitting on donkeys; but a little was steeper, which it was necessary to ascend laboriously on foot; as was also done.

9. This place was in the Wadi Ayun Musa. On Egeria's use of the term "ascetic," see the commentary on 3.4.
11 1. For "kindly," see the commentary on 3.1. For *eulogiae*, see the commentary on 3.6.
2. On water from the rock, see the commentary on 10.8. The references to the abundance of water here may suggest that the incident as recounted in Numbers is at the forefront, as the version in Exodus does not dwell on the quantity of water produced by the rock.
3. On worship in the holy places, see the Introduction, pp. 53–57. Very likely the reading was Ex 17:1-7 or Num 20:1-13; see also the commentary on 10.8.
4. Further confirmation that Egeria usually rode rather than walked: see the commentary on 3.2.

12 ¹So we arrived at the summit of that mountain, where there is now a church, not a large one, on the very summit of Mount Nebo. Inside that church, in the place where the ambo is, I saw a slightly raised place, occupying as much space as graves are accustomed to have. ²So, I then asked those holy ones what this was; they replied, "Holy Moses was placed here by the angels, because, as it is written, 'no one knows his burial,' because it is certain that he was buried by the angels. For his grave, where he was laid, is not shown [*sic*] to this day; for as the place was shown to us by our predecessors who lived here, so also we point it out to you; and our predecessors said that it had been handed down to them by their predecessors."

³Thus, prayer was soon made and everything that we had been accustomed to do in order in each of the holy places was also done here; and so we began to go out of the church. Then those who knew the place, that is, the presbyters and holy monks, said to us, "If you wish to see the places that are written in the books of Moses, come outside the door of the church and pay heed and see from the summit, but from the side that they can be visible from here, and we will tell you what all these places are that are visible." ⁴Then we were very pleased and immediately went outside. For from the door of that church we saw the place where the Jordan enters the Dead Sea; the place was visible below us as we stood. We also saw from the other side not only Livias, which was this side of the Jordan, but also Jericho, which was across the Jordan, so high did the place where we stood rise, that is, before the door

12 1. This is the only reference to an ambo or pulpit in the diary.

2. Although the Hebrew of Deut 34:6 says, "No one knows his tomb," the LXX uses the Greek word *taphē*, which can mean "act of burial," which also seems to be the meaning of the Latin word *sepultura* used here; otherwise, it would be difficult to make sense of the claim that Moses's place of burial was visible. In any case, the negative "is not shown" seems to be a scribal error, as the grave was being shown, unless, as Wilkinson, 121 n. 3, suggested, what was shown was simply a memorial and not the grave itself. See further Maraval, 174, n. 1.

3. On worship in the holy places, see the Introduction, pp. 53–57.

4. For "from the other side," see the commentary on 2.7.

of the church. [5]The greatest part of Palestine, which is the land of promise, was seen from there, as well as the whole land of Jordan, at least as much as could be seen with the eyes.

On the left side we saw all the lands of the Sodomites as well as Segor; but Segor alone of those five [cities] remains today. [6]For there is a monument there, but of the rest of those cities nothing else appears except a heap of ruins, as they were turned to ashes. The place where there was the inscription of Lot's wife was also shown to us—the place is also read in the Scriptures. [7]But believe me, revered ladies, that the pillar itself is not visible, but only the place is shown: the pillar itself is said to have been covered over by the Dead Sea. Certainly [when] we saw the place, we did not see the pillar, and so I cannot deceive you over this matter. For the bishop of that place, that is, of Segor, told us that it has already been some years that the pillar has not been visible. For from Segor that place where the pillar stood, which the water has now completely covered, [is] about six miles.

[8]Then we went to the right side of the church, but outside, and there were shown to us from there on the other side two cities,

---

5. The expression "land of promise" occurs in Heb 11:9. Segor is the LXX and Latin form of Zoar, the only one of the five cities of the plain slated for destruction by God to be spared: see Gen 19:20-25. There has been considerable debate about its location: see Gingras, 192, n. 156; Maraval, 176, n. 2.
6. The biblical reference is to Gen 19:26.
7. On the address "revered ladies," see the commentary on 3.8. Both Josephus, *Ant. Jud.* 1.203, and Irenaeus, *Adv. haer.* 4.31.3, claimed to have seen the pillar; but note Egeria's caution in accepting the account of what had happened to it ("is said to have been covered"): see also 8.2; 15.2; 17.2; 37.2. On this episode, see further Blake Leyerle, "Lot's Wife on the Border," *Harvard Theological Review* 107 (2014): 59–80. A bishop of Segor is not otherwise known: could Egeria have really meant the bishop of Zoara, a city south of the Dead Sea that Jerome, *Ep.* 108.11, identified with the biblical Segor? But where did she encounter him? As Maraval, 178, n. 2, observed, it could hardly have been at Nebo, or he would have contradicted what she was told by her guides about the true location of Segor. Could it have been while she was in Jerusalem? Or was the bishop she met actually the bishop of Livias?
8. For "on the other side," see the commentary on 2.7. The form "Exebon" is not otherwise known. By "Safdra," Egeria probably means Edrei (Num 21:33; Deut 1:4; 3:1, 10; Josh 12:4; 13:12, 31), although it was too far away to have been visible; but see R. Hill, "Aetheria XII 9 and the Site of the Biblical Edrei,"

that is, Heshbon, which belonged to King Sihon, king of the Amorites, which is now called Exebon, and the other to Og, king of Bashan, which is now called Safdra. Then from the same place was shown to us on the other side Fogor, which was a city of the kingdom of Edom. [9]All these cities that we saw were located in the mountains, but a little down below the place seemed to us to be more level. Then we were told that in those days when holy Moses and the children of Israel had fought against those cities, they had fixed their camp there; for signs of the camp were also visible there. [10]Indeed, on that side of the mountain that I said [was] on the left, which was above the Dead Sea, there was shown to us a very steep mountain that was called previously *Agri specula*. This is the mountain where Balak, the son of Beor, placed Balaam the diviner to curse the children of Israel and God was unwilling to allow it, as it is written. [11]Thus, having seen everything that we desired, returning in the name of God through Jericho and the whole route by which we had come, we came back to Jerusalem.

13 [1]Then after some time I wished also to go to the region of Ausitis in order to see the grave of holy Job for the sake of prayer. For I

Vetus Testamentum 16 (1966): 412–19. Fogor (= Peor) is mentioned in Num 23:28, although there Peor designates a mountain not far from Nebo and the city is Beth-peor (Deut 3:29; 4:46; 34:6; Josh 13:20). But Egeria or her guides probably had confused it with the Peor that was a city in the kingdom of Edom far to the south and mentioned in Gen 36:39 and 1 Chr 1:50.

9. These conflicts are described in Num 21:21-35; Deut 2:24–3:11.

10. *Agri specula* = "Viewpoint of the field," which is what Pisgah is called in the LXX of Num 23:14. Balak is described as son of Zippor and Balaam as the son of Beor in Num 22:2-5, the whole story being told in Num 22–24 (but cf. the LXX of Gen 36:32 and the LXX ending of Job 42:17d, which do present Balak as the son of Beor). It has been thought by some that because the same misidentification is made in the *Onomasticon* of Eusebius translated by Jerome, and because it too calls Balaam the diviner, Eusebius must have been the source of the information. This was denied by Maraval, 181, n. 3, who claimed that the word "diviner" came from Josh 13:22. Perhaps this alternative identification of Balak was just something that was said to Egeria by her guides.

11. For "in the name of God," see the commentary on 5.11.

13 1. Ausitis is used for Uz in the LXX of Job 1:1.

used to see many holy monks from there coming to Jerusalem to see the holy places for the sake of prayer; when they informed me all about those places, they increased my desire to take upon me the labor of also going to those places, if it can be called labor where someone sees their desire fulfilled. [2]Thus, I set out from Jerusalem with the holy ones who were gracious enough to give me their company on my journey, they themselves also [going] for the sake of prayer. So, making my way from Jerusalem as far as Carneas, going through eight staging posts—the city of Job is now called Carneas, which before was called Dinhaba, "in the land of Ausitis, on the borders of Idumaea and Arabia."

Going on this route, I saw on the bank of the River Jordan a very beautiful and pleasant valley, abounding in vines and trees because there was plenty of excellent water there. [3]For in that valley was a large village that is now called Sedima. So, in that village, which is located in the middle of a plain, is in the center a little hill of no great size, but shaped like tombs are accustomed to be, but large; so, there on the top is a church and below, around the hill, are visible large ancient foundations, but in the village itself some crowds now remain. [4]When I saw such a pleasing

2. "Going through eight staging posts" meant eight days of travel, presumably staying overnight at each post. For Dinhaba, see Gen 36:32; 1 Chr 1:43. Egeria's statement here fuses two different traditions about the place of Job's tomb, one locating it at Carneas, twenty-five miles east of the Sea of Galilee, the other reflected in her quotation at the end from the Syriac appendix to the LXX book of Job, locating it south of the Dead Sea in northwest Arabia. See Gingras, 196, n. 170; Maraval, 182–83, n. 1.

3. The word "crowds" (*turbae*) seems odd. Gingras, 197, n. 171, treated it as a scribal error for *tumbae*, "tombs"; Maraval, 185, and Wilkinson, 126, translated it as "communities," Brodersen, 131, as *Trümmerhaufen*, "heaps of rubble."

4. Those who had told Egeria would have been the guides accompanying her. See Gingras, 197, n. 172, and Maraval, 184, n. 1, for the variant ancient traditions about where the city of Melchizedek had been and the dissension among modern scholars about the exact location of Sedima. The transliterated Greek words simply mean "where Melchizedek," the opening words of the statement that follows, "where Melchizedek offered . . .," apparently used as the name of the church; see "on Horeb" at 4.1. The biblical reference is to Gen 14:18, but the addition of the expression "pure victims" reflects common early Christian eucharistic language: see, for example, *Didache* 14; Justin Martyr, *Dialogue with Trypho* 41.2; 117; Tertullian, *De or.* 28.

place, I asked what such a pleasant place was. Then I was told, "This is the city of King Melchizedek, which was previously called Salem; from this through the corruption of language the village is now called Sedima. For on that little hill that is located in the middle of the village, on its summit the building that you see is a church, which is now called in the Greek language *opu Melchizedek*. For this is the place where Melchizedek offered pure victims to God, that is, bread and wine, as it is written that he did."

14 ¹So, as soon as I heard this, we dismounted from the animals, and behold, the holy presbyter of that place and the clergy were gracious enough to meet us, and receiving us, immediately led us up to the church. When we had come there, immediately according to custom prayer was first made, then the passage from the book of holy Moses was read, one psalm relevant to that place was recited, and then after prayer was made, we came down.

²So, when we had come down, that holy presbyter spoke to us. He was already old and well instructed in the Scriptures, that is, he had been in charge of that place after having been a monk and, as we learned afterward, very many bishops also bore great witness to his life as a presbyter, for they said this about him, [that he was] worthy to be in charge of that place where holy Melchizedek was the first to offer pure victims to God when holy Abraham came. So, when we came down from the church, as I said above, that holy presbyter said to us: "Behold, these foundations around this little hill that you see, these are from the palace of King Melchizedek. For from then till now if any wish to make a house for themselves close nearby and they hit the foundations from there, they will sometimes also find small fragments of silver and bronze there. ³For behold, that road that you see going between

14   1. The reference to dismounting confirms once again that Egeria normally rode: see the commentary on 3.2. This is the first instance in which other clergy besides a presbyter are mentioned as being at a church: on the use of "clergy" in this sense, see the commentary on 7.2. On worship in the holy places, see the Introduction, pp. 53–57. The biblical passage that was read here is likely to have been Gen 14:18-20 or even the whole chapter.

2. As at 9.2, Egeria seems to be implying that his proficiency in the Scriptures arose from his monastic training rather than from his ordination. On "pure victims," see 13.4.

3. The biblical reference is to Gen 14:17-18. Egeria applies the title "King of nations" to Chedorlaomer, whereas Gen 14:1, 9 ascribes it to Tidal.

the River Jordan and this village, this is the road by which holy Abraham came back from the slaughter of Chedorlaomer, King of nations, returning to Sodom, where holy Melchizedek, King of Salem, met him."

15 ¹Then, because I remembered that it is written that holy John had baptized in Aenon near Salim, I asked how far away that place was. Then that holy presbyter said, "Behold, it is within two hundred paces. For if you wish, behold, I will straightaway lead you on foot there. For this abundant pure water that you see in this village comes from that spring." ²Then I began to thank him and to ask him to lead us to the place; as was also done. So we immediately began to go with him on foot all through the most pleasant valley until we came to a very pleasant orchard garden, where he showed us in the middle a spring of excellent pure water that sent out a single continuous stream. The spring had in front of it as it were a pool, where it appeared that holy John the Baptist had ministered.

³Then that holy presbyter said to us, "To this day this garden is called in the Greek language nothing other than *cepos tu agiu Iohanni*, that is, as you say in Latin, the garden of holy John." For many brothers, holy monks, coming from various places, head here to wash in that place. ⁴Then at that spring, as also in every place, prayer was made and the reading read, a suitable psalm was also recited and we also did there everything that it was our custom to do wherever we came to holy places.

---

15 1. The reference is to John the Baptist in Jn 3:23, Salim being identified with Salem.

2. Because Egeria uses the same Latin adjective *sanctus* in relation to Old Testament figures and the clergy and monks that she met as she does for John the Baptist and all Christian saints, we have translated it as "holy" in all cases. Note her apparent caution in accepting that here was where John had baptized ("it appeared that"): see also 8.2; 12.7; 17.2; 37.2.

3. Egeria attempts to reproduce the Greek, κῆπος του ἁγίου Ἰωάννου. She finds it necessary to qualify the word "brothers" to show that she means monks: see the commentary on 2.7. The washing would have been for spiritual cleansing, of course, rather than for physical hygiene.

4. For worship in holy places, see the Introduction, pp. 53–57.

⁵The holy presbyter also told us that down to the present day at Pascha all those who were to be baptized in that village, that is, in the church that is called *opu Melchizedek*, were always baptized in that spring, then they returned early by candlelight with the clergy and monks, reciting psalms and antiphons; and thus all who had been baptized were led early from the spring to the church of holy Melchizedek. ⁶So, receiving from the presbyter *eulogiae*, that is, from the orchard of holy John the Baptist, similarly also from the holy monks who had monastic cells there in that orchard garden, and constantly giving thanks to God, we set out on our way that we were going.

16 ¹Thus, going for a while through the valley of the Jordan along the bank of that river, as our route was there for a while, we suddenly saw the city of the holy prophet Elijah, that is, Tishbe, from which he had the name of Elijah the Tishbite. There down to this day is the cave in which that holy one sat, and there is the grave of holy Jephtha, whose name we read in the book of Judges. ²Thus, also giving thanks to God there according to custom, we continued our route. Then going on that route, we saw a most pleasant valley coming to us on the left. The valley was immense, sending a great

---

5. Egeria does not mention candles in her admittedly brief reference to the baptisms in Jerusalem at Pascha (= Easter; see 38.1). It is possible that their use here may have been for purely practical reasons, to illuminate a walk in the dark from the spring to the church, rather than for any symbolic effect. By "early" she must mean in the early hours of the morning, when the Easter vigil was moving to its culmination in the Eucharist.

6. For *eulogiae*, see the commentary on 3.6.

16 1. At some point along this route Egeria would have crossed the Jordan to its east bank. Maraval, 191, n. 2, suggested that she probably viewed Tishbe merely from a distance as she did not mention any of the customary elements of the worship that accompanied her visits to holy places. However, the reference in the following verse to "giving thanks to God there according to custom" should probably be understood as a shorthand expression for that activity: see the Introduction, p. 54. For the description "the Tishbite," see 1 Kings 17:1. The cave is mentioned in 1 Kings 19:8-9, but it was on Mount Horeb. For Jephtha, see Judg 11:1–12:7, where he is said to have been buried in one of the cities of Gilead.

2. Egeria again finds it necessary to qualify the word "brother" to show that she means a monk: see the commentary on 2.7.

stream into the Jordan. And there in that valley we saw the cell of a certain brother now, that is, a monk.

³Then, as I am very curious, I began to ask what was this valley where a holy monk had now made a cell; for I did not think this was without a reason. Then the holy ones who were making the journey with us, that is, knowing the place, said to us, "This is the valley of Corra, where holy Elijah the Tishbite lived in the time of King Ahab, when there was a famine and at God's bidding a raven used to bring him food and he used to drink water from that stream. For this stream that you see flowing from that valley into the Jordan, this is Corra." ⁴Thus, once again giving thanks to God who was gracious enough to show us, undeserving ones, everything that we desired, we began to go on our journey as on other days. Thus, making our journey each day, there suddenly appeared on the left side, from where on the other side we saw parts of Phoenicia, a huge and immensely high mountain that extended in length. . . .

⁵"This holy monk, an ascetic man, found it necessary, after so many years in which he lived in the desert, to move and go down to the city of Carneas in order to advise the bishop and clergy of that time, according to what had been revealed to him, that they should dig in that place that had been shown to him; as it was also done. ⁶When they dug in the place that had been shown, they

---

3. Corra = Cherith: see 1 Kings 17:2-6.
4. For the expression of unworthiness and gratitude, see the commentary on 5.12; and for "on the other side," see 2.7. What Egeria saw would have been Mount Hermon. A folio is missing from the manuscript after this. A few fragments from two ninth/tenth-century manuscripts (see Appendix C, pp. 207–8) apparently belong in this lacuna, but they are too brief to offer much illumination as to its overall contents.
5. On Egeria's use of the term "ascetic," see the commentary on 3.4. Wilkinson, 129, n. 3, noted that she is the sole witness to the existence of a bishop at Carneas.
6. "To this Job," i.e., in honor of Job. The expression in the second person "that you see" seems to indicate that the whole of this section from the lacuna onward was part of an explanation delivered to Egeria, quite probably by the bishop mentioned in the following verse, and hence we have introduced quotation marks around it.

found a cave; they followed it for about a hundred paces, when suddenly as they dug, a tombstone became visible; when they had completely uncovered the tombstone, they found carved on its cover 'Job.' To this Job the church that you see was then built in that place, but in such a way that the tombstone with the body was not moved to another place but located there where the body had been found and that the body should lie under the altar. But that church, which an unknown tribune built, stands thus unfinished to this day."

⁷Thus, the next morning we asked the bishop to make the oblation, as he also was gracious enough to do, and with the bishop blessing us we set out. So, receiving Communion there also, constantly giving thanks to God, we returned to Jerusalem, making our way through each of the staging posts through which we had gone for three years.

17 ¹Then in the name of God, having passed some time, when there had now been three full years since I came to Jerusalem, also having seen all the holy places to which I had headed for the sake of prayer, my intention was to return to my country. I wished, God willing, to go also to Mesopotamia of Syria to see the holy monks who were said to be very numerous there and of such exemplary life as could hardly be described, as well as for the sake of prayer at the martyrium of holy Thomas the Apostle, where his entire body is laid, that is, at Edessa. Our God Jesus promised in a letter

---

7. Another instance, like 4.8, of the Eucharist being celebrated at the request of the visitors. Egeria only mentions bishops bestowing a blessing, and never presbyters or others (see 19.16; 20.3; 21.1; 24.2 and passim in the Jerusalem liturgy). The final words "for three years" seem to be a scribal error, perhaps as a result of their occurrence in the next verse, as it is most improbable that she had passed that way going to Jerusalem three years earlier.

17 1. For "in the name of God," see the commentary on 5.11; and on "our God Jesus," see the commentary on 10.2. Mesopotamia of Syria is used in the LXX of Gen 28:2, 5-7 to translate Paddan-aram. According to the apocryphal *Acts of Thomas* 170, the relics of St. Thomas were transferred to Edessa from India. The purported letter from Jesus to King Abgar (see Appendix B, pp. 205–6) states only that Jesus would send one of his disciples to Edessa, and Eusebius reports (*Hist. eccl.* 1.13.4, 10), not that Thomas was sent, but that Thomas sent Thaddeus, one of the seventy (Lk 10:1). There was either a variant tradition, or Egeria confused the one sending with the one sent.

that he sent to King Abgar by the messenger Ananias that he would send him there after he had ascended into heaven. This letter is kept with great reverence in the city of Edessa, where the martyrium is. ²For I wish your affection to believe me that there is no Christian who has arrived at the holy places, that is, in Jerusalem, who does not head there for the sake of prayer, and this place is at the twenty-fifth staging post from Jerusalem. ³And as Mesopotamia is nearer from Antioch, it was very convenient for me, God willing, that, as I was returning to Constantinople, because the route was through Antioch, I should go from there to Mesopotamia; as was also done by God's will.

18 ¹Thus, in the name of Christ our God I set out from Antioch to Mesopotamia, having my route through various staging posts and cities of the province of Coele-Syria, which is [the province] of Antioch, and from there having entered the borders of the province of Augustophratensis, I arrived at the city of Hierapolis, which is the capital city of that province, that is, of Augustophra-

2. There is insufficient evidence about the volume of pilgrimage at this time to know how much of an exaggeration Egeria's claim might have been, but such a lengthy journey would have taken up a large part of the time that an average pilgrim would have spent in the Holy Land. Does her request that her sisters should believe her suggest that someone had told her this and even she found it hard to accept? See also 8.2; 12.7; 15.2; 37.2. Alternatively, is she merely trying to justify her detour and delayed return to her sisters, on the grounds that simply every pilgrim to Jerusalem must also visit Edessa? 3. For "your affection," see the commentary on 5.8.

18 1. For "in the name of Christ our God," see the commentary on 5.11. Maraval, 200, n. 1, estimated that there would have had to be four or five staging posts on this journey. Coele-Syria, with Antioch as its capital, was the northern part of the ancient province of Syria, divided into two at the end of the second century. In the fourth century, probably in 341, it was further subdivided, with the eastern part being named Augusta Euphratensis, which Egeria renders as Augustophratensis. Hierapolis is mentioned in Col 4:13. Maraval, 201, n. 3, judged that her reference to making a "stop" (*stativa*) there rather than the usual "staging post" meant that she must have spent a day or two there. He also remarked that, unusually, she made no mention of a church or any martyria there. This was probably because Hierapolis was still a great center of pagan religion and had not yet acquired the status of a major Christian city that it was to have later.

tensis. And as this city is very beautiful and rich and abounds in all things, it was necessary for me to make a stop there, as the borders of Mesopotamia were not far from there. ²So, setting out from Hierapolis, at the fifteenth mile in the name of God I arrived at the River Euphrates, of which it has been very well written that it is "the great River Euphrates," and it is huge and almost terrifying; for it so flows having a force like the River Rhône has, except the Euphrates is even larger. ³Thus, as it was necessary to cross it in boats, and only in large boats, I stayed there for more than about half a day; and from there having crossed the River Euphrates, in the name of God I entered the borders of Mesopotamia of Syria.

19 ¹So, making my way then through several staging posts, I arrived at a city, the name of which we read stated in Scripture, that is, Batanis; this city exists to this day. For it has both a church with a truly holy bishop, both a monk and a confessor, and several martyria. The city also abounds in the number of people; for the military are stationed there with their tribune. ²Then, setting out

---

2. For "in the name of God," see the commentary on 5.11. The quotation is from Gen 15:18. The mention of the Rhône is one of the factors that has encouraged some to think that Egeria came from Gaul, although she could also have crossed it coming from Spain: see the Introduction, pp. 20–21.

3. For "in the name of God," see the commentary on 5.11. For Mesopotamia of Syria, see the commentary on 17.1.

19 1. Batanis is not mentioned in the Bible: was Egeria supposing that it was Beten, mentioned in Josh 19:25? The term "confessor" was used by early Christians of someone who had suffered for the faith but had not been martyred. Egeria uses the word only three times, here and at 19.5 and 20.2, in each case of a bishop who was also a monk and had received the title of confessor through having been exiled by the Arian emperor Valens (364–378), a fact that has been used by scholars to help date Egeria's visit: see the Introduction, p. 23. This bishop appears to have been Abraham, who was said by Basil of Caesarea, *Ep.* 132, to have been in exile in 375 and is known to have attended the Council of Constantinople in 381. There is no testimony to the existence of martyria in this city other than from Egeria herself.

2. For "in the name of Christ our God," see the commentary on 5.11. Edessa was one of the great centers of Eastern Christianity. Whether by "to the church and to the martyrium" Egeria means one building or two has been the subject of much discussion by scholars: see Gingras, 205, n. 204. Maraval, 202, n. 5, opted for two buildings; Wilkinson, 132, n. 4, favored one. On the implications for dating Egeria's journey, see the Introduction, p. 25. The use

from there, we arrived in the name of Christ our God at Edessa. When we had arrived there, we immediately proceeded to the church and to the martyrium of holy Thomas. So, according to custom having made prayers and the rest that was the custom to do in holy places, we also read there something from holy Thomas himself.

[3]The church that is there is huge and very beautiful and of new construction, so that it is truly worthy to be a house of God; and as there were many things that I desired to see there, it was necessary for me to make a three-day stop there. [4]Thus, I saw in that city very many martyria as well as holy monks, some living by the martyria, others having their cells further from the city in more secluded places. [5]And the holy bishop of that city, a truly pious man, both a monk and a confessor, receiving me willingly, said to me, "As I see, daughter, that you have taken on yourself such great labor for the sake of piety that you have come to these places from the farthest distant lands, therefore, if you are willing, we will show you whatever places here are pleasant for Christians to see." Then, giving thanks to God first, I asked him very much that he would be gracious enough to do as he said.

---

of the plural "prayers" rather than the singular commonly found elsewhere is not significant: see the Introduction on worship in the holy places, pp. 53–57. Maraval, 203, n. 6, argued that the use of the active verb "we read," rather than Egeria's normal passive expression "was read," indicated a private reading instead of a liturgical one, but this is hardly convincing. The reading may have been from the apocryphal *Acts of Thomas*. For further discussion concerning this reading, the role of Thomas in the "apostolic geography" of late antiquity, and Egeria as a collector of texts, see Johnson, *Literary Territories*, 82–88.

3. The phrase "of new construction" might mean that the church had recently been built, or it could mean that it was of a kind that Egeria had not seen before.

4. For the identity of these martyria, see Maraval, 204, n. 1.

5. On "confessor," see 19.1. Eulogios, bishop of Edessa from 379 to his death in 387, had previously been exiled in Egypt by the Arian Emperor Valens: see Theodoret, *Hist. eccl.* 4.15. The words "from the farthest distant lands" have been cited by scholars as testimony that Egeria came from Western Europe: see the Introduction, pp. 21–22; and for the suggestion that they may reflect Egeria's own perception of her travels as much as what the bishop actually said, see p. 22, n. 65.

⁶Thus, he led me first to the palace of King Abgar and there showed me a huge statue of him, very much like him, as they said, of marble, of such luster as if it were made of pearl. In Abgar's face from the front it appeared that this man had been very wise and honorable. Then the holy bishop said to me, "Behold King Abgar, who before he saw the Lord, believed in him, that he was truly the Son of God." For there was also nearby a statue similarly made of the same marble, which he said was of his son Magnus, and similarly also having something of grace in the face. ⁷Then we went into the inner part of the palace; and there were springs full of fish, such as I never saw before, that is, of such size, and so bright and of such a good taste. For the city has no other water at all now except that which comes out of the palace, which is like a huge silver river.

6. There had been several kings of Edessa named Abgar. Although the bishop attributed the construction of the palace to Abgar V (reigned 4 BCE–7 CE and 13–ca. 40 or 50), who had allegedly been in correspondence with Jesus, it was Abgar VIII (reigned ca. 177–212), Edessa's first Christian king, who is said to have built two palaces, the winter one on higher ground and the summer one near a spring: see 19.14-15. Both Abgar V and Abgar VIII had sons named Magnus. While Gingras, 78, and Brodersen, 147, translated the word *archiotipa* as "statue," both Maraval, 205, and Wilkinson, 133, preferred "portrait." For "from the front" (*de contra*), see the commentary on 2.7; Gingras, 206, n. 210, admitted that it could hardly be translated here as "at a distance." The bishop's words here seem to be influenced by the wording of the alleged letter of Jesus to Abgar: see Appendix B, pp. 205–6. Since Abgar does not see Christ directly in any legendary account of this exchange, some scholars interpret Egeria's words as an allusion to the story of an image of Christ's face miraculously impressed in cloth first mentioned in connection with Abgar and Edessa in the Syriac *Doctrine of Addai* ca. 400. This later became famous as the Image of Edessa or Mandylion, which the messenger Ananias was said to have brought with him: see further Mark Guscin, *The Tradition of the Image of Edessa* (Newcastle-upon-Tyne: Cambridge Scholars Publishing, 2016).
7. Maraval, 206, n. 3, was surely correct that it was the brightness and taste of the water that Egeria was admiring here and not that of the fish (*pace* Gingras, 78, and Wilkinson, 133), especially as she regularly commented on the quality of water: see 4.7; 11.2; 13.2; 15.1-2. Her statement that it was the only water source in the city has surprised scholars because it is known that a river crossed the city. Various explanations have been offered: that her visit must have been after the Emperor Justinian had diverted the river in the

⁸And then the holy bishop told me about the water, saying, "At some time after King Abgar had written to the Lord and the Lord had replied to Abgar by the messenger Ananias, as is written in the letter itself, after some time had passed the Persians came against the city and surrounded it. ⁹But immediately Abgar, carrying the letter of the Lord to the gate with all his army, prayed publicly. And he said, 'Lord Jesus, you had promised us that no enemy should enter this city, and behold, now the Persians are attacking us.' When the king had said this, holding the letter open in his upraised hands, suddenly such darkness fell, but outside the city before the eyes of the Persians when they were already drawing so near to the city that they were about three miles from the city; but soon they were so confused by the darkness that they scarcely pitched their camp and surrounded the whole city three miles away. ¹⁰The Persians were so confused that they never saw afterward on which side to enter the city but they kept the city surrounded with troops three miles away, and kept it for several months.

¹¹"But afterward, when they saw that they could by no means enter the city, they wished to kill with thirst those who were in

---

sixth century in an attempt to eliminate its periodic flooding; that she was there in a season when the riverbed was dry; or simply that she was misinformed: see Gingras, 206, n. 213; Maraval, 207, n. 4; but cf. Palmer, "Egeria the Voyager," 45–46, who argued that the bishop's story that follows involved a deliberate deception that hid the river as the true source of the water in order to present its miraculous origin.

8. Because of its position, Edessa was often caught up in wars between the Romans and the Persians and had been occupied by the Persians in 259–260: see Maraval, 208, n. 1.

9. The final sentence of the Syriac version of Jesus's letter to Abgar, not present in the text Eusebius translated into Greek (see Appendix B, pp. 205–6), promises, "And your fortress shall be blessed and no enemy shall rule over it for ever": see Wilkinson, 135, n. 2. This version of the story must have originated later than the incursion in 260 mentioned above: see also 19.13. After Eusebius, Egeria is the next literary witness to the Abgar correspondence.

10. It is unclear whether there was any particular significance to the three-mile distance mentioned three times in the story.

11. Diverting the water supply was a common siege tactic in the ancient world.

the city. For that little hill that you see above this city, daughter, at that time supplied water to this city. Then seeing this, the Persians diverted that water from the city and made it run down the opposite way to that place where they had pitched their camp. [12]On that day and at that hour when the Persians had diverted the water, immediately these springs, which you see in that place, at God's command at once burst forth; from that day until today these springs remain here by the grace of God. But the water that the Persians had diverted dried up at that hour, so that those who were besieging the city did not have anything to drink for even one day, as is also apparent down to this day; for afterward no moisture whatsoever has ever appeared there down to this day. [13]So, by the will of God who had promised this would be, it was necessary for them immediately to return to their own land, that is, to Persia. For afterward also, whenever enemies have wanted to come and capture this city, this letter has been brought out and read at the gate, and immediately by the will of God all enemies have been driven back."

[14]The holy bishop also related that [the place] where these springs burst forth had before been a level place within the city lying below Abgar's palace. "Abgar's palace had been located in a somewhat elevated place, as is also visible now, as you see. For the custom was such at that time that palaces, whenever they were built, were always in elevated places. [15]But after these springs burst forth in that place, then Abgar himself built this palace in that place for his son Magnus (that is, the one whose statue you see set up next to his father) so that these springs would be included within the palace."

---

12. This etiological story was obviously intended to provide a miraculous basis for the emergence of the pools.

13. The end of the story also attributes invincibility to the city because of the divine promise contained in the Syriac version of the letter: see the commentary on 19.9.

14. Wilkinson, 135, n. 6, reported that this low-lying place had originally been the riverbed. A palace had had been built there, but was destroyed by flooding in the year 201.

15. As Gingras, 297, n. 217, observed, in reality the palace at the higher elevation was most probably built after, and not before, this palace, as a winter palace intended to avoid the effects of winter floods.

[16]After the holy bishop had related all this, he said to me, "Let us now go to the gate through which the messenger Ananias entered with that letter of which I had spoken." So, when we had come to that gate, the bishop, standing, made a prayer and read to us there those letters, and then blessing us, another prayer was made. [17]The holy one also related this to us, saying, "From that day when the messenger Ananias entered through that gate with the Lord's letter down to the present day it has been maintained that no one unclean, no mourner should go through that gate, nor should the body of any dead person be carried out through that gate."

[18]The holy bishop also showed us the grave of Abgar and of all his family, very beautiful but done in the ancient style. He also led us to that upper palace that King Abgar had had first, and showed us whatever other places there were. [19]It was also very gratifying to me that I should receive for myself from that holy one the letters themselves whether of Abgar to the Lord or of the Lord to Abgar, which the holy bishop had read to us there. And although I had copies of them at home, yet it seemed more gratifying to me that I should also receive them there from him, lest

16. On bishops alone bestowing blessings, see the commentary on 16.7.

17. Maraval, 212, n. 1, argued that the real reason for this prohibition on mourners and corpses going through that gate would have been to prevent the use of the cemeteries on that side of the city; and that the unclean (*immundi*) would probably have been lepers, as that word is often used in the Latin Bible in relation to such people (e.g., Lev 15:13), or at least those who had been rendered ritually unclean by their contact with the dead bodies that they had accompanied (e.g., Num 19:11).

18. Wilkinson, 136, n. 3, observed that the tomb that Egeria was shown before going to the upper palace is not the same one as exists currently, as that is on a hill.

19. As noted in 19.9, the Greek version of the letter lacked the final sentence of the Syriac text, and so what Egeria already possessed may have been a translation of the former. In any case, if Egeria's visit is correctly dated to the fourth century, it must have been an older Latin translation than the one known to have been made by Rufinus in 403. We can presume that Egeria meant that she received original *copies* of the letters from Edessa's bishop: see Guscin, *The Tradition of the Image of Edessa*, 15. On "our God Jesus," see the commentary on 10.2; and on the address "ladies, my souls," see the commentary on 3.8.

perhaps something less had reached us at home; for what I received here is indeed fuller. If our God Jesus shall will it and I shall come home from here, you will read them, ladies, my souls.

20 ¹Thus, having spent three days there, it was necessary for me to go even further to Carrhae, as it is so called. For in the holy Scriptures it is called Charra, where holy Abraham stayed, as it is written in Genesis, the Lord saying to Abraham, "Leave your country and your father's house and go to Charra," and the rest. ²So, when I had come [there], that is, to Charra, there I immediately went to the church that is within the city itself. I also soon saw the bishop of that place, truly holy and a man of God, and himself both a monk and a confessor, who was quickly gracious enough to show us all the places there that we desired. ³For he immediately led us to a church that is outside the city in the place where the house of holy Abraham was, that is, on the same foundations and of the same stone, as the holy bishop said. So, when we had come into that church, prayer was made and that passage from Genesis read, also one psalm was recited, and another prayer was said, and then the bishop blessing us, we went outside.

⁴Then he was gracious enough to lead us to the well from which holy Rebecca used to carry water. And the holy bishop said to us, "Behold the well from which holy Rebecca watered the camels of holy Abraham's servant, that is, Eleazar"; and so he was gracious enough to show us each thing. ⁵For at the church that I said was

20 1. What Egeria recalls as from Genesis is actually influenced by Acts 7:2-4. In Gen 12:1-4, Abraham was already in Haran (= Charra in the LXX) when God's call came to him. Egeria engaged multiple layers of history and religious practices in her account of her visit to Carrhae; for an analysis of her narrative technique, see Johnson, *Literary Territories*, 23–25.

2. On "confessor," see 19.1. Protogenes, like Eulogios (see 19.5) having previously been exiled in Egypt by the Arian Emperor Valens, was then made bishop of the city of Carrhae: see Theodoret, *Hist. eccl.* 4.15; 5.4. For "man of God," see the commentary on 2.3.

3. On bishops alone bestowing blessings, see the commentary on 16.7.

4. The biblical reference is to Gen 24:15-28. The servant is only named as Eleazar or Eliezer in Gen 15:2.

5. On the address "ladies, revered sisters," see the commentary on 3.8 above. The feast of St. Helpidius was on April 23 or 24, depending upon how one reads the date that Egeria gives, whether in apposition to "the day before"

outside the city, ladies, revered sisters, where originally Abraham's house was, now a martyrium is also located there, that is, of a certain holy monk by the name of Helpidius. It turned out very gratifyingly for us that we came there the day before the martyr's day, that is, of holy Helpidius himself, the ninth day before Kalends of May, on which day it was necessary for all the monks from everywhere and from all the borders of Mesopotamia to go down to Charra, even also those greater ones who live in solitude, whom they call ascetics, for that day which is marked there with great grandeur, and on account of the memorial of holy Abraham, as it was his house where is now the church in which is placed that holy martyr's body.

⁶Thus, it turned out very gratifyingly beyond expectation for us that we saw there holy monks of Mesopotamia, truly men of God and also those whose reputation and way of life were heard about far away, but whom I did not think I would ever be able to see, not because it was impossible for God, who was gracious enough to grant all things, to grant this also to me, but I had heard that they did not come down from their places except for the day of Pascha and except for this day, both because they are such that they do many wonders, and because I did not know in which

---

or to "the martyr's day." He is otherwise unknown. If he really had been a martyred monk, because monasticism did not really take root until the fourth century when Roman persecution ceased, this suggests that he may have suffered under persecution from the Persians; see also the commentary on 20.6. In contrast to English translators, Maraval, 217, and Brodersen, 157, understood "greater" here as "the oldest" (cf. also 20.13), but there is no reason to suppose that those who lived in solitude were always the aged and Egeria's category of "ascetics" (see the commentary on 3.4) suggests instead that they were more outstanding in some way. Although she normally uses the Latin word *memoria* to denote a grave, that cannot be its meaning in this case, as Abraham was buried at Machpelah (Gen 49:31), and so we have translated it as "memorial" here and in 20.8.

6. For "men of God," see the commentary on 2.3. That these solitaries only assembled together for Pascha (=Easter) and for this one feast day indicates their adherence to the most ancient liturgical calendar that excluded any more recently established annual festivals. Does this suggest that Helpidius was actually a martyr from more ancient times, or did they observe his day because he was the sole martyr in that locality? Also, it is not clear what they did with regard to the Eucharist. Did a presbyter visit them weekly, or perhaps less often? Or did they receive Communion from preconsecrated elements?

month was the day of this martyr whom I have spoken about. And so at God's will it turned out that I came there on a day that I did not expect. ⁷So we stayed there two days for the sake of the martyr's day and for the sake of seeing those holy ones, who were gracious enough to receive me very willingly, to greet me and to address me, which I did not deserve. For they were not seen there immediately after the martyr's day but soon in the night sought the desert and each of them their cells where they lived.

⁸In that city, apart from a few clergy and holy monks, if any live in the city, I found no Christian person at all, but they are entirely pagan. For as we venerate with great reverence that place where originally holy Abraham's house was for the sake of his memorial, so also about a thousand paces from the city those pagans venerate with great reverence the place where the graves of Nahor and Bethuel are. ⁹And because the bishop of that city was well instructed in the Scripture, I asked him, saying, "I ask you, my lord, to tell me what I desire to hear," and he said, "Say, daughter, what you wish, and I will tell you, if I know." Then I said, "I know from the Scriptures that holy Abraham came to this place with his father Terah and Sarah his wife and Lot his brother's son; but I have not read when Nahor and Bethuel came to this place, except that this alone I know, that afterward Abraham's servant came to Charra to search for Rebecca, the daughter of Bethuel the son of Nahor, for the son of his master Abraham, that is, Isaac." ¹⁰Then the holy bishop said to me, "Truly, daughter, it

---

7. The two days were presumably the day before the festival (see 20.5) and the martyr's day itself, as the solitaries disappeared immediately afterward.
8. Nahor is mentioned in Gen 11:22-29; 22:20; 24:10; 29:5; 31:53; Bethuel in Gen 22:22; 24:50; 25:20; 28:2, 5; both of them in Gen 22:23; 24:15, 24, 47. Why they should have been the objects of veneration by pagans is a mystery.
9. As in 8.4; 9.2; and 14.2, Egeria seems to attribute proficiency in the Scriptures to those bishops and presbyters who had been monks (see 20.2), but in this case some external confirmation is supplied by Theodoret, *Hist. eccl.* 4.15, who reports that while in exile Protogenes had opened a school for boys that included scriptural and doctrinal teaching. The biblical references are to Gen 11:31; 24.
10. This is the only place where Egeria employs the word "canon" in relation to Scripture, the term having only come into use in this sense since the mid-fourth century. The biblical references are to Gen 24; 28:1-5; 29, although the text only states that Abraham's servant went to Nahor's city and does

is written, as you say, in Genesis that holy Abraham came here with his family, but canonical Scripture does not say when Nahor with his family or Bethuel passed this way. But plainly they also did pass this way afterward; indeed their graves are also here, about a thousand paces from the city. For truly Scripture testifies to this, that the servant of holy Abraham came here to take away holy Rebecca and then holy Jacob came here when he took the daughters of Laban the Syrian."

[11] Then I asked where was the well where holy Jacob watered the flocks that Rachel, the daughter of Laban the Syrian, was feeding. And the bishop said to me, "Six miles from here is the place, next to the village that was then the farm of Laban the Syrian, but when you wish to go, we will go with you and show you, for many very holy monks and ascetics are both there, and a holy church is there." [12] I also asked the holy bishop where that place of the Chaldeans was where Terah first lived with his family. Then the holy bishop said to me, "That place, daughter, that you seek is at the tenth staging post from here, going into Persia. For from here to Nisibis there are five staging posts, and from there to Ur, which was the city of the Chaldeans, are another five staging posts; but now there is no access there for Romans, for the Persians occupy the whole of it. This part is especially called the Eastern [province]; it is on the borders of the Romans and the Persians and the Chaldeans."

[13] And many other things he was gracious enough to relate, as the other holy bishops and holy monks also were gracious enough to do, but everything from the Scriptures of God or the deeds of

---

not explicitly name the place. Laban is described as "the Syrian" in the LXX and Old Latin of Gen 25:20; 31:20, 24; in the Hebrew text he is "Laban the Aramean."

11. The biblical reference is Gen 29:2-10. On Egeria's use of the term "ascetic," see the commentary on 3.4.

12. Terah was said to come from Ur of the Chaldeans (Gen 11:28). Nisibis and the territory east of the River Tigris had been abandoned to the Persians by the Emperor Jovian in 363, which provides evidence that Egeria's visit must have been no earlier than that date: see the Introduction, p. 22.

13. For "still in the body," see 2 Cor 12:3 and 23.10 below; on Egeria's use of the term "ascetic," see the commentary on 3.4; and for "your affection," see the commentary on 5.8. Maraval, 223, understood "greater" here as "old," in line with his translation of 20.5, but Brodersen, 161, as "earlier."

holy men, that is, of monks, either what miracles those who had already died had done or what those who are still in the body do daily, those who are ascetics. For I do not wish your affection to think that there were ever any other stories from the monks except either from the Scriptures of God or the deeds of the greater monks.

21 ¹After the two days that I spent there, the bishop led us to the well where holy Jacob watered the flocks of holy Rachel, which is six miles from Carrhae; in honor of this well a very huge and beautiful holy church has been built nearby there. When we had come to the well, prayer was made by the bishop, also that passage from Genesis was read, also one psalm suitable to the place was recited, and after another prayer, the bishop blessed us. ²We also saw, lying in a place next to the well, that very immense stone that holy Jacob moved from the well, which is shown to this day.

³There around the well no others live except the clergy of the church that is there and monks having their cells nearby, whose truly unheard-of way of life the holy bishop related to us. Thus, after prayer had been made in the church, I went with the bishop to the holy monks in their cells, giving thanks both to God and to those who were gracious enough to receive me with a willing mind in their cells wherever I entered and to address me with those words which were worthy to proceed out of their mouth. For they were also gracious enough to give *eulogiae* to me and to all who were with me, as is the custom for monks to give to those whom they receive with a willing mind into their cells.

⁴And as that place is on a large plain, a large village on the other side was shown to me by the holy bishop about five hundred paces from the well; through this village we had our route. This

21 1. On bishops alone bestowing blessings, see the commentary on 16.7. On worship in the holy places, see the Introduction, pp. 53–57.
2. The biblical reference is to Gen 29:2-10, which was probably the passage read in 21.1.
3. Although apparently in an unpopulated area, the church had several clergy attached to it and not just a sole presbyter as seems to have been the case with the churches around Sinai (see the commentary on 3.4). For *eulogiae*, see the commentary on 3.6.
4. For "on the other side," see the commentary on 2.7. Fadana is the Latin version of Paddan-aram (Gen 25:20; 28:2, 5, 6). Rachel's theft is in Gen 31:19, 34-35.

village, as the bishop said, was once the farm of Laban the Syrian; the village is called Fadana. For there was shown to me in that village the grave of Laban the Syrian, Jacob's father-in-law; also shown to me was the place where Rachel stole her father's images. ⁵Thus, having seen everything, in the name of God, bidding farewell to the holy bishop and holy monks who had been gracious enough to lead us to that place, we returned by the route and the staging posts by which we had come from Antioch.

22 ¹When I had returned to Antioch, I stayed for a week afterward until the things that were necessary for the journey were prepared. And so setting out from Antioch, making the journey through several staging posts, I arrived at the province that is called Cilicia, which has Tarsus as its capital city, where indeed I had already been when going to Jerusalem. ²But as the martyrium of holy Thecla is at the third staging post from Tarsus, that is, in Isauria, it was very gratifying also to go there, especially when it was so close.

23 ¹For setting out from Tarsus, I arrived at a certain city by the sea still in Cilicia, which is called Pompeiopolis. And from there, already having entered the borders of Isauria, I stayed in a city called Corycus. On the third day I arrived at a city that is called

---

5. This would presumably have meant returning via Edessa, even though that was a detour from the most direct route. For "in the name of God," see the commentary on 5.11.

22 1. Egeria says nothing here about the martyria and churches of Antioch, presumably because she had already done so in the missing part of the text that described her journey to Jerusalem. She speaks of going through several staging posts; the pilgrim from Bordeaux specifies seven to Tarsus.
2. According to the apocryphal *Acts of Paul and Thecla*, dating from the second century, Thecla was a young woman from Iconium who was so impressed by St. Paul's teaching on virginity that she broke off her engagement and lived as a virgin and hermit for the rest of her life, after escaping attempts to put her to death. See further Davis, *The Cult of Saint Thecla*, esp. chap. 2; Egeria's experience at Thecla's shrine is discussed specifically on 55–56, 59–60, and 64–69; and also Johnson, *Literary Territories*, 88–91.

23 1. Maraval, 227, n. 2, asserted that Corycus was in the province of Cilicia, in spite of what Egeria said, though close to the border with Isauria. The bishop may have been Symposios, present at the Council of Constantinople in 381, or his successor, Samos.

Seleucia in Isauria. When I had arrived there, I went to the bishop, truly holy from the time he was a monk; I also saw a very beautiful church there in that city. ²And as from there to holy Thecla, which place is outside the city on a hill, but flat, is about fifteen hundred paces from the city, so I preferred to go there to make the stay there that I was going to make. But there is nothing else there at the holy church except numberless monastic cells of men and of women. ³For I found there someone very dear to me, and to whose way of life everyone in the east bore witness, a holy deaconess by the name of Marthana, whom I had known at Jerusalem, where she had gone up for the sake of prayer; she was governing cells of *apotactitae* or virgins. When she had seen me, surely I cannot write down what her joy and mine could have been?

⁴But to return to the point, there are very many monastic cells there on that hill and in the middle a huge wall that surrounds the church, in which is the martyrium; the martyrium is very beautiful. The wall was built to protect the church because of the Isaurians, as they are very evil and frequently commit robbery, lest perhaps they should try to do anything against the monastery that is established there. ⁵So, when I had come there in the name of God, prayer having been made at the martyrium as well as all the Acts of holy Thecla read, I gave endless thanks to Christ our

2. Seleucia is the only place, outside Jerusalem, where Egeria explicitly mentions the existence of women among the monastic communities she encountered. She presumably lodged with them.

3. Marthana is the only person Egeria met for whom she supplied a name. She may perhaps have been the same person mentioned by Basil of Seleucia: see the Introduction, p. 26. Deaconesses usually ministered to women, especially in connection with the administration of baptism, and it is unusual to find one in charge of a community of women. Egeria seems to treat the term *apotactitae* (from the Greek, meaning "those set apart") as a synonym for monks and nuns, though perhaps indicating those among them who followed a more austere way of life: see 23.6; 28.3; 39.3; 40.1; 44.3; 49.1.

4. She quickly recognizes that her personal comments about Marthana are a digression from her narrative and returns "to the point": see also 25.10.

5. On worship in the holy places, see the Introduction, pp. 53–57. For the *Acts of Thecla*, see the commentary on 22.2, and for "Christ our God," see 5.11.

6. For *apotactitae*, see the commentary on 23.3. Might the absence of any explicit mention of a Eucharist mean that Communion was received from the reserved sacrament?

God, who was gracious enough to fulfill for me, unworthy and undeserving, my desires in all things.

⁶Thus, having spent two days there, also having seen the holy monks or *apotactitae*, both men and women, who were there, and prayer having been made and Communion received, I returned to Tarsus to my route, where I made a stay of three days, and set out from there on my route in the name of God. So, arriving on the same day at a staging post that is called Mansocrenae, which is below Mount Taurus, I spent the night there. ⁷And from there on the next day climbing Mount Taurus and taking the route I already knew through every province that I had crossed as I went, that is, Cappadocia, Galatia, and Bithynia, I arrived at Chalcedon, where on account of the most famous martyrium of holy Euphemia that is there, already known to me from before, I spent the night in the place.

⁸Thus, crossing the sea on the next day, I arrived at Constantinople, giving thanks to Christ our God because he had been gracious enough to grant such grace to me, unworthy and undeserving, that is, that he had been gracious enough to grant not only the wish to go but also the ability to visit the places I desired and at last to return to Constantinople. ⁹When I had come there, in all the churches, or the Apostles, as well as in all the martyria, which are very many there, I did not cease to give thanks to our God Jesus, who had been so gracious to bestow his mercy on me.

¹⁰From this place, ladies, my light, while I send this [letter] to your affection, I have already decided, in the name of Christ our

7. Egeria's list of provinces through which she had previously gone doubtless refers to the route taken when she first traveled to Jerusalem, which would have been described in the missing opening part of the manuscript. St. Euphemia was martyred in 303 or 304 during the Diocletian persecution. Egeria furnishes the earliest attestation of her martyrium at Chalcedon.
8. For "Christ our God," see the commentary on 5.11, and for the expression of unworthiness and gratitude, see 5.12.
9. The reference to the Apostles appears to be to the church dedicated to the Apostles built there by the Emperor Constantine in 337: see Eusebius, *Vita Constantini* 4.58. On "our God Jesus," see the commentary on 10.2.
10. On the address "ladies, my light," see the commentary on 3.8; for "Christ our God," see 5.11; and for "your affection," see 5.8. By Asia, Egeria means Asia Minor. The phrase "in the body or out of the body" is an allusion to

God, to travel to Asia, that is, to Ephesus, for the sake of prayer at the martyrium of the holy and blessed Apostle John. And if after this I remain in the body, if I am able to visit other places besides, I will either relate them to your affection in person, if God shall be gracious enough to grant it, or certainly, if something else shall be resolved in my mind, tell you in writing. You, ladies, my light, only be gracious enough to be mindful of me, whether I shall be in the body or out of the body.

24 ¹So that your affection may know what is the regular ritual each day in the holy places, I must make you aware, knowing that you would eagerly wish to know this. For each day before cockcrow all the doors of the Anastasis are opened and all the *monazontes*

---

2 Cor 12:3; see also 20.13. Egeria's reference here to sending the account to her sisters and the abrupt change of location and subject in the following chapter onward suggest that this first part of the text was sent to them separately from what now follows, which she may already have dispatched to them earlier in the journey, with the two parts being united later, probably by someone other than their author. On the practicalities of conveying letters from one place to another in the ancient world and the challenge of finding reliable mail carriers, see Stanley K. Stowers, *Letter Writing in Greco-Roman Antiquity* (Philadelphia: Westminster Press, 1986) and the shorter overview in Dietz, *Wandering Monks, Virgins, and Pilgrims*, 20–21.

24 1. For "your affection," see the commentary on 5.8, and for the Anastasis and for the daily services in general, see the Introduction, pp. 61, 70–75. Cockcrow would have been about three hours before sunrise. The words *monazontes* and *parthenae* are Greek for monks and virgins, respectively. Cyril of Jerusalem uses the same terms (*Baptismal Catecheses* 4.24; 16.22), but Egeria does not use these Greek words at all outside her description of the Jerusalem church, and on all other occasions in that description seems to employ *monazontes* to cover both males and females. This is also one of only three occasions on which she uses the term "lay people" (see also 24.12; 25.12), each time adding that there were both men and women. On the meaning of "come down" to the Anastasis in this chapter (24.1, 3, 4, 9), see the Introduction, p. 61. The alternation of psalms and prayer was characteristic of "monastic" night offices, but the prayers elsewhere were normally led by a member of the monastic community itself. Here the deacons would presumably pronounce each bidding to pray and the presbyters recite the prayer. While some ancient monastic communities rose for prayer in the middle of the night, others, as here, began their day with a vigil from cockcrow till morning: see John Cassian, *De inst. coen.* 3.5; *Apostolic Constitutions* 8.34; John Chrysostom, *Hom. in I Ep. ad Tim.* 14.4.

and *parthenae*, as they say here, come down; and not only these but also lay people besides, men and women, those who wish to keep the earlier vigil. And from that hour until daybreak hymns are recited and psalms with refrains, similarly also antiphons; and between each hymn a prayer is made. For two or three presbyters, similarly also deacons, are there in turn each day with the *monazontes* to recite the prayers between each hymn or antiphon.

[2]When it begins to get light, then they begin to recite the morning hymns. Behold, the bishop also arrives with his clergy and immediately goes into the cave and from inside the enclosure he first recites the prayer for all; he also commemorates the names of those whom he wishes; then he blesses the catechumens. Then he says a prayer and blesses the faithful. And after this, as the bishop comes out from inside the enclosure, all come to his hand, and he blesses them one by one as he comes out, and so the dismissal is done when it is already light.

[3]Then at the sixth hour all similarly come down into the Anastasis and psalms and antiphons are recited while the bishop is sent for; he similarly comes down and does not sit but immediately goes inside the enclosure in the Anastasis, that is, inside the cave where also [he was] earlier, and from there he similarly first makes a prayer; he then blesses the faithful and then as he comes

2. "Morning hymns" appear to be the "urban monastic" morning office: see the Introduction, p. 71. Egeria does not identify what the contents might have been, but practice in other places suggests that they may have included some or all of the following: Pss 51, 63, 148–50, and the canticle *Gloria in excelsis*: see Taft, *Liturgy of the Hours*, 31–56. The cave is Christ's tomb, which apparently had a waist-high enclosure at its entrance. From it, the bishop led the intercessory prayer himself, naming those for whom he wanted the people to pray. For the dismissal and the meaning of "come to his hand," see the Introduction, p. 69, and for the meaning of "the catechumens" and "the faithful," see p. 84.

3. Prayer at the sixth and ninth hours follows the same pattern as the morning office. For the meaning of "antiphons," see the Introduction, p. 74. The absence of any explicit mention of the blessing of catechumens at these services does not necessarily mean that they were not present, although that might have been the case, as in 25.2. It is not until Egeria describes the Lenten daily pattern that she also refers to the different service that took place on Wednesdays and Fridays at the ninth hour during the rest of the year: see 27.5.

out from the enclosure, they similarly come to his hand. The ninth hour is also done as at the sixth hour.

⁴At the tenth hour—what they call here *Licinicon*, for we say *Lucernare*—a whole crowd similarly gathers at the Anastasis; all the lamps and candles are lit, and the light is immense. The light is not brought from outside but is taken from inside the cave, that is, from inside the enclosure, where a lamp is always burning night and day. The *Lucernare* psalms and also antiphons are recited for some time. Behold, the bishop is also sent for, and he comes down and takes his seat, and the presbyters as well sit in their places; hymns and antiphons are recited. ⁵And when they have finished them according to the custom, the bishop rises and stands in front of the enclosure, that is, the cave, and one of the deacons makes the commemoration of individuals, as is the custom, and when the deacon says the names of the individuals, very many children always stand, constantly responding, *Kyrie eleison*, as we say, "Lord have mercy." Their voices are immense. ⁶And when the deacon has finished all that he has to say, the bishop first says

4. The evening gathering seems to feature a "monastic" evening office followed by "cathedral" evening hymns/psalms for which the bishop and clergy arrive and sit: see the Introduction, p. 72. Elsewhere the psalms would commonly include Ps 141. Egeria's use of the word "crowd" suggests that it was attended by more people than the other daily services, perhaps because it took place after the working day was over. Thanksgiving at the time of evening lamplighting was a domestic ceremony that formed the basis of the evening church service almost everywhere, and hence the name *Lucernarium* or *Lucernare*, or its Greek equivalent *Lychnikon* (which Egeria transcribes as *Licinicon*), referring to the lighting of lamps. In some places it may have involved the hymn *Phos hilaron*, often thought to be quoted by Basil, *De Spiritu Sancto* 73; but see also *Apostolic Constitutions* 7.48; 8.37. Bringing the light from Christ's tomb here seems intended to symbolize that the thanksgiving was not just for the natural light of the day and for candlelight to illuminate the night but also for the light that Christ brought to the world.

5. The intercessions at evening prayer take a different form from the other services of the day: a litany in which a deacon invited prayer for various individuals and groups by name; a choir of children responded to each one with *Kyrie eleison* (a Greek response apparently unknown to Egeria and her community); and the bishop recited the concluding prayer.

6. *Apostolic Constitutions* 8.6 includes a similar litany for catechumens and their dismissal from the eucharistic liturgy, as well as instructions and texts for evening prayer in 8.35-37.

a prayer and prays for all; and thus all pray, both the faithful and also the catechumens alike. Then the deacon bids all the catechumens to bow their heads where they are standing, and the bishop, standing, then says a blessing over the catechumens. Then a prayer is made, and then the deacon raises his voice and bids each of the faithful, standing, to bow their heads; then the bishop blesses the faithful, and so the dismissal is done at the Anastasis. [7]And individuals begin to come to his hand.

And afterward the bishop is led from the Anastasis to the Cross with hymns, and all the people go with him. When he has arrived, he first makes a prayer, then he blesses the catechumens; then another prayer is made, then he blesses the faithful. And after this both the bishop and all the people then go behind the Cross, and the same is done there as also before the Cross. And they similarly come to the bishop's hand both before the Cross and behind the Cross, as at the Anastasis. Very many large glass lamps hang everywhere, and there are very many candles, both before the Anastasis and also before the Cross and behind the Cross. So all this ends as darkness falls. This regular ritual is held on the six days at the Cross and at the Anastasis.

[8]On the seventh day, that is, the Lord's Day, a whole crowd gathers before cockcrow, as many as can be in that place, as if at

7. After evening prayer is over, there is a further devotional act, or rather a double act centered around the site of the Cross, once in front of it and then again behind it. This was something unique to Jerusalem, and it is not clear why it was repeated, nor how everyone could have been accommodated in the small space behind the Cross, unless they simply streamed in and out to receive the blessing.

8. Egeria calls Sunday the seventh day only because she has just been speaking about the preceding six days and not because it was a regular designation for that day. It involved a change in the usual daily pattern of services because a special vigil occupied the time of the regular "monastic" office at cockcrow. Both the contents and the ministers of the earlier outdoor gathering suggest that it was really that displaced night office rather than an informal community singing event while waiting for the doors to open, as Egeria apparently understood it (*pace* Maraval, 242, n. 2). The use of the word "basilica" to describe the space outside the Anastasis here and even the Anastasis itself at 24.10 and 25.2 is odd, as Egeria, unlike the pilgrim from Bordeaux, never uses the word to describe any other church buildings. Was she trying to indicate that the tomb was enclosed within a building (see the Introduction, p. 61)?

Pascha, at the basilica that is next to the Anastasis, but outdoors, where lights are hung for this. For while they fear that they may not arrive at cockcrow, they come early and sit there. And hymns as well as antiphons are recited, and prayers are made between each hymn and antiphon. For both presbyters and deacons are always ready in that place for the vigil because of the crowd that gathers there. For it is the custom that the holy places are not opened before cockcrow.

[9]As soon as the first cock has crowed, the bishop immediately comes down and goes into the cave at the Anastasis. All the doors are opened and the whole crowd goes into the Anastasis, where very many lights are already lit, and when the people have entered, one of the presbyters recites a psalm and all respond; after this a prayer is made. Then one of the deacons recites a psalm, similarly a prayer is made; a third psalm is also recited by one of the clergy, a third prayer is also made and the commemoration of all. [10]So

9. This "cathedral" vigil at cockcrow is clearly a weekly commemoration of Christ's resurrection on the day and in the very place where it was said to have happened. It was also imitated elsewhere; it is, for example, mentioned in *Apostolic Constitutions* 2.59. There the three psalms are said to symbolize the three days in the tomb, but it was actually a normal Christian custom to arrange psalms in groups of three. In contrast to her more common use of the term, by "clergy" here Egeria may specifically mean someone in minor orders (subdeacons or readers: see the commentary on 7.2), or she may simply mean that any member of the clergy might recite the third psalm. The "commemoration of all" seems to be the equivalent of the "prayer for all" at the daily morning service.

10. This is one of the earliest references to the use of incense in Christian worship. It has been suggested that its presence here was intended to symbolize the spices that women brought to anoint the body of Jesus (Mk 16:1; Lk 23:56–24:1), as that certainly was the interpretation given in later tradition, even if that might seem unlikely for this early date. On the other hand, no other convincing explanation exists as to why incense was used at this service and no other at this time in Jerusalem. The story of the women at the tomb could have been one of the motivations that attracted women to make the pilgrimage there: see Elm, *'Virgins of God,'* 273. The emotional response of the people to the bishop's gospel reading indicates that it was the passion as well as the resurrection narrative that was read each week. Egeria records a similar response to some of the gospel readings in Holy Week (34; 36.3; 37.7). Were people so deeply moved every time they heard it, or was there a cultural expectation that accounts of suffering should receive this response? For "basilica," see the commentary on 24.8.

when these three psalms have been recited and the three prayers made, behold, censers are brought into the cave of the Anastasis, so that the whole Anastasis basilica is filled with the smell. And then where the bishop stands inside the enclosure, he takes the gospel and comes to the door, and the bishop himself reads [the account of] the Lord's resurrection. When he has begun to read it, there is such a groaning and moaning from everyone and such tears that the hardest person could be moved to tears that the Lord had undergone such things for us. ¹¹So, when the gospel has been read, the bishop comes out and is led with hymns to the Cross and all the people with him. There one psalm is then recited and a prayer is made. Then he blesses the faithful and the dismissal is done. And as the bishop comes out, all come to his hand.

¹²The bishop soon retires to his house, and from that time all the *monazontes* return to the Anastasis and psalms and antiphons are recited until daybreak, and between each psalm and antiphon a prayer is made, for the presbyters and deacons keep the vigil by turns every day at the Anastasis with the people. Those of the lay people also who wish, men and women, stay there until daybreak; those who do not wish return to their houses and retire to bed.

25 ¹When it is daybreak, as it is the Lord's Day, they assemble in the major church that Constantine built, the church that is on Golgotha

11. Unlike the devotions at the Cross on weekdays, where there was a blessing and dismissal from the evening service that preceded it, the action here follows on directly, suggesting that it was viewed as an integral part of the passion/resurrection vigil. Once more the absence of explicit mention of catechumens does not necessarily mean that they were excluded from the service.

12. The bishop's house was very probably part of the complex of buildings on Golgotha. The monastic communities complete the night office that they had apparently begun prior to the vigil.

25 1. On "the major church," see the Introduction, p. 62. Egeria's reference to what was done everywhere on Sundays implies that this assembly was for a celebration of the Eucharist, although she does not actually say so. Apparently, the only element in it unfamiliar to her was the preaching of multiple sermons, as she does not comment on anything else. There is no mention of a service of morning prayer preceding it: Did the earlier vigil substitute for it, or was it just part of what was done everywhere and so did not merit a comment? All editors of the Latin text have assumed that the word "not" must have fallen out of the final sentence because it scarcely makes sense without it.

behind the Cross, and everything is done according to the custom by which it is also done everywhere on the Lord's Day. But it is the custom here that as many of all the presbyters seated who wish preach, and after them all, the bishop preaches. These sermons are always done on the Lord's Days, so that the people may always be instructed in the Scriptures and in the love of God. While these sermons are being delivered, there is a long delay before the dismissal from the church is done and so it is [not] before the fourth or even the fifth hour that the dismissal is done.

²But when the dismissal from the church has been done according to the custom by which it is also done everywhere, then the *monazontes* lead the bishop with hymns from the church to the Anastasis. And as the bishop begins to come with hymns, all the doors of the Anastasis basilica are opened; all the people enter— but the faithful, not the catechumens. ³And when the people have entered, the bishop enters and immediately goes inside the enclosure of the cave of the martyrium. First, thanks are given to God, and then the prayer for all is made. Afterward, the deacon bids everyone bow their heads where they are standing and the bishop then blesses them standing inside the enclosure, and afterward

2. Elsewhere, e.g., 27.6, Egeria says that the people, rather than the *monazontes*, lead the bishop in procession. Some have supposed that the service in the middle of the day was a second celebration of the Eucharist, even though Egeria never describes the Eucharist as giving thanks but as the oblation: see Baldovin, *Liturgy in Ancient Jerusalem*, 21–22; Gingras, 221–22, n. 298. Wilkinson, 70, following some earlier scholars (see Gingras, 221, n. 295), improbably proposed that only the liturgy of the word had taken place in the Martyrium and that it was the Eucharist proper that was being held in the Anastasis, even though Egeria never describes such a division of the Eucharist anywhere else. Instead, what took place in the Anastasis seems to be a more primitive version of the weekday prayer at the sixth hour. Catechumens are explicitly excluded from it, not because it was a sacramental rite that they were not permitted to attend, but because it was adhering to the earlier Christian tradition that the unbaptized did not pray together with the faithful. For "basilica," see the commentary on 24.8.

3. The service consisted of a simple thanksgiving (rather than psalmody) and general intercession. This is the only place where Egeria applied the term "martyrium" to Christ's tomb, although it was also used in the same sense by Eusebius, *Vita Constantini* 3.28.

he comes out. [4]As the bishop comes out, all come to his hand. So it is that the dismissal is delayed until nearly the fifth or sixth hour. Then *Lucernare* is done in a similar way to the daily custom.

So this custom is observed every day throughout the whole year, except on feast days, and how it is done on those days we will describe below. [5]Among all this what is quite remarkable is that they arrange that appropriate psalms and antiphons are always recited, both those recited at night, those in the early morning, and those during the day at the sixth or ninth hours or at *Lucernare*, always so appropriate and so reasonable that they are relevant to what is being done.

[6]And all year always on the Lord's Day they assemble at the major church, that is, the one that is on Golgotha, that is, behind the Cross, the one Constantine built; only on one Lord's Day, that is, the fiftieth day of Pentecost, do they assemble on Sion, as you will find noted below; but that they may go on Sion before it is the third hour, the dismissal is done first in the major church. . . .

"Blessed is the One who comes in the name of the Lord," and the rest that follows. And since for the sake of the *monazontes*, who go on foot, it is necessary to go more slowly, they arrive at Jerusalem at that hour when one person can begin to be able to recognize another, that is, near daybreak but before it becomes light.

---

4. Prayer at the ninth hour seems not to have been celebrated on Sundays, as was also true during the Easter season and apparently during the octave of Epiphany (see 25.10; 41), thereby leaving the much more ancient tradition of prayer just three times a day, even if the morning worship had by now become rather protracted.

5. Egeria's pleased surprise at the suitability of the psalms and antiphons might suggest that her community at home followed a traditional "monastic" pattern of psalms recited consecutively from the Psalter without regard for time or season.

6. For Pentecost on Sion, see 43.1-3. Even on that day, there was still a celebration of the Eucharist in the Martyrium, before the one on Sion. A folio is then missing from the manuscript here, and the narrative resumes apparently after Egeria has described the celebration of the eve of the Epiphany in Bethlehem. The chant of the *Benedictus qui venit* (Ps 118:26 = Mt 21:9) seems to have accompanied the nighttime journey of over five miles back to Jerusalem in some way, but there is no mention in AL of a liturgical procession here. The reference to the monks walking implies that others probably rode.

⁷When they have arrived there, the bishop immediately goes into the Anastasis, and everyone with him. There a great number of lights are already burning. One psalm is recited there; a prayer is made; first the catechumens, then the faithful are blessed by the bishop. The bishop retires and everyone goes to their lodgings in order to rest. But the *monazontes* are there until daybreak and recite hymns.

⁸But when the people have rested, they all gather at the beginning of the second hour at the major church that is on Golgotha. It would be impossible to describe how adorned on that day is the church or the Anastasis or the Cross or at Bethlehem. You see there nothing other than gold and jewels and silk; for if you look at the veils, they are entirely of silk with gold stripes; if you look at the curtains, they are similarly entirely of silk with gold stripes. All kinds of vessels of gold and jewels are brought out that day. Surely the number or the weight of the candles or the tapers or the lights or the various vessels could not be estimated or described? ⁹For what shall I say about the decoration of the buildings themselves, which Constantine, with his mother's presence and as far as the resources of his empire extended, adorned with gold, mosaic, and precious marble, both the major church and the Anastasis, at the Cross, and the other holy places in Jerusalem?

¹⁰But to return to the point: the dismissal is done on the first day in the major church that is on Golgotha. And when they

7. The journey concludes with a brief liturgical rite in the Anastasis. While others rest, the monastic community apparently celebrates its regular night office.
8. The Eucharist is held a little later than on a Sunday, at the beginning of the second hour rather than at daybreak, presumably to give the people time for a rest after their night's journey.
9. Eusebius credits Constantine's mother, the empress Helena, with assisting the emperor in the erection of the churches on the Mount of Olives and at Bethlehem (*Vita Constantini* 3.42-43), but says nothing of any connection with Golgotha. By the 390s, however, she was being associated with the discovery of the wood of the cross and the consequent construction of the Martyrium (Ambrose, *De obitu Theodosii* 41–47; Rufinus, *Hist. eccl.* 10.7-8), and Egeria may perhaps be aware of the beginnings of that legend.
10. Egeria quickly recognizes that her enthusiastic description of the adornment of the churches was a digression from her narrative and returns "to the point": see also 23.4. According to AL, the same psalm and epistle reading

preach or read the individual lessons or recite hymns, all are appropriate for the day itself; and from there afterward, when the dismissal from the church has been done, they go with hymns to the Anastasis, according to the custom, and so the dismissal is done about the sixth hour. [11]And on this day *Lucernare* similarly is also done according to the daily custom.

Then on the next day they similarly assemble at the church on Golgotha, the same also on the third day. So, for three days they celebrate with all this rejoicing until the sixth hour in the church that Constantine built. On the fourth day on Eleona, that is, in the very beautiful church that is on the Mount of Olives, everything is similarly decorated and they celebrate there; on the fifth day at the Lazarium, which lies about fifteen hundred paces from Jerusalem; on the sixth day on Sion; on the seventh day at the Anastasis; on the eighth day at the Cross. Thus, for eight days they celebrate with all this rejoicing and decoration in all the holy places that I have named above.

---

were used at this Eucharist on January 6 as had been used in Bethlehem the night before, Ps 2 and Titus 2:11-15, but the gospel was Mt 1:18-25, the account of the nativity, rather than Mt 2:1-12, the visit of the Magi, that had been read at the Eucharist at Bethlehem, implying that this might have been the original Epiphany celebration before the visit to Bethlehem was added. As on Sundays, the service included preaching; and also seemingly like Sundays and the Easter season, there was a service in the middle of the day in the Anastasis but not one at the ninth hour, probably also throughout the Epiphany octave.

11. For discussion of the locations of the daily Eucharist during the octave, see the Introduction, pp. 98–99. In AL, there had been some changes to these stations, and the propers for each day were: (2: at the martyrium of St. Stephen, built after Egeria's visit) Ps 5; Acts 6:8–8:2; Titus 2:11-15; Jn 12:24-26; (3: the Martyrium) Ps 2; Heb 1:1-12; Mt 2:13-23; (4: Sion) Ps 110; Gal 4:1-7; Lk 1:26-38; (5: Eleona) Ps 99; Heb 12:18-27; Lk 1:39-56; (6: Lazarium) Ps 30; 1 Thess 4:13-18; Jn 11:1-46; (7: Golgotha) Ps 96; Rom 1:17; Lk 2:1-7; (8: Anastasis; feast of Christ's circumcision) Ps 98; Col 2:8-15; Lk 2:21. The introduction of the station at the martyrium of St. Stephen has obviously resulted in the addition of the Acts reading and a change to the gospel (perhaps from Mt 2:1-12), just as the station at the Lazarium has affected the readings there: see Baldovin, *Liturgy in Ancient Jerusalem*, 36–37.

¹²In Bethlehem throughout all the eight days every day is celebrated with decoration and rejoicing by the presbyters and by all the clergy of that place and by the *monazontes* who have been assigned to that place. For from that time when all return by night to Jerusalem with the bishop, then the monks of that place, all that there are, keep vigil until daybreak in the church in Bethlehem, reciting hymns and antiphons, because it is necessary for the bishop always to keep these days in Jerusalem. Because of the solemnity and rejoicing of that day, immense crowds gather from everywhere in Jerusalem, not only *monazontes* but also lay people, men and women.

26 The fortieth day after Epiphany is certainly celebrated here with the greatest honor. For on that day the procession [*processio*] is in

12. For "clergy" used to mean those other than presbyters, see the commentary on 7.2. The vigil at Bethlehem appears to be a special all-night vigil for the festival rather than the normal daily "monastic" night office, as Egeria records the existence of a similar vigil elsewhere for the festival: see 9.1. Her remark about the necessity for the bishop to keep Epiphany and its octave in Jerusalem seems to support the suggestion we made in the commentary on verse 10 that the visit to Bethlehem was a later addition to an original celebration in Jerusalem.

26 The fortieth day after Epiphany would have been February 14. This account is the oldest evidence that exists for a festival celebrating the presentation of Christ in the Temple, later known in the East in Greek as the *Hypapante*, meaning "meeting," and referring to the meeting of Simeon and Anna with the infant Jesus (Lk 2:22-40). Although Luke does not specify the fortieth day for the event but only the completion of "the days of her [Mary's] purification according to the Law of Moses," that would have been the fortieth day after the birth for a male child (Lev 12:2-5). AL gives Ps 98, Gal 3:24-29, and Lk 2:22-40 as the propers. See further Nicholas Denysenko, "The Hypapante Feast in Fourth to Eighth Century Jerusalem," *Studia Liturgica* 37 (2007): 73–97. It is not clear from Egeria's expression "celebrated here with the greatest honor" whether she intended to contrast the degree of honor accorded to the Jerusalem festival with her own community's simpler celebration or to highlight a feast that was entirely unknown in her home region. Although Maraval, 255, n. 3, believed that the reference to the Anastasis only meant that the first office of the day took place there and that the Eucharist itself would actually have been held in the Martyrium as on a Sunday (and as was the case in AL), that seems to be ruled out by Egeria's choice of the terms *processio* and *procedo* here in relation to the Anastasis. This was the only occasion on which she used the noun *processio* and it is very doubtful that she

the Anastasis and all assemble [*procedunt*] and everything is done in its order with the greatest rejoicing, as at Pascha. All the presbyters also preach and then the bishop, drawing on that passage in the gospel where on the fortieth day Joseph and Mary brought the Lord into the Temple and Simeon and Anna the prophetess, the daughter of Phanuel, saw him, and about their words that they spoke when they saw the Lord and about the offering that his parents made. And after everything that is customary has been celebrated in order, the sacrament is administered and then the dismissal is done.

27 ¹Then when the paschal days approach, they are celebrated thus: For as among us forty days before Pascha are observed, so here eight weeks are observed before Pascha. Eight weeks are observed because on the Lord's Day and the Sabbath they do not fast, except for the one Sabbath day when it is the paschal vigil and it is obligatory to fast; so, apart from that day, there is never any fasting here on the Sabbath in the whole year. Thus, taking away eight Lord's Days and seven Sabbaths from the eight weeks, because it is obligatory to fast on the one Sabbath as I said above, there remain

---

really meant "procession," even though we have translated it thus. It should probably be rendered as "assembly," especially as she regularly employed the related verb *procedo* to mean "assemble for a Eucharist with a liturgy of the word" and not for any other service: see the Introduction, pp. 82–83. For the phrase "in its order," see the commentary on 3.6. The use of the Anastasis for the Eucharist rather than the Martyrium on this occasion was probably because the Anastasis was viewed as symbolically representing the Temple: see Baldovin, *Liturgy in Ancient Jerusalem*, 36. It was also the only time when Egeria described the Eucharist as the "sacrament," although using the word in the plural (*sacramenta*).

27 1. Egeria's own community would doubtless have followed the common Western practice of keeping Lent for a total of only six weeks with fasting every day except Sunday, and hence her need to comment on the very different custom in Jerusalem. For more on the length of Lent, see the Introduction, pp. 88–90. The use of the Greek word *heortae*, "festivals," as the local term for Lent is not otherwise attested. Egeria might have misunderstood what she was told, though Maraval, 259, n. 1, defended it as authentic on the grounds that Lent "was experienced as an integral part of the paschal season, in an atmosphere of spiritual exultation." Quadragesima is the Latin word for "fortieth" and was used as the standard name for Lent in the West.

forty-one days when they fast, which here they call the "Festivals," that is, Quadragesima.

²The various days of the several weeks are kept thus; that is, on the Lord's Day after first cockcrow the bishop reads the passage from the gospel about the Lord's resurrection inside the Anastasis, as is also done all year on the Lord's Day, and similarly up to daybreak they do at the Anastasis and at the Cross what is also done all year on the Lord's Day. ³Afterward in the morning, as always on the Lord's Day, they assemble and do what it is custom to do on the Lord's Day in the major church that is called the Martyrium, which is on Golgotha behind the Cross. And similarly, when the dismissal from church has been done, they go to the Anastasis with hymns, as is always done on the Lord's Day. So, while they are doing this, the fifth hour is reached. *Lucernare* is done at its same time as always at the Anastasis and at the Cross, as is done also in the various holy places, for on the Lord's Day the ninth hour is [not] done.

⁴Then on the second day of the week similarly at first cockcrow they go to the Anastasis as also in the rest of the year and do until morning as always. Then at the third hour they go to the Anastasis and do what in the rest of the year they are accustomed to do at the sixth hour, because in the days of Quadragesima it is added that they go at the third hour. Then at the sixth hour and the ninth hour and *Lucernare* they do as it is the custom always to do in the rest of the year in the holy places.

⁵Similarly also on the third day of the week everything is done as also on the second day. On the fourth day they similarly go by night to the Anastasis and do as always until morning; similarly

2. The sole point of this verse and the longer one that follows is to say that the services on Sundays during Lent are exactly the same as in the rest of the year.

3. Although the text says that the ninth hour is done, there is general agreement among scholars that "not" was in the original and has fallen out: see the commentary on 25.4.

4. In Lent the public celebration of the third hour was added to the weekday cycle, which was otherwise unchanged. The third hour, however, was almost certainly observed throughout the year by the monastic communities separately.

5. Here Egeria reveals the existence of a service of the word on Sion at the ninth hour on Wednesdays and Fridays throughout the year, unless they

also at the third hour and at the sixth hour. But at the ninth hour, as the custom is always, that is, in the rest of the year, on the fourth and sixth days of the week to assemble on Sion at the ninth hour—because in these places, unless a martyr's day intervenes, there is always fasting on the fourth and sixth days of the week, even also by catechumens—and so they assemble at the ninth hour on Sion. For if by chance a martyr's day does intervene on the fourth or sixth day of the week in Quadragesima, [. . .?], still they assemble at the ninth hour on Sion.

⁶In the days of Quadragesima, as I said above, on the fourth day of the week they assemble at the ninth hour on Sion according to the custom of the rest of the year and do everything that it is the custom to do at the ninth hour, except for the oblation. For so that the people may constantly learn the law, both the bishop and the presbyter[s] preach assiduously. When the dismissal has been done, the people lead the bishop with hymns from there to the Anastasis; thence it happens that when he enters the Anastasis, it

---

happened to coincide with a festival honoring a martyr. These two days were the regular weekly occasions for fasting in early Christianity, ending at the ninth hour. Does Egeria's explicit mention of catechumens' participation in the fasting imply that this was not the case where she came from? In the sentence about a martyr's day falling on a Wednesday or Friday in Lent, Maraval, 261, n. 2, followed several commentators in suspecting that there had been a lacuna in the text (marked here by [. . .?]) which would have alluded to the suspension of fasting on those days, just as in the rest of the year, but he believed that the service was nevertheless retained, although perhaps the Sion location was not. Gingras, 228, n. 328, and Brodersen, 191, on the contrary, followed other scholars in rejecting the alleged lacuna but changing the Latin word *atque*, "and," to a negative, meaning that the ninth-hour service was also suspended, as on martyrs' days in the rest of the year. The abandonment of fasting on such days in Lent seems very improbable, however, as it would have resulted in less than forty fasting days, and it is to be noted that the Council of Laodicea (380), canon 51, directed that "in Lent the *natalia* of martyrs must not take place." Hence we have preferred to follow Wilkinson, 149, in rendering *atque* as "still," meaning that both fasting and the service were retained even on a martyr's day in Lent.
6. Whether by "except for the oblation" Egeria means that the service included the celebration of the Eucharist outside Lent, see the Introduction, pp. 80–81. Although not noted by Maraval or others, the singular "presbyter" is surely an error for the plural, as multiple sermons by presbyters were a feature of the Eucharist on Sundays and festivals (see 25.1; 26; 42) and so seem to be intended here.

is already the hour for *Lucernare*; then they recite hymns and anti-phons, prayers are made, and the dismissal from *Lucernare* is done in the Anastasis and at the Cross. [7]The dismissal from *Lucernare* in these days, that is, in Quadragesima, is always done later than in the rest of the year.

On the fifth day of the week everything is done in the same way as on the second and third days of the week. On the sixth day of the week everything is done in the same way as on the fourth day of the week, and they likewise go to Sion at the ninth hour and likewise the bishop is led from there with hymns to the Anastasis. But on the sixth day of the week a vigil is celebrated from the time when they have come from Sion with hymns until the morning, that is, from the time of *Lucernare* until the beginning of the morning of the next day, that is, the Sabbath. The oblation is made earlier in the Anastasis, so that the dismissal may be done before sunrise. [8]Throughout the night are recited in turn respon-sorial psalms, antiphons, and various readings, which all last until the morning. The dismissal, which is done on the Sabbath at the Anastasis, is done before sunrise, this is the oblation, so that the dismissal also may be done at the time when the sun begins to rise. Thus are each of the weeks of Quadragesima celebrated.

[9]As I said, the dismissal is done earlier on the Sabbath, that is, before sunrise; it is done in order that those whom they call

7. It is not clear why *Lucernare* would end later in Lent than in the rest of the year, especially as Egeria has said that the previous service would have ended at the time for *Lucernare*. Did she really mean to say that the previous service went on longer in Lent, perhaps because of more preaching (and an extra reading on Fridays? See the Introduction, p. 90), and so *Lucernare* actually started and finished later than usual? Here and at 29.1 and 3 are the only explicit references she makes to the celebration of the Eucharist on Saturdays: see the Introduction, p. 81.

8. For more detail of the structure of an identical Friday vigil practiced year-round by the Palestinian monastic communities described by John Cassian, see the Introduction, pp. 76–77. This suggests that the Jerusalem church had adopted as a Lenten discipline a custom that was already practiced by the local monastic communities on their own throughout the year.

9. Egeria explains that the celebration of the Eucharist takes place earlier to shorten slightly the week of fasting undertaken in Lent by a particular group of ascetics who do not eat from Sunday onward until they have received Communion the following Saturday.

hebdomadarii here may finish sooner. For the custom of fasting here in Quadragesima is such that those whom they call *hebdomadarii*, that is, "those who do the week," eat on the Lord's Day when the dismissal is done at the fifth hour. And when they have breakfasted on the Lord's Day, they do not eat until the Sabbath morning as soon as they have received Communion in the Anastasis. So for their sake, in order that they may finish sooner, the dismissal is done in the Anastasis on the Sabbath before sunrise. I said that for their sake the dismissal is done in the morning, not that they alone receive Communion but all who wish to receive Communion that day in the Anastasis receive Communion.

28 ¹For the custom of fasting here in Quadragesima is such that some, when they have eaten on the Lord's Day after the dismissal, that is, at the fifth or sixth hour, do not eat for the whole week until the coming Sabbath, after the dismissal at the Anastasis; these [are] "those who do the week." ²After they have eaten in the morning of the Sabbath, they do not eat in the evening, but on the next day, that is, the Lord's Day, they breakfast after the dismissal from the church at the fifth hour or later, and afterward do not eat until the coming Sabbath, as I said earlier.

³For the custom here is such that all who are, as they say here, *apotactitae*, men and women, not only in the days of Quadragesima but also the whole year eat once a day, when they do eat. But if there are any of these *apotactitae* who cannot do complete weeks of fasting, as we said above, throughout Quadragesima they dine in the middle, on the fifth day. But anyone who cannot do this does a two-day fast throughout Quadragesima; and any who [cannot do] even this eat every evening.

28 1. Egeria here effectively repeats herself in describing what the *hebdomadarii* do.

2. She then explains that they only eat one meal on Saturday and another on Sunday during the weeks of Lent.

3. For *apotactitae*, see the commentary on 23.3; the term obviously covers a range of ascetics who have in common that they eat only one meal a day throughout the rest of the year, but differ in the degree to which they fast in Lent: some are *hebdomadarii*, while others break their weekly fast once in the middle of the week. When Egeria speaks of those who fast only two days at a time and those who eat one meal every day, she may possibly still be referring to yet other *apotactitae*, but it seems more likely that she has ordinary Jerusalem Christians in mind here.

⁴No one compels how much anyone ought to do, but everyone does what they are able; those who have done much are not praised, nor are those who have done less reproached. For such is the custom here. Their food in the days of Quadragesima is this: they taste neither bread—even that cannot be sampled—nor oil nor anything that grows on trees, but only water and a little broth made with flour. Quadragesima is done thus, as we said.

29 ¹At the end of these weeks there is a vigil in the Anastasis from the time of *Lucernare* on the sixth day, when they come from Sion with psalms, to the morning of the Sabbath, when the oblation is made in the Anastasis. The second, third, fourth, fifth, and sixth weeks are like the first week of Quadragesima.

²When the seventh week has come, that is, when with this one two weeks remain until it is Pascha, on each day everything indeed is done as also in the other weeks that have passed, except that the vigil, which was done in those six weeks in the Anastasis, in the seventh week, that is, on the sixth day of the week, is done on Sion according to the same custom with which it was done in the Anastasis during the six weeks. During the whole vigil psalms and antiphons appropriate to the place and the day are always recited.

4. Egeria here appears to be implicitly contrasting the freedom allowed to Jerusalem Christians with what was seemingly a more regimented discipline of fasting in her own community. The phrase "even that cannot be sampled" is one conjecture among several offered by scholars for an uncertain Latin text, although none of them is very satisfactory: see Gingras, 231, n. 340; Maraval, 266, n. 3. Abstinence from even a little bread during a fast would have been relatively rare. *Apostolic Constitutions* 5.18, for example, directed that only bread, salt, herbs, and water were to be consumed from Monday to Thursday during Holy Week. Broth made with flour is what is called gruel in English. Egeria must surely be referring to the Lenten food of the *apotactitae* in this instance and not to Jerusalem Christians in general!

29 1. Egeria repeats here what she had said at 27.7-9, merely clarifying that this was also true of the other weeks in Lent.
2. The fact that the Friday vigil in this penultimate week before Easter is on Sion rather than in the Anastasis like the rest may be an indication that it is a more ancient custom. Had it originally belonged to the Friday night before Pascha, as part of an older extended fast and vigil, and then was moved back one week when Lent became distinguished from Great Week? Egeria does not explicitly mention readings in her summary of the contents of this vigil, but she probably did not intend to make any distinction from the form she described in 27.8.

[3]When the Sabbath morning begins to grow light, the bishop offers and makes the oblation on the Sabbath morning. As the dismissal is being done, the archdeacon raises his voice and says: "Let us all be ready today at the seventh hour in the Lazarium." Thus, when the seventh hour begins to approach, everyone comes to the Lazarium. The Lazarium, that is, Bethany, is about two miles from the city. [4]Going from Jerusalem to the Lazarium, about five hundred paces from that place there is a church on the road in that place where Mary, the sister of Lazarus, met the Lord. So, when the bishop comes there, all the monks meet him and the people enter there; one hymn is recited and one antiphon and that passage from the gospel is read where the sister of Lazarus meets the Lord. And then when prayer has been made and all have been blessed, they go from there to the Lazarium with hymns.

[5]When they have come into the Lazarium, a whole crowd gathers there so that not only the place itself but also all the fields around are full of people. Hymns and antiphons appropriate to the day and place are also recited, similarly also readings all ap-

3. Offering was not understood as done by the bishop alone: see 4.3, "we made the oblation"; 4.8, "we were not able to make the oblation." This is one of the oldest references to the office of archdeacon; it appears that making such announcements was one of his functions: see 30.2; 35.1; 43.3. Egeria says nothing about prayer at the third and sixth hours: Was she simply taking them for granted, or were they omitted because of the other services that day? For the Lazarium, see the Introduction, p. 68.

4. A station is made on the way to the Lazarium at this church in the place where Mary was believed to have met Jesus, the relevant passage from John being read, presumably something like 11:17-30. There is no trace of this station in AL.

5. The Lazarium church was probably quite small, and hence not large enough to accommodate the crowds that gathered there for this celebration. Although the bishop himself read the gospel at least at the weekly Sunday vigil (24.10) and apparently at the special Holy Week services (33.2; but cf. 34), here a presbyter is said to do so: Was that because it formed part of the dismissal rite? In AL the vigil-like structure of the service that Egeria describes has disappeared, and in its place are Ps 30; 1 Thess 4:13-18; Jn 11:55–12:11, although Egeria implies that the gospel read at the dismissal began at 12:1. Does this pattern mean that the service in AL was a Eucharist? While the first reading seems to relate to the raising of Lazarus, the gospel indicates that the focus of the event had already shifted to the later visit of Jesus to Bethany: see the Introduction, p. 91.

propriate to the day are read. As the dismissal is being done, Pascha is announced, that is, a presbyter ascends to a higher place and reads that passage that is written in the gospel, "When Jesus had come to Bethany six days before the Pascha," and the rest. So, when that passage has been read and Pascha announced, the dismissal is done. [6]This is done on that day because, as it is written in the gospel, this was done in Bethany six days before Pascha; for from the Sabbath to the fifth day of the week, when after supper the Lord was arrested by night, are six days. So all return to the city straight to the Anastasis and *Lucernare* is done according to the custom.

30 [1]So, on the next day, that is, the Lord's Day, when the paschal week begins, which they call here Great Week, having celebrated from cockcrow those things that are customary to do in the Anastasis and at the Cross until morning, in the morning of the Lord's Day they assemble according to the custom in the major church, which is called the Martyrium. It is called the Martyrium for the reason that it is on Golgotha, that is, behind the Cross where the Lord suffered, and hence the Martyrium. [2]So, when everything has been celebrated according to the custom in the major church, and before the dismissal is done, the archdeacon raises his voice and says first, "All this week, that is, from tomorrow, let us all come together at the ninth hour at the Martyrium," that is, in the major church. Then he raises his voice again and says, "Today let us all be ready

6. Pascha here must mean the Jewish Passover (as in Jn 12.1) rather than the Christian Easter. The same dating is used in AL. This special service must have replaced the usual daily service at the ninth hour.

30 1. The later Western term "Holy Week" is obviously not yet known to Egeria, nor does she seem familiar with the name "Day of Palms" for the Sunday. The latter is found in AL, which gives the propers for the Eucharist in the Martyrium as Ps 98; Eph 1:3-10; Mt 20:29–21:17. This gospel reading included the entry into Jerusalem, but it seems unlikely that it was used at this Eucharist in Egeria's day, as she records it being read on the Imbomon at the eleventh hour, prior to the procession (see 31.2), which is not mentioned in AL. This is the first time that she offers a rationale for the church being called the Martyrium.

2. The archdeacon makes his announcements at the end of the Eucharist and not at the following service in the Anastasis. Was this simply because it was the traditional place for announcements or is it an indication that not everybody would stay on for the gathering in the Anastasis?

at the seventh hour on Eleona." [3]So, when the dismissal has been done at the major church, that is, at the Martyrium, the bishop is led with hymns to the Anastasis and when they have completed there what it is the custom to do on the Lord's Day in the Anastasis after the dismissal at the Martyrium, everyone hurries home to eat so that at the beginning of the seventh hour all may be ready in the church that is on Eleona, that is, the Mount of Olives, where there is the cave in which the Lord taught.

31 [1]So, at the seventh hour all the people ascend the Mount of Olives, that is, on Eleona, in the church. The bishop sits, hymns and antiphons appropriate to that day and place are recited, similarly also readings. And when the ninth hour begins to approach, they go up with hymns to the Imbomon, that is, the place from which the Lord ascended into heaven, and there they sit, for all the people are always bidden to sit when the bishop is present, and the deacons alone always stand. Hymns and antiphons appropriate to the place and day are also recited there; similarly also readings and prayers are interspersed.

[2]And when the eleventh hour begins, there is read that passage from the gospel where children with branches and palms meet the Lord, saying, "Blessed is the One who comes in the name of the Lord." And immediately the bishop rises and all the people go forward from there entirely on foot from the summit of the Mount of Olives. For all the people [go] before him with hymns

---

3. For Eleona and the cave, see the Introduction, pp. 66–67.

31 1. For the Imbomon, see the Introduction, p. 67. AL preserves this vigil-type service, but does not mention going to the Imbomon but only to the Mount of Olives from the ninth hour until the eleventh hour, during which time the people sing psalms and pray. There is no reference to readings in AL, and it is difficult to imagine what readings "appropriate" to the Imbomon on this day might have been. If Egeria really means by "always" that on every single occasion when the bishop is present at any liturgy all the people sit rather than stand, this is something that she has not indicated elsewhere.

2. None of the gospels mention children in this particular context, but Mt 21:15 does refer to children in the Temple crying out, "Hosanna to the Son of David," and so it seems likely that it was the Matthean account of the entry into Jerusalem that was read (Mt 21:1-9 or 1-17). AL does not mention the reading of the gospel passage but only the procession to the Anastasis, singing Ps 118 with verse 26 as its refrain, "Blessed is the One who comes in the name of the Lord."

and antiphons, continually responding, "Blessed is the One who comes in the name of the Lord." ³And there are very many children in these places—including those who cannot walk on foot; because they are to be carried, their parents carry them on their shoulders—all carrying branches, some of palm, others of olive; and so the bishop is led in the same way as the Lord was led then.

⁴And from the summit of the Mount to the city and from there through the whole city to the Anastasis all, even any who are noble ladies and gentlemen, lead the bishop entirely on foot, responding thus, going very slowly lest the people become tired, and so at a late hour arrive at the Anastasis. When they have arrived there, even though it is late, *Lucernare* is still done, then prayer is made at the Cross, and the people are dismissed.

32 ¹Then on the next day, that is, the second day of the week, they do what it is customary to do from first cockcrow until morning

3. The association of children with the carrying of palms must have been a long-established Jerusalem tradition, because the pilgrim from Bordeaux was shown the palm tree from which it was said that children had taken branches and spread them in Christ's path (see Appendix A, p. 202), and Cyril of Jerusalem, *Baptismal Catecheses* 10.29, similarly referred to the palm tree that supplied the branches to the children. For more on this connection, see Bruce N. Beck, " 'Out of the Mouth of Babes': Prophetic Children of Palm Sunday in Patristic-Liturgical Tradition," *Revue Scriptura: Nouvelle Série* 10, no. 1 (2008): 23–34. The statement that the bishop was led in the same way as Christ had been does not necessarily mean that he also rode on a donkey, as some have supposed, but only that he too was escorted by children carrying branches.

4. It appears to have been an important act of piety for the journey to be made on foot; see also 36.2-3 for another descent from the Imbomon on foot in the early hours of Good Friday.

32 1. On Monday in Holy Week the normal Lenten services are held until the afternoon. Then, in place of the usual prayer at the ninth hour in the Anastasis, there is a vigil service in the Martyrium, lasting for four hours like the one on Palm Sunday. AL places its beginning at the tenth hour rather than the ninth, and provides the following readings: Gen 1:1–3:24; Prov 1:1-9; Isa 40:1-8; Ps 65; Mt 20:17-28. This would hardly be sufficient for a long vigil, and suggests that it had been reduced by then to a more moderate service of the word comparable in structure to AL's Friday services in Lent at the tenth hour, except for the addition of a gospel reading (see the Introduction, p. 90). See also Lages, "Étapes de l'évolution du Carême à Jérusalem," 90–96, for a possible earlier arrangement of these readings of Holy Week.

at the Anastasis; similarly both at the third and at the sixth hours they do what is done all through Quadragesima. At the ninth hour all gather in the major church, that is, at the Martyrium, and there until the first hour of the night hymns and antiphons are continually recited, readings also appropriate to the day and place are read, prayers always interspersed. [2]*Lucernarium* also takes place there when the hour approaches; so it is already nightfall when the dismissal is done at the Martyrium. When the dismissal has been done there, the bishop is led with hymns from there to the Anastasis. When he has entered into the Anastasis, one hymn is recited, prayer is made, the catechumens are blessed, then the faithful, and the dismissal is done.

33 [1]Then on the third day of the week everything is done just as on the second day of the week. This alone is added on the third day of the week, that late at night after the dismissal has been done at the Martyrium and they have gone to the Anastasis and then the dismissal has been done in the Anastasis, all go at that hour of the night to the church that is on Mount Eleona. [2]When they have come to that church, the bishop enters into the cave in which the Lord was accustomed to teach the disciples, and he takes the gospel book, and, standing, the bishop himself reads the words of the Lord that are written in the Gospel according to Matthew,

---

2. For some reason, Egeria switches from *Lucernare* to *Lucernarium* as her name for the evening office from this point until after her description of the Easter octave in Chapter 40, when she reverts to *Lucernare*. There is a change in the location of this service during Holy Week from the rest of the year. Instead of going to the Anastasis, they stay in the Martyrium for it, and then go to the Anastasis rather than to the Cross for the usual devotion afterward.

33 1. Tuesday is the same as Monday, apart from the addition of a late-night visit to the Mount of Olives. AL again locates the afternoon service at the tenth hour, but this time on Eleona, and so it appears that the late evening service that Egeria describes was subsequently transferred to this earlier hour.

2. Egeria uses the Latin word *codex* for "book" here: see 10.7 above. The gospel verse to which Egeria refers is Mt 24:4, the beginning of the discourse that the evangelist says was delivered by Jesus on the Mount of Olives two days before the Passover (Mt 26:2). AL confirms the gospel reading at its afternoon service as Mt 24:1–26:2, but prefaces it with three Old Testament readings, from the same books as at the same service on Monday. They are: Gen 6:9–9:17; Prov 9:1-11; Isa 40:9-17; together with Ps 25.

that is, where he says, "See, let no one lead you astray." And the bishop reads through that whole discourse. And when he has read through it, prayer is made, the catechumens are blessed, then also the faithful, the dismissal is done and everyone returns from the Mount to their homes as it is already quite late at night.

34 Then on the fourth day of the week everything is done throughout the day from first cockcrow as on the second and third days of the week, but after the dismissal has been done at night at the Martyrium and the bishop has been led with hymns to the Anastasis, the bishop immediately enters into the cave that is in the Anastasis and he stands inside the enclosure; but a presbyter stands outside the enclosure and takes the gospel and reads that passage where Judas Iscariot went to the Jews and determined what they should give him to betray the Lord. When that passage has been read, there is such a groaning and moaning from all the people that there is no one who could not be moved to tears at that time. Afterward prayer is made, the catechumens are blessed, afterward the faithful, and the dismissal is done.

35 [1]Then on the fifth day of the week they do those things that are customary from first cockcrow until the morning in the Anastasis;

34 The Wednesday services are the same as those on Monday and Tuesday, except that the visit to the Anastasis after *Lucernarium* in the Martyrium is not just for the usual brief devotion as on the other evenings, but includes a reading of the account of the betrayal of Jesus by Judas in Mt 26. On this occasion the gospel is unusually read by a presbyter rather than by the bishop. The only other instance Egeria records of a presbyter reading the gospel is at the Lazarium on the Saturday before Holy Week (29.5), but there it was part of a dismissal rite. For similar emotional responses to a gospel reading, see 24.10; 36.3; 37.7. Once again AL provides three Old Testament readings for a service in the Martyrium at the tenth hour, Gen 18:1–19:30; Prov 1:10-19; Zech 11:11-14, followed by Ps 41; and then Mt 26:3-16 was read at the Anastasis.

35 1. The services on Holy Thursday are the same as on the other days in Holy Week until the afternoon, when the service is at the eighth hour rather than the ninth, presumably in order to allow time for two celebrations of the Eucharist. It is difficult to know whether Egeria's expression "they do what is to be done" refers to more than just a normal celebration of the Eucharist (though presumably without the multiple sermons that were usual on Sundays as the whole service was much shorter). AL certainly includes more. There the assembly is at the seventh hour rather than the eighth, and includes similarly at the third and at the sixth hours. At the eighth hour all the people gather at the Martyrium according to custom, but earlier than on other days because it is necessary for the dismissal to be done sooner. Thus, when all the people have gathered, they do what is to be done; that day the oblation is made at the Martyrium and the dismissal is done there about the tenth hour. But before the dismissal is done, the archdeacon raises his voice and says, "At the first hour of the night let us all come together at the church that is on Eleona, because the greatest labor awaits us today, this very night." [2]When the dismissal has been done at the Martyrium, they come behind the Cross, one hymn only is recited there, prayer is made, and the bishop offers the oblation there and all receive Communion. For except on that one day it is never offered behind the Cross throughout the whole year except on that day only. So the dismissal also having been done there, they go to the Anastasis, prayer is made, the catechumens are blessed according to the custom and then the faithful, and the dismissal is done.

---

two Old Testament readings (rather than the three of the services earlier in the week), Gen 22:1-18 and Isa 61:1-6 (not Isa 61:14, as in Wilkinson), continuing the sequence begun at those services, but adding Acts 1:15-26 as a third reading, followed by Ps 55. It then states: "After the psalm they sit down for the commentaries, and the catechumens are dismissed." What are translated here as "commentaries" were apparently patristic homilies that were read. The eucharistic liturgy of the word then follows, with Ps 23; 1 Cor 11:23-32; and Mt 26:17-30. The archdeacon makes his announcement at the end of this first Eucharist and not the second. As in 30.2, does this mean that everyone did not stay for the second celebration, or was he just following an older tradition when there was only one Eucharist on this day?

2. For the discussion of reasons for the second celebration of the Eucharist, see the Introduction, pp. 92–94. Egeria's unusually explicit statement that "all" received Communion on this occasion must have some particular significance: Did she mean that this was not always the case on other occasions? The visit to the Anastasis is for the usual brief devotional act as on the earlier evenings of this week. Egeria gives no indication that *Lucernarium* was held either there or elsewhere on this day, but AL states that both the evening office and the vigil are celebrated on the Mount of Olives. If "everyone" is to be taken literally, even those who have fasted for the whole week in Lent break their fast on this day, between what would originally have been the end of the Lenten fast as such on this day and the beginning of the paschal fast proper.

And then everyone hurries to return to their home to eat, because as soon as they have eaten, they all go to Eleona, to the church in which there is the cave in which on this day the Lord was with the apostles. [3]And there until about the fifth hour of the night hymns and antiphons appropriate to the day and place are continually recited, similarly also readings; prayers are interspersed; those passages also from the gospel are read in which the Lord addressed the disciples that very day, sitting in the same cave that is in that church. [4]And from there at about the sixth hour of the night they go up with hymns to the Imbomon, to that place where the Lord ascended into heaven. And there again similarly readings and hymns and antiphons appropriate to the day are recited; also whatever prayers there are that the bishop says are always appropriate both to the day and to the place.

36 [1]Thus, when the cocks begin to crow, they come down from the Imbomon with hymns and come to that place where the Lord

3. This vigil during the first part of the night lasts for about four hours, like those at the ninth hour on the other days of this week, and with similar contents. In AL, however, there are only psalms and prayers and not readings, with five groups of three psalms, a prayer being said after each three-psalm unit. Jn 13:16–18:1 then followed at midnight. Was this what Egeria described as the "passages [plural] . . . in which the Lord addressed the disciples," even though that address really belonged to the Supper, rather than the much shorter passage, Mt 26:31-35, said to have been spoken on the Mount of Olives?

4. The vigil continues at the Imbomon, but in AL there is simply one psalm (109) and the reading of Lk 22:1-65 there. This reading breaks the historical sequence represented by the other gospel readings during this night and duplicates what is in them, suggesting that it is a later addition.

36 1. Egeria misquotes Lk 22:41 here, which has "withdrew" and not "approached." This is the only place in which Egeria uses the adjective *elegans*, which we have translated as "fine." Archaeological excavation has revealed that the nave of that church covered an area of less than 4,000 square feet, which means that if everyone in the procession could really have been accommodated within it, they would have numbered in hundreds rather than thousands: see also Baldovin, *Urban Character*, 52–53. Egeria states that the gospel passage read here included Mk 14:38. AL has the reading of Mk 14:27-72, and this could have been what was read in Egeria's day, although it may have been shorter and not included the arrest and trial. In AL it is said to have been read in the "Room of the Disciples," which Gingras, 237, n. 372, and Wilkinson, 186, n. 40c, identified as being the cave in the Eleona, though this seems an odd designation for that place.

prayed, as it is written in the gospel: "And he approached a stone's throw and prayed," and the rest. For in that place there is a fine church. The bishop and all the people enter, a prayer appropriate to the place and day is recited there, an appropriate hymn is also recited and that passage from the gospel is read where he said to his disciples, "Watch, lest you enter into temptation." And the whole of that passage is read through there and then prayer is made. ²And from there with hymns, even down to the smallest child, they come down on foot with the bishop to Gethsemane, where on account of the large size of the crowd both wearied from the vigil and weak from the daily fasting, because they have to come down such a large mountain, they come very slowly with hymns to Gethsemane. More than two hundred church candles are prepared to give light to all the people.

³So, when they have arrived at Gethsemane, first an appropriate prayer is made, then a hymn is recited; then is read that passage from the gospel where the Lord was arrested. When that passage has been read, there is such a groaning and moaning from all the people, with weeping, that the lamentation of all the people is heard about as far away as the city. And from that hour they go to the city on foot with hymns; they arrive at the gate at that time when one person begins to recognize another; from there right through the middle of the city all as one, older and younger, rich, poor, all [are] ready there; especially on that day no one withdraws from the vigil until morning. Thus the bishop is led from Geth-

---

2. Once again, as on Palm Sunday (31.4), it seems important that the journey was made on foot. It appears that the Jerusalem church understood the place in which Jesus prayed as being on the Mount of Olives, as in Lk 22:39-46 (see also Cyril of Jerusalem, *Baptismal Catecheses* 10.19; 13.38) and Gethsemane as the scene of his arrest, in contrast to Mt 26:36-56 and Mk 14:32-50, which locate both events in the Garden of Gethsemane. It is not clear whether the designation "church candles," also in 43.7, merely indicated the source from which they came or also something else distinctive about them.

3. AL gives the gospel read at Gethsemane as Mt 26:31-56, but again it may have been shorter in Egeria's time. See 24.10; 34; 37.7 for similar emotional responses to a gospel reading. AL also adds a further stop at "the Court of the High Priest, the place of Peter's repentance," where Mt 26:57-75 is read. Then Ps 118 is sung in procession to the gate of the city, and a group of three psalms (79–81) as they go through the city to Golgotha.

semane as far as the gate and from there through the whole city as far as the Cross.

⁴When they have arrived before the Cross, the daylight is already beginning to be bright. Then is read there that passage from the gospel where the Lord is brought before Pontius Pilate, and everything that is written that Pilate said to the Lord and to the Jews is read in full. ⁵Afterward the bishop addresses the people, comforting them because they have labored all night and will labor that day, that they should not be weary but have hope in God who will repay them a greater reward for their labor. And so comforting them, as he is able, addressing them, he says, "Go now meanwhile, each of you, to your homes, sit down a little while, and just before the second hour of the day all be ready here, so that from that hour until the sixth you can see the holy wood of the cross, each of us believing it will be profitable for our salvation. For from the sixth hour we must all then come together here in this place, that is, before the Cross, so that we may give heed to readings and prayers until nightfall."

37 ¹So, after this the dismissal from the Cross is done, that is, before the sun rises, and everyone immediately goes eagerly to Sion to

4. Maraval, 282, seemed to identify this reading as Mt 27:1-26, but AL gives it as Jn 18:2-27, followed at dawn by Ps 109 and Jn 18:28–19:16. It is possible that only this second passage from John, the trial before Pilate, was read in the time of Egeria. Her reference to "everything that is written that Pilate said to the Lord and to the Jews [being] read in full" certainly suggests that reading from John.

5. This is the only indication that Egeria gives of some sort of short homily or exhortation during this lengthy vigil.

37 1. According to Matthew, Jesus was scourged by Pilate (27:26) and simply ill-treated at the house of Caiaphas the High Priest (26:67), but the pilgrim from Bordeaux noted that this pillar was at the site of Caiaphas's house (see Appendix A, p. 202). On some subsequent occasion, it was moved to the church. In a letter written in 404 but describing the pilgrimage made by Paula some twenty years earlier, Jerome spoke of it as a "bloodstained column holding up the portico of the church" (*Ep.* 108.9). The visit was obviously an individual act of piety rather than a formal part of the stational procession of the previous night. The clause "where he now stands" is an emendation by Maraval, 284, n. 2, to the manuscript reading, "which is now standing," that seems to some to make better sense, although others believe that the manuscript was correct and a representation of the cross itself was erected

pray at that pillar at which the Lord was scourged. Having returned from there, they sit down a little while in their homes, and soon all are ready. And then a chair is placed for the bishop on Golgotha behind the Cross, where he now stands; the bishop sits in the chair; a table covered with a linen cloth is placed before him; the deacons stand around the table and a silver-gilt casket is brought, in which is the holy wood of the cross; it is opened and [the wood] is brought out; both the wood of the cross and the inscription are placed on the table.

²So, when it has been placed on the table, the bishop, sitting, grips the ends of the holy wood with his hands, and the deacons who stand around guard it. It is guarded thus because the custom is that all the people coming one by one, both the faithful and the catechumens, bowing at the table, kiss the holy wood and pass through. And because, I don't know when, someone is said to have bitten off and stolen a piece of the holy wood, therefore it is now thus guarded by the deacons who stand around lest anyone dares to come and do so again.

³Thus, all the people pass through one by one, all bowing, touching the cross and the inscription first with their forehead, then with their eyes, and then kissing the cross, they pass through, but no one raises a hand to touch. When they have kissed the cross and passed through, a deacon stands holding Solomon's ring and the horn with which kings were anointed. They kiss the horn also and venerate the ring . . . less the second . . . until the sixth hour all the people pass through, entering through one of the doors,

---

there for the occasion. The normal daily services were apparently suspended on this day.

2. Cyril of Jerusalem provides the earliest explicit attestation of the existence of the "holy wood of the cross" (see the Introduction, p. 65, n. 187), and Egeria the first reference to the inscription. In the fifth century Paulinus of Nola reported that some pilgrims who requested might be permitted to view the wood of the cross on other occasions (*Ep.* 31.6). Egeria appears to show hesitation over the veracity of the story about someone having bitten off a piece of the wood ("is said to have"): see also 8.2; 12.7; 15.2; 17.2.

3. Presumably touching the cross was forbidden in case someone tried to grab a piece of it. There is a small hiatus in the manuscript here, with the words "less the second" in the middle of it. It has been conjectured that it may well have read something like "and from more or less the second hour and thus."

going out through another, as this is done in the place in which on the previous day, that is, on the fifth day of the week, the oblation was made.

⁴When the sixth hour has come, they go before the Cross, whether it is rainy or hot, because that place is out of doors, that is, like a rather large and quite beautiful court which is between the Cross and the Anastasis. There all the people gather, such that it cannot be opened. ⁵A chair is placed for the bishop before the Cross and from the sixth to the ninth hour nothing else is done except that readings are read thus, that is, first there are readings from the Psalms, wherever they speak of the passion; there are also readings from the Apostle, either from the letters of the Apostles or from the Acts, wherever they speak of the Lord's passion; and also passages from the gospels where he suffered are read; so they read from the prophets where they say that the Lord will suffer and then they read from the gospels where he speaks of his passion.

⁶So, from the sixth hour to the ninth hour readings are read and hymns recited continually, to show all the people that whatever the prophets foretold concerning the Lord's passion is shown to have been done both from the gospels and also from the writings of the Apostles. And so during those three hours all the people are taught that nothing had been done that had not been foretold, and nothing had been told that had not been completely fulfilled. Prayers that are appropriate to the day are always interspersed. ⁷To each of the readings and prayers there is such emotion and

4. The location of this principal service before the Cross rather than in the Martyrium was very probably intended to provide a symbolic focus for the worship on this day. The clause "such that it cannot be opened" doubtless means that the crowd was so great and so tightly packed together that there was not even room to open a door.
5. On the contents of this service, see the Introduction, p. 79. As Egeria explains, "the Apostle" was the standard term for the section of the New Testament containing the Acts of the Apostles and the Epistles.
6. Egeria here adds to her description of the contents that there were "hymns" and prayers interspersed.
7. The emotional response to the readings here resembles those in 24.10; 34; 36.3. According to AL, the final reading was Jn 19:17-37, which includes the verse (19:30) cited by Egeria.

lamentation from all the people that it is astonishing; for there is no one, either older or younger, who on that day in those three hours does not bewail more than can be reckoned that the Lord had suffered those things for us. After this, when the ninth hour has already begun to approach, that passage from the Gospel according to John is read where he gave up his spirit. When it has been read, a prayer and the dismissal are done.

[8]When the dismissal has been done from before the Cross, immediately everyone [gathers] in the major church, at the Martyrium, and everything is done that they are accustomed to do during this week from the ninth hour when they gather at the Martyrium until late during this week. When the dismissal from the Martyrium has been done, they come to the Anastasis. And when they have come there, that passage from the gospel is read where Joseph asks for the Lord's body from Pilate [and] places it in a new tomb. When this has been read, prayer is made, the catechumens are blessed, then [the faithful, and then] the dismissal is done. [9]On this day no announcement is made that they will keep vigil at the Anastasis because it is known that the people are tired, but it is the custom that they do keep vigil there. So, those of the people who wish, or rather who are able, keep vigil; those who are not able do not keep vigil there until the morning, but the clergy keep vigil there, that is, those who are stronger or younger, and throughout the night hymns and antiphons are recited there until morning. A very large crowd keeps vigil, some from the evening, others from the middle of the night, as they are able.

8. "Everything is done that they are accustomed to do" must mean another four-hour vigil-type service as on the other days of Holy Week. As on those other days, AL reduces it to a shorter service, with just two readings rather than the usual three: Jer 11:18–12:8 and Isa 53:1-12, together with Ps 22. Gingras, 240, n. 392, and Maraval, 288, appeared to believe that the reading at the following visit to the Anastasis was the Johannine version of the burial of Jesus, Jn 19:38-42, but it seems more likely to have been Mt 27:57-61, as prescribed in AL.

9. Because this was a voluntary vigil, it does not appear in AL, and presumably for the same reason did not have a formal liturgical rite as its conclusion (*pace* Gingras, 240, n. 394).

38 ¹The next day, the Sabbath, the third hour is done according to the custom, then the sixth hour is done, the ninth hour is not done on the Sabbath, but the paschal vigil is prepared in the major church, that is, in the Martyrium. The paschal vigil is done in the same way as with us; but this alone is different, that the "infants," when they have been baptized and clothed, as they come out of the font, are first led along with the bishop to the Anastasis. ²The bishop goes inside the enclosure of the Anastasis, one hymn is recited, and the bishop makes a prayer for them, and then he comes to the major church with them, where according to the custom all the people are keeping vigil. They do there what is also customary with us, and after the oblation has been made, the dismissal is done. And after the dismissal from the vigil in the major church has been done, they immediately come with hymns to the Anastasis and there that passage of the gospel about the resurrection is then read, prayer is made, and then the bishop makes the oblation there; but all is done quickly on account of the

38 1. Egeria makes no mention of a morning service prior to the third hour. Previous Saturdays in Lent would have begun with the Eucharist, but it does not look as if anything replaced that here. AL begins the day with a brief service at dawn in the Anastasis at which Ps 88 was sung and Mt 27:62-66, the setting of a watch at the tomb, was read. Unusually, although there was the customary service at the third hour, there was not one on this particular day at the ninth hour, and Egeria makes no mention of an evening service prior to the vigil. AL, however, begins the evening with what was seemingly an embryonic form of *Lucernarium* in the Anastasis involving Ps 113: see Renoux, "Liturgie de Jérusalem," 182. The vigil was then held in the Martyrium: for the readings, see the Introduction, p. 78. The "infants" here are not babies, but all who had been born again through baptism (see also 39.3); this was a common Christian expression: see, for example, Augustine, *Sermo* 228.1. The simple word "clothed" does not reveal whether they had put on special baptismal robes or merely their own clothing after being baptized naked.

2. AL gives as the propers for the Eucharist at midnight Ps 65; 1 Cor 15:1-11; Mt 28:1-20. As in Egeria's account, a second Eucharist was then celebrated in the Anastasis, apparently without its own liturgy of the word, nor even necessarily with people receiving Communion again. Presumably there was a desire to have a celebration in the very place of the resurrection. In AL a reading from Jn 19:38–20:18 followed the Eucharist there, and then a third Eucharist in the Martyrium at dawn, with Ps 65; Acts 1:1-14; Mk 15:42–16:8.

people, in order that they are not delayed longer, and so the people are dismissed. The dismissal from the vigil on that day is done at the same hour as also with us.

39 ¹The eight paschal days are kept in the same way as also with us, and the dismissals are done in their order throughout the eight paschal days, as is also done everywhere at Pascha through the octave. Here the adornment and the arrangement throughout the eight days of Pascha is the same as during Epiphany, both in the major church and at the Anastasis and at the Cross and on Eleona, but also in Bethlehem as well as in the Lazarium and everywhere, because they are the paschal days. ²They assemble on this first Lord's Day in the major church, that is, at the Martyrium, and on the second and third days of the week, but always so that when the dismissal from the Martyrium is done, they come to the Anastasis with hymns. On the fourth day of the week they assemble on Eleona, on the fifth day of the week at the Anastasis, on the sixth day of the week on Sion, on the Sabbath before the

39 1. Egeria is clearly familiar with an Easter octave at home, marked by a daily Eucharist. The Lazarium is said to be decorated, even though it is not used for any of the services in the Easter octave. For the phrase "in their order," see the commentary on 3.6.

2. For differences in the locations of the daily Eucharist in this octave from those of the Epiphany octave in 25.11, see the Introduction, pp. 98–99. "They come to the Anastasis with hymns" for the bishop's postbaptismal addresses each day (see 47.1-2). According to AL (where changes had been made in some of the stations), successive portions of Acts 2:22–6:7 constituted the first reading at the Eucharist each day of the octave, and successive portions of Jas 1:1–3:13 formed a second reading from Wednesday onwards, with portions of Lk 23:50–24:40 being the gospel from Monday to Wednesday, Mt 5:1-12 on Thursday, Jn 21:1-14 on Friday, Jn 21:15-25 on Saturday, and Jn 1:1-17 on Sunday. Baldovin, *Liturgy in Ancient Jerusalem*, 41, explained the surprising choice of the Beatitudes as the Thursday gospel by observing that the station for that day was now Eleona, perhaps thought of as where the Sermon on the Mount had been delivered; the addition of the readings from James from Wednesday onward he attributed to the Wednesday station being on Sion, the traditional seat of James, as the first bishop of Jerusalem; and the choice of the prologue of John's Gospel for the octave Sunday as the result of a desire to capture the whole sweep of salvation history at this solemn season. In other Eastern Christian traditions John's prologue was read on Easter Day itself, perhaps once having been the beginning of a course reading of the Fourth Gospel during the fifty-day season.

Cross, and on the Lord's Day, that is, the octave, again in the major church, that is, at the Martyrium.

³On these eight paschal days every day after breakfast the bishop goes up to Eleona with all the clergy and all the "infants," that is, those who have been baptized, and all who are *apotactitae*, men and women, as well as any of the people who wish. Hymns are recited, prayers are made both in the church that is on Eleona, in which is the cave in which Jesus taught the disciples, and also at the Imbomon, that is, in that place from which the Lord ascended into heaven. ⁴And after the psalms have been recited and prayer has been made, they come down from there to the Anastasis with hymns at the hour of lamplighting: this is done throughout the eight days.

Now on the Lord's Day during Pascha, after the dismissal from *Lucernarium*, that is, from the Anastasis, all the people lead the bishop with hymns to Sion. ⁵When they come there, hymns

---

3. Egeria does not explicitly refer to prayer at the sixth hour during this week, even though she says in 41 that it did take place every day from Pascha to Pentecost. We do not know at what time the daily Eucharist was celebrated in this octave. During the Epiphany octave it seems to have lasted from the second till the sixth hour (25.8, 10-11), rather than from daybreak until the fourth or fifth hour as on Sundays (25.1). The latter seems more likely here, as there would need to have been enough time after the Eucharist for the bishop's daily address to the newly baptized and others in the Anastasis (see 47.1) before they could go home to eat their breakfast (apparently toward the middle of the day). Egeria states that on the octave day, the gathering on Eleona takes place immediately after the sixth hour (40.1), and very likely this was also so on the other days. This vigil-like daily assembly on Eleona primarily for the newly baptized seems a strange sort of ascetic exercise for the season of Easter joy, but perhaps it was because Eleona was regarded as the place where Jesus taught his disciples. For *apotactitae*, see the commentary on 23.3.

4. AL includes a similar, though much shorter, gathering on Eleona on Easter Day at the ninth hour and on the octave Sunday at the tenth hour (though not during the week) for a time of psalm-singing before going to the Anastasis, presumably for the evening office. The "Lord's Day during Pascha" must mean Easter Day, as Egeria refers to the Lord's Day "on the octave of Pascha" in 40.1.

5. As Egeria indicates, this evening gathering is to commemorate the gathering of the disciples "in the evening on the first day of the week" (Jn 20:19-25), which AL also records as the reading for this occasion.

appropriate to the day and place are recited, prayer is made, and that passage from the gospel is read where on the same day in the same place where the church is now on Sion, with the doors closed, the Lord came in to the disciples, that is, when one of the disciples was not there, that is, Thomas, and when he returned and the other apostles told him that they had seen the Lord, he said, "I do not believe unless I shall see." When this has been read, then prayer is made, the catechumens are blessed, then the faithful, and everyone returns to their home late, about the second hour of the night.

40 [1]Then on the octave of Pascha, that is, the Lord's Day, immediately after the sixth hour all the people go up to Eleona with the bishop; first they sit for a while in the church that is there; hymns are recited, antiphons appropriate to the day and place are recited, prayers likewise appropriate to the day and place are made. Then they go up from there with hymns to the Imbomon, and they similarly do there what was also done in the former place. And when it begins to be the time, all the people and all the *apotactitae* lead the bishop with hymns to the Anastasis. They arrive at the Anastasis at the time when *Lucernarium* is accustomed to be done.

[2]So *Lucernarium* is done both at the Anastasis and at the Cross, and from there all the people as one lead the bishop with hymns to Sion. When they have come there, hymns appropriate to the place and day are similarly recited, then that passage from the gospel is also read where on the octave of Pascha the Lord entered where the disciples were and reproved Thomas because he had been unbelieving. And then the whole of that reading is read; afterward prayer is made; when the catechumens and the faithful

---

40 1. This appears to be the same gathering that Egeria has said took place on every day of the octave, but perhaps it was a more formal part of the liturgical life of the church on the octave day itself and so attracted a larger congregation because it was not a work day. As noted above, AL includes this assembly too, but at the tenth hour. For *apotactitae*, see the commentary on 23.3.

2. Presumably Egeria does not mean that *Lucernarium* is done twice, at the Anastasis and at the Cross, but that the usual devotion at the Cross follows *Lucernarium* in the Anastasis. The evening gathering on Sion parallels that on Easter Day, this time commemorating the meeting of the disciples "after eight days" (Jn 20:26-31). Both Egeria and AL record this as the reading that was used.

have been blessed according to the custom, everyone returns to their home just as on the Lord's Day of Pascha at the second hour of the night.

41 From Pascha until the fiftieth day, that is, Pentecost, no one at all fasts here, not even those who are *apotactitae*. For on those days just as in the rest of the year the customary things are always done at the Anastasis from first cockcrow until morning, similarly at the sixth hour and at *Lucernare*. On the Lord's Days they always assemble according to the custom in the Martyrium, that is, the major church, and from there they go to the Anastasis with hymns. On the fourth and sixth days of the week, because no one at all fasts on those days, they assemble on Sion, but in the morning; the dismissal is done in its order.

42 On the fortieth day after Pascha, that is, the fifth day of the week, all go on the previous day, that is, on the fourth day of the week, after the sixth hour to Bethlehem to celebrate the vigil. The vigil is done in the church in Bethlehem, the church in which there is the cave where the Lord was born. The next day, that is, the fifth day of the week, the fortieth day, the dismissal is celebrated in its order, such that both the presbyters and the bishop preach, saying what is appropriate to the day and place, and afterward everyone returns late to Jerusalem.

43 [1]On the fiftieth day, that is, the Lord's Day, when there is very great labor for the people, everything is done from first cockcrow

---

41 Just as on Sundays, so throughout the fifty days of the Easter season the ninth hour of the day is not observed, but all the other daily and Sunday services remain the same. Because there is no fasting, the Wednesday and Friday services on Sion are moved to the mornings, but were they services of the word only, or celebrations of the Eucharist? See the Introduction, pp. 80–81, and also the commentary on 3.6. AL makes no provision for these services, nor for any propers for the Sunday Eucharists during this season.

42 Although scholars are now mostly agreed that this was not the celebration of Christ's ascension, it is unclear what it might have been: see the Introduction, p. 97. It was obviously important enough not only for the Jerusalem church to go to Bethlehem for it but also for it to be preceded by an all-night vigil, like Epiphany and Easter, though not given an octave. For the phrase "in its order," see the commentary on 3.6.

43 1. Those things that "are then done in the Anastasis that are customary" must be the completion of the "monastic" night office when the resurrection vigil is over (see 24.12).

according to the custom: they keep vigil in the Anastasis, so that the bishop may read that passage of the gospel that is always read on the Lord's Day, that is, the Lord's resurrection, and afterward those things are then done in the Anastasis that are customary, as in the rest of the year.

²When morning has come, all the people assemble in the major church, that is, the Martyrium, everything also is done that it is customary to do; the presbyters preach, afterward the bishop; all that is proper is done, that is, the oblation is made according to the custom by which it is customary to be done on the Lord's Day, but the dismissal is hastened in the Martyrium so that it may be done before the third hour. For when the dismissal has been done at the Martyrium, all the people as one will lead the bishop with hymns to Sion, but [so that] they will be on Sion at the full third hour.

³When they have come there, that passage from the Acts of the Apostles is read where the Spirit descends so that all tongues that were spoken might be understood; afterward the dismissal is done in its order. For the presbyters read there from the Acts of the Apostles from this that is read, because that is the place on Sion— another church is there now—where once after the Lord's passion

---

2. This is the only place where Egeria explicitly says that the regular Sunday morning service in the Martyrium was indeed a Eucharist, although it finished earlier on this particular day. AL gives the propers at this service as Ps 143; Acts 2:1-21; Jn 14:15-24.

3. The assembly occurs at the third hour so that the descent of the Holy Spirit at Pentecost may be commemorated not only in the place in which it was believed to have happened but also at the same hour of the day (see Acts 2:15). Egeria mentions only the reading from Acts 2:1-21, but AL provided the full set of propers for the Eucharist that Egeria says was then celebrated there. These were identical to those it listed for the service in the Martyrium, except that the gospel was Jn 14:25-29. The structure of service that Egeria describes suggests that it might once have been a brief station to which the Eucharist was added later. For the phrase "in its order," occurring twice, see the commentary on 3.6. The loose syntax of the sentence beginning "For the presbyters read . . ." has caused translators some difficulties, and especially the clause that we have translated "another church is there now." If we have caught its sense correctly, is Egeria alluding to the existence there of a previous building where the earliest Christians used to meet? See the Introduction, pp. 59–60.

a crowd had gathered with the apostles when this was done, as we said above. Afterward the dismissal is done in its order, the oblation is also made there, and as the people are dismissed, the archdeacon raises his voice and says, "Today immediately after the sixth hour let us all be ready on Eleona [at] the Imbomon."

⁴So, all the people return each to their home, and immediately after breakfast they ascend the Mount of Olives, that is, on Eleona, each one as they are able, so that no Christian remains in the city but they all go. ⁵So, when they have gone up the Mount of Olives, that is, on Eleona, they go first to the Imbomon, that is, to the place from which the Lord ascended into heaven, and there the bishop and presbyters sit, but also all the people; readings are read there, in between hymns are recited, also antiphons appropriate to that day and place; prayers also that are interspersed always have such expressions that are fitting to both the day and the place. That passage from the gospel is also read where it speaks of the Lord's ascension; then there is a reading from the Acts of the Apostles where it speaks of the Lord's ascension into heaven after the resurrection.

⁶When this has been done, the catechumens are blessed, then the faithful, and at the ninth hour they come down from there and go with hymns to that church which is also on Eleona, that is, in the cave where the Lord sat and taught the apostles. When they have come there, it is already past the tenth hour. *Lucernare* is done there, prayer is made, the catechumens and then the faithful are blessed. And they come down from there with hymns, all the people completely as one reciting with the bishop the hymns and

4. Egeria's claim that no Christian remains in the city may be an indication that the afternoon gathering attracted more people than the morning one.

5. The shape of this rite suggests that it was a kind of short vigil. AL instead places it at the tenth hour, the usual time for *Lucernarium*, and gives as the propers Ps 143 (for the third time this day), Acts 2:1-21 (also yet again), and Jn 16:5b-15. Egeria, however, seems to imply that the gospel reading she heard was Lk 24:50-53, and clearly indicates that the reading from Acts included at least 1:6-11, if not more from that chapter. These readings were no doubt changed later when the Jerusalem church began to celebrate Christ's ascension on the fortieth day instead.

6. As the Imbomon was in the open air at this time, Eleona would have been the nearest church in which to celebrate the evening office.

antiphons appropriate to that day; so they come very slowly to the Martyrium.

7When they arrive at the gate of the city, it is already night and about two hundred church candles are available for the people. Because it is some distance from the gate to the major church, that is, to the Martyrium, they arrive about the second hour of the night, because they go all the way very slowly for the sake of the people, lest their feet are tired. And the great doors that are on the side of the *Quintana* having been opened, all the people enter the Martyrium with hymns and with the bishop. Having gone into the church, hymns are recited, prayer is made, the catechumens are blessed and then the faithful; and then from there they go with hymns to the Anastasis.

8Similarly when they have come to the Anastasis, hymns and antiphons are recited, prayer is made, the catechumens are blessed, then the faithful; the same is also done at the Cross. And then from there all the Christian people as one lead the bishop with hymns to Sion. 9When they have come there, appropriate readings are

---

7. On church candles, see the commentary on 36.2. Although Egeria does not emphasize that everyone made the journey on foot, as she does on Palm Sunday (31.4) and Good Friday (36.2), it appears that they did so. The *Quintana* (literally, "of the fifth") was the street in a Roman military camp where the market was located, and hence came to be used as a term for the market in a city.

8. It is not obvious why the day of Pentecost ended with such an extensive series of stations after *Lucernarium*—at the Martyrium, at the Anastasis, and at the Cross—before they went on to Sion, when compared with other festivals in the year. Perhaps it was a way of marking the close of the fifty days of the Easter season. AL has rather the enigmatic statement at the service at the Imbomon (43.5) that "immediately after the Gospel they kneel and this canon is performed three times—in the same way in all the holy places." The act of kneeling at this point appears to be a symbolic marking of the close of the Easter season and the resumption of the practice of kneeling for prayer. As the word "canon" is regularly used in AL to denote a set of propers, could the "three times" originally have been a reference not to a triple genuflection (as it became in later Eastern practice), but to a similar stational liturgy with the same propers as at the Imbomon that was held at the first three of the places that Egeria mentions?

9. The final assembly on Sion is the most substantial of the stations, with readings as well as the hymns and antiphons used in the other places. This station is corroborated in AL, which gives as the propers Ps 143 (yet again!)

read, psalms and antiphons are recited, prayer is made, the catechumens are blessed and then the faithful, and the dismissal is done. When the dismissal has been done, all come to the bishop's hand and then everyone returns to their home about the middle hour of the night. Thus, they endure very great labor that day, because they kept vigil from first cockcrow at the Anastasis and from there never stopped for the whole day; every celebration lasts so long that all return to their homes in the middle of the night after the dismissal that was done on Sion.

44 ¹From the day after the fiftieth day all fast according to the custom as in the rest of the year, as they are able, except on the Sabbath day and the Lord's Day, when there is never fasting in these places. Also afterward on the rest of the days everything is done as in the whole year, that is, vigil is always kept from first cockcrow at the Anastasis. ²For if it is the Lord's Day, from first cockcrow the bishop first reads the gospel according to the custom inside the Anastasis, the passage about the Lord's resurrection, which is always read on the Lord's Day, and afterward hymns and antiphons are recited in the Anastasis until daybreak. But if it is not the Lord's Day, only hymns and antiphons are similarly recited in the Anastasis from first cockcrow until daybreak. ³All the *apotactitae* go, and those of the people who are able go, and the clergy in turn each day go from first cockcrow; but the bishop always comes as it begins to get light so that the morning dismissal may be done with all the clergy, except on the Lord's Day, when it is necessary for him to go from first cockcrow so that he may read the gospel in the Anastasis. Then at the sixth hour they do what is customary in the Anastasis, similarly also at the ninth

---

and Jn 14:15-24, the same gospel that had been used at the Martyrium in the morning. Although Wilkinson lists the propers in his translation of AL, he fails to mention this evening assembly on Sion to which they belong.

44 1. Egeria does not mean that everyone fasts from the Monday after Pentecost onward, but only that normal fasting was resumed, which meant that the *apotactitae* would fast during the day every weekday, eating only one meal in the evening (28.3), and others would do the same on Wednesdays and Fridays (27.5).

2. She summarizes what she had said earlier (24.1-2, 8-10) about the differences between the weekday night office and the Sunday vigil.

3. She amplifies her summary here, adding what was done in the rest of the day (24.3-7). For *apotactitae*, see the commentary on 23.3.

hour, similarly also at *Lucernare* according to the custom which it is customary to do the whole year. But on the fourth and sixth days of the week the ninth hour is always done on Sion according to the custom.

45 ¹And I ought also to write how those who will be baptized at Pascha are instructed. For those who give in their names give them in on the day before Quadragesima, and a presbyter writes down the names of all, that is, before those eight weeks for which I have said Quadragesima is kept here. ²When the presbyter has written down the names of all, afterward on the next day of Quadragesima, that is, when the eight weeks begin, a chair is placed for the bishop in the middle of the major church, that is, at the Martyrium, the presbyters sit in chairs on each side and all the clergy stand. And then the *competentes* are brought forward one by one; if they are males, they come with their "fathers," but if females, with their "mothers." ³And then the bishop asks the neighbors of each one who has entered, saying, "Is this person of a good life, obedient to their parents, not a drunkard or a liar?"

45　1. Egeria appears belatedly to remember that she has not said anything about the teaching that baptismal candidates receive during Lent. On this and on the process of baptismal preparation in general, see the Introduction, pp. 83–85.

2. The phrase "the next day of Quadragesima" seems to mean the first day of Lent, which would have been a Monday (see 27.1). The word *cathedra*, "chair," is not being used in a technical sense as referring to the bishop's seat alone, as the presbyters also sit in *cathedris*. "All the clergy" who stand must comprise deacons and those in minor orders: for its use in this sense, see the commentary on 7.2. Egeria uses the standard Latin term *competentes* to denote those of the catechumens enrolled in the final period of preparation for baptism, although at Rome they were known instead as *electi*, "those who have been chosen": the equivalent Greek term used in the East was *photizomenoi*, "those being enlightened" (see Cyril of Jerusalem, *Procatechesis* 12). The "fathers" and "mothers" mentioned here are not the biological parents of infant candidates, but the sponsors or godparents of all candidates (see also 38.1; 39.3), although it is true that parents often acted as sponsors for their children: see Augustine, *Ep.* 98.5-7.

3. The "neighbors" mentioned must include those who had sponsored them for baptism. A similar questioning of sponsors is attested by other sources from elsewhere: Theodore of Mopsuestia, *Baptismal Homilies* 1.14-15; *Apostolic Tradition* 20.1-2.

And he makes inquiry about particular vices that are more serious in people. ⁴And if they prove to be without blame in all these matters in which he has made inquiry of the witnesses present, he himself writes down their names with his own hand. But if they are accused in any matter, he orders them to go outside, saying, "Let them amend themselves, and when they have amended themselves, then let them come to the bath." He speaks thus when making inquiry both of the men and of the women. If someone is a stranger, unless they have testimonies from those who know them, they do not so easily come to baptism.

46 ¹I must write this, lady sisters, lest you think that it is done without explanation. For the custom here is such that those who come to baptism during those forty days in which there is fasting are first exorcized by the clergy early, as soon as the morning dismissal from the Anastasis has been done. And a chair is immediately placed for the bishop at the Martyrium, in the major church, and all who are to be baptized, both male and female, sit in a circle around the bishop; the "fathers" and "mothers" stand there also, and also all those of the people who wish to listen—but [only] the faithful—come in and sit. ²A catechumen does not enter there then

4. Cyril of Jerusalem, *Procatechesis* 1, 4, 13; *Baptismal Catecheses* 3.2, also refers to the inscription of names. "Bath" was commonly used to denote baptism, and the "strangers" here were no doubt mainly those pilgrims to Jerusalem who wanted to be baptized there. For the translation of *peregrinus* as "stranger," see the Introduction, pp. 33–34.

46 1. On the address "lady sisters," see the commentary on 3.8. Daily exorcism in preparation for baptism is also attested by Cyril of Jerusalem, *Procatechesis* 9, 13, 14, and was standard elsewhere in Syria at this time: see John Chrysostom, *Baptismal Instructions* (Stavronikita series) 2.12-14; Theodore of Mopsuestia, *Baptismal Homilies* 2.1-4. These churches did not possess a formal order of exorcists, in contrast to those in the West, and hence it is unclear whether the "clergy" whom Egeria says performed the rite were presbyters or deacons, or possibly subdeacons or readers: see the commentary on 7.2. Before the fourth century exorcism seems to have been limited to those candidates displaying more obvious signs of what was understood to be demon possession, but it was later extended to all seeking baptism.
2. Christian tradition kept certain teachings hidden from the unbaptized, including catechumens who had not yet become *competentes*: see, for example, Cyril of Jerusalem, *Procatechesis* 12. Catechesis seems to be an unfamiliar

when the bishop teaches them the law, that is, thus: beginning from Genesis he goes through all the Scriptures during those forty days, first explaining them literally and then interpreting them spiritually. They are also taught both about the resurrection and similarly everything about the faith during those days; this is called catechesis.

³And when five weeks have been completed in which they are taught, then they receive the Creed; he explains to them the meaning of the Creed in a similar way to the meaning of all the Scriptures, each article first literally and then spiritually; so also he explains the Creed. And so it is that in these places all the faithful follow the Scriptures when they are read in church, because they are all taught during those forty days, that is, from the first hour to the third hour, because catechesis is done for three hours. ⁴God knows, lady sisters, that the voices of the faithful who come in to listen to the catechesis are louder at those things that are said or explained by the bishop than at those things that are explained in this way when he sits and preaches in church. The dismissal from the catechesis having been done at the third hour, the bishop is immediately led from there with hymns to the Anastasis and the dismissal takes place at the third hour; and so they are taught for three hours a day for seven weeks, for in the eighth week of Quadragesima, that is, what is called Great Week, there is no time for them to be taught so that those things that [are] above may be carried out.

---

word to Egeria, and is not found in earlier Latin Christian literature. On its contents here, see the Introduction, pp. 84–85. The expression "the resurrection and similarly everything about the faith" appears to refer to the teaching of the Creed in the sixth and seventh weeks.

3. Egeria seems implicitly to be contrasting the degree of learning that Jerusalem Christians had with that of Christians back home. "They are all taught" could mean that everyone was taught or that all the Scriptures were taught: the Latin is ambiguous.

4. On the address "lady sisters," see the commentary on 3.8. It is interesting to note that the bishop normally sat to preach in liturgical services. The catechesis is followed by the usual Lenten service at the third hour in the Anastasis. "Those things that are above" are the extensive Holy Week services that Egeria has described earlier (30–38).

⁵When seven weeks have passed, there remains that one paschal week that they call here Great Week; then the bishop comes in the morning into the major church at the Martyrium. A chair is placed for the bishop at the back in the apse behind the altar, and there they come one by one, males with their "fathers" and females with their "mothers," and repeat the Creed to the bishop. ⁶After the Creed has been repeated to the bishop, he addresses them all and says: "For these seven weeks you have been taught all the law of the Scriptures and you have also heard about the faith; you have also heard about the resurrection of the flesh and also the whole meaning of the Creed, as far as you can hear while still catechumens: but those things that are of a higher mystery, that is, of baptism itself, you cannot hear, being still catechumens. And lest you should think that anything is done without explanation, when you have been baptized in the name of God, you will hear during the eight paschal days in the Anastasis when the dismissal from the church has been done: because you are still catechumens, the more secret mysteries of God cannot be told to you."

47 ¹When the days of Pascha have come, during those eight days, that is, from Pascha to the octave, when the dismissal from the

5. It was normal at this time for those about to be baptized to be required to learn the Creed by heart and to recite it back to the bishop, the custom being known in the West as the *redditio symboli*: see, for example, Augustine, *Sermo* 58; Theodore of Mopsuestia, *Baptismal Homilies* 1.26-28; 2.1. Egeria is not specific about the day or time when this took place.

6. In some other places too, including Milan, it had also become the practice to reserve the explanation of baptism and the Eucharist until after the candidates had experienced them so that the secrecy might increase the sense of drama and the psychological impact of the experience. Noting some similarities between the bishop's words on this occasion and part of Cyril of Jerusalem's final *Baptismal Catechesis* (18.32-33), even though first delivered more than thirty years before, Maraval, 312, n. 1, suggested that this was a standard liturgical formulary recited every year rather than an extempore homily that Egeria heard.

47 1. The "dismissal from the church" refers to the daily eucharistic celebration that took place during the Easter octave: see 39.2. The faithful alone are blessed, because catechumens were excluded from the addresses that follow. Cyril, *Baptismal Catecheses* 18.33, confirms that the teaching took place in the Anastasis rather than in the Martyrium, where the prebaptismal instruction had been given, perhaps as an indicator of the new status of the baptized.

church has been done and they go with hymns to the Anastasis, soon prayer is made, the faithful are blessed, and the bishop stands leaning on the inner enclosure that is in the cave of the Anastasis, and explains everything that is done in baptism. [2]For at that time no catechumen comes into the Anastasis; only the neophytes and the faithful who wish to listen to the mysteries enter the Anastasis. The doors are closed lest a catechumen heads there. While the bishop discusses and relates each item, the voices of those praising are such that their voices are heard far outside the church. For indeed he interprets all the mysteries in such a way that no one cannot be moved at those things that they hear so explained.

[3]And because in that province some of the people know both Greek and Syriac, others Greek alone, and others only Syriac, and because the bishop, though he may know Syriac, however always speaks Greek and never Syriac, therefore a presbyter always stands by, who, when the bishop is speaking in Greek, translates into Syriac so that everyone may hear what is being explained. [4]The readings also that are read in church, because they must be read in Greek, someone always stands there to translate into Syriac for the sake of the people, so that they may always learn. Indeed, those who are Latin here, that is, who know neither Syriac nor

---

2. The newly baptized are neophytes ("newborns"). It would have been during this week that the *Mystagogical Catecheses* attributed to Cyril of Jerusalem would have been delivered. For the days on which this teaching would have happened, see the Introduction, p. 86, n. 230. The Latin verbs *disputare*, "discusses," and *narrare*, "relates," were technical terms used in relation to preaching, the latter meaning to narrate the Scriptures and the former to explain their meaning: see Bastiaensen, *Observations*, 101–105. Cyril, *Baptismal Catecheses* 13.23, also refers to his hearers responding with a shout of praise.

3. Whatever the native language of the participants, the liturgy and preaching of the Jerusalem church remained consistently in Greek. What Egeria describes as Syriac should probably be more accurately called a Palestinian Aramaic dialect.

4. The need to translate all the readings must have lengthened the services somewhat. "Brothers and sisters" are not necessarily monks and nuns: the words could just mean fellow Christians, although it is likely that included in that number of Latin speakers were some Christians from the West who had joined monastic communities in Jerusalem as well as pilgrims who spoke both languages.

Greek, lest they be disheartened, also have things explained to them, because there are other brothers and sisters who are bilingual who explain to them in Latin. ⁵Above all it is very pleasing and very admirable here that both the hymns and the antiphons and the readings as well as the prayers that the bishop recites always have such expressions that they are always appropriate and suitable both to the day that is being celebrated and to the place in which it is being done.

48 ¹It is called the day of the Encaenia when the holy church that is on Golgotha, which they call the Martyrium, was consecrated to God; but also the holy church that is at the Anastasis, that is, in that place where the Lord rose after the passion, was also consecrated to God on that day. Thus the Encaenia of these holy churches is celebrated with the greatest honor because the cross of the Lord was found on that day. ²And so for this reason it was so ordained that when the holy churches listed above were first consecrated, it was that day when the cross of the Lord was found, so that they should be celebrated together with all rejoicing on

5. Egeria repeats once more the point she has made many times during her description of the Jerusalem liturgy.

48 1. On the meaning of Encaenia ("Dedication") and its date, see the Introduction, pp. 100–101. Eusebius described the original dedication of the church in 335, in which he himself participated, in his *Vita Constantini* 4.43-47. Although Egeria does not state on what days in the year the Encaenia was celebrated, AL reveals it to have been September 13 and 14, with the same propers being used each day, Ps 65; 1 Tim 3:14-16; Jn 10:22-42. The feast of dedication mentioned in this gospel reading, however, was that of the re-dedication of the Temple in 165 BCE (Hanukkah) and not that of the original dedication of Solomon's Temple.

2. Although the festival commemorated all three events—the dedication of the Martyrium, the dedication of the Anastasis, and the discovery of the cross—it is at least questionable whether all three did originally occur on the same day, especially as the rotunda over the tomb seems to have been built much later than the Martyrium. See Stephan Borgehammar, *How the Holy Cross Was Found: From Event to Medieval Legend* (Stockholm: Almquist & Wiksell, 1991), 100–101, who suggested that the dedication of the Martyrium was originally celebrated with a veneration of the cross on September 13, and that when the Anastasis was completed, it was celebrated on this day and the celebration of the dedication of the Martyrium moved to September 14. The biblical reference is to 2 Chr 5:1–7:9.

the same day. And this is found in the holy Scriptures that this day of the Encaenia is when holy Solomon also, having completed the house of God that he had built, stood before the altar of God and prayed, as it is written in the books of Chronicles.

49 ¹So, when these days of the Encaenia have come, they are kept for eight days. For crowds begin to gather from everywhere very many days before, not only of monks or *apotactitae* from various provinces, that is, from Mesopotamia and Syria and from Egypt and the Thebaid, where there are very many *monazontes*, but also from all sorts of places and provinces; for there is no one who does not head for Jerusalem on that day for such rejoicing and for such honorable days; and lay people, both male and female, with faithful mind similarly gather in Jerusalem on those days from all provinces on account of the holy day. ²Bishops, when they are few, are more than forty or fifty in Jerusalem on those days; and with them come many of their clergy. And—what more [shall I say]?—those who have not been present on these days at such a solemnity think themselves to have committed a very great sin if there has been no contrary necessity that holds someone back from a good intention.

³So on these days of the Encaenia the adornment of all the churches is like that both during Pascha and during Epiphany, and they assemble each day at various holy places as during Pascha and Epiphany. For they assemble on the first and second day in the major church, which is called the Martyrium; then on the third day on Eleona, that is, in the church that is on that mount

49 1. In AL the celebration lasts only two days. This was obviously the greatest pilgrimage festival of the year in Jerusalem, not least because it was not in competition with other local celebrations on these days. For *apotactitae*, see the commentary on 23.3.

2. Egeria may have thought forty or fifty bishops were few, but it would have been a surprisingly large number, greater than the attendance at many ecclesiastical councils.

3. The manuscript breaks off before she has finished listing all the stations of the octave. At Easter and Epiphany the Eucharist was at the Martyrium on the first three days (25.10-11; 39.2), but here it was on Eleona on the third day. According to AL, the celebration was in the Anastasis on the first day and the Martyrium on the second.

from which the Lord ascended into heaven after the passion, the church within which is that cave in which the Lord taught the apostles on the Mount of Olives; on the fourth day. . . .

Appendix A:
The Pilgrim from Bordeaux

The travel diary (*itinerarium*) was a well-established genre from the pre-Christian period of the Roman Empire. Representative documents typically recorded distances traveled and places visited.[1] The oldest extant description of a Christian journey to the Holy Land, by an anonymous pilgrim beginning from Bordeaux, largely follows that pattern. It documents an overland journey from Bordeaux to Constantinople, continuing through Syria and Palestine, and then a return route by sea via the Adriatic and Mediterranean and onward by land through Italy. Since the pilgrim records the names of the current consuls at Constantinople, it is clear that this trip occurred in the year 333. Nothing is known about the identity of the pilgrim, not even his or her gender. Although it was traditionally assumed that the writer was male, there are at least some grounds for considering the possibility that, like Egeria, the pilgrim might have been a

---

[1] For a more extensive account of travel narratives in antiquity and the *itinerarium* genre in particular, see Scott Fitzgerald Johnson, "Travel, Cartography, and Cosmology," in *The Oxford Handbook of Late Antiquity* (Oxford: Oxford University Press, 2012), 562–94; also Jaś Elsner, "The *Itinerarium Burdigalense*: Politics and Salvation in the Geography of Constantine's Empire," *Journal of Roman Studies* 90 (2000): 181–95, esp. 183–86. For discussions of gender differences and the portrayal of travel by women and men in travel narratives, see James Clifford, "Travelling Cultures," in *Cultural Studies*, ed. L. Grossberg, C. Nelson, and P. Treichler (New York: Routledge, 1992), 96–116, here at 105–6; J. Wolff, "On the Road Again: Metaphors of Travel in Cultural Criticism," *Cultural Studies* 7 (1993): 224–39, here at 229.

woman.[2] And we conclude that he or she came from Bordeaux only because that is where the itinerary begins. Written in Latin, it is preserved in four manuscripts, all dating between the eighth and tenth centuries, two of which cover only the journey through the Holy Land, which is the most detailed part of the pilgrim's account and the most interesting for our purposes. The rest consists almost entirely of a listing of the many places through which the pilgrim passed, with indications of the distances between them and whether each one necessitated an overnight stay or merely a change of horses for the carriage.[3] In these sections, there is only occasional brief commentary about significant events, people, or characteristics associated with a particular site.

Upon reaching Jerusalem and its environs, however, where scriptural connections are much more prevalent, "a bureaucratic list of places and mileages is transformed into the description of a journey into the biblical past, where every location visited and named in Jerusalem and its environs is identified by a scriptural label—it is biblical *historia* run riot."[4] Like Egeria, this pilgrim is most concerned with the topography of Palestine and any built features added to the natural landscape as the backdrop where the sacred biblical drama played out in the past and "lives" again in the traveler's beholding of these sites. Some "new" features of the Jerusalem landscape, like the four recently constructed basilicas sponsored by the emperor Constantine, also drew the Bordeaux pilgrim's attention as the ascent of the "new Jerusalem" in the Christian era, a tangible witness to the ongoing establishment of God's intentions for the city and, by extension, the whole world as set forth in the Scriptures.[5] Comparing the Bordeaux pilgrim's account with Egeria's, it is striking how little attention Egeria devotes to describing distances. She sometimes men-

---

[2] Recent debate on this point rests largely on the significance of the author's references to sites associated with biblical women, fertility, and children. See Laurie Douglass, "A New Look at the *Itinerarium Burdigalense*," *Journal of Early Christian Studies* 4 (1996): 313–33; Susan Weingarten, "Was the Pilgrim from Bordeaux a Woman? A Reply to Laurie Douglass," *Journal of Early Christian Studies* 7 (1999): 291–97.

[3] This mode of transport implies that the traveler may have been part of an official party eligible to use the *cursus publicus*: see above, p. 29.

[4] Hunt, "Space and Time Transcended," 71.

[5] Ibid., 72.

tions how many days it took to travel to a particular place but mentions precise mileage much more rarely than the Bordeaux pilgrim and certainly does not seem concerned to document all the stages of her journey methodically. Furthermore, Egeria's descriptions of the holy sites are much more extensive and not just confined to places in the Holy Land proper. While her account certainly can be categorized as a travelogue, the religious significance of the travel she undertakes stands out much more strongly in it than her overviews of the travel itself.

Our translated extract from the Bordeaux pilgrim's *itinerarium* commences at the point where the account becomes more detailed, as what is observed on the way begins to be more regularly recorded and described, and ends when it reverts to being simply a list of places and distances.[6] Numbers in brackets indicate the accepted divisions of the text, and we have also added biblical references and some other notes in brackets.

[583] . . . City of Sidon, 8 miles.

From there to Sarepta, 9 miles.

There Elijah went up to the widow and asked for food for himself [1 Kings 17:9-16].

Change at "ad Nonum" [at the ninth milestone?], 4 miles.

[584] City of Tyre, 12 miles.

Total from Antioch to Tyre, 174 miles, 20 changes, 11 stays.

Change at Alexandroschene, 12 miles.

Change at Ecdeppa, 12 miles.

City of Ptolemais, 9 miles.

Change at Calamon, 12 miles.

Stay at Sycaminos, 3 miles.

---

[6] Latin text ed. Paul Geyer and Otto Cuntz, in *Itineraria et Alia Geographica*, Corpus Christianorum Series Latina 175 (Turnhout: Brepols, 1965), 1–26; Brodersen, 26–72; ET of the complete text in Aubrey Stewart and C. W. Wilson, *Itinerary from Bordeaux to Jerusalem: 'The Bordeaux Pilgrim', 333 A.D.* (London: Palestine Pilgrims' Text Society, 1887). For a more recent study of the work, see Oded Irshai, "The Christian Appropriation of Jerusalem in the Fourth Century: The Case of the Bordeaux Pilgrim," *Jewish Quarterly Review* 99 (2009): 465–86.

[585] There is Mount Carmel, where Elijah offered sacrifice [1 Kings 18:19-40].

Change at Certa, 8 miles.

Frontier of Syria, Phoenicia, and Palestine.

City of Caesarea Palestina, that is, Judaea, 8 miles.

Total from Tyre to Caesarea Palestina, 73 miles, 2 changes, 3 stays.

There is the bath of Cornelius the centurion, who gave many alms [Acts 10:2, 47-48].

At the third milestone from there is [586] Mount Syna, where there is a spring, in which, if a woman bathes, she becomes pregnant.

City of Maximianopolis, 18 miles.

City of Stradela [Jezreel], 10 miles.

There King Ahab reigned and Elijah prophesied [1 Kings 16:29–17:7]; there is the plain where David slew Goliath [1 Sam 17:32-51].

City of Scythopolis, 12 miles.

[587] Aser, where was the estate of Job, 16 miles.

City of Neapolis, 15 miles.

There is Mount Gerizim, where the Samaritans say that Abraham offered sacrifice, and one ascends to the top of the mountain by steps, in number thirteen hundred. From there at the foot of the mountain itself is a place, the name of which is Sichem.

There is a tomb, where is laid [588] Joseph in the estate that his father Jacob gave to him [Josh 24:32].

From there Dinah, Jacob's daughter, was carried off by the sons of the Amorites [Gen 34].

A mile from there is the place by the name of Sychar, from where the Samaritan woman came down to the same place where Jacob had dug the well to draw water from it, and our Lord Jesus Christ spoke with her [Jn 4:5-26]; where are also plane trees that Jacob planted and a bath [baptistery] that is watered from that well.

Twenty-eight miles from there going toward Jerusalem is an estate on the left side that is called Bethar.

A mile from there is the place where Jacob slept when he was going into Mesopotamia [Gen 28:10-22], and there is the almond tree, and he saw the vision and the angel wrestled with him [Gen 32:22-32].

There was King Jeroboam, to whom the prophet was sent that he should be turned to God [589] most high; and the prophet had been ordered not to eat with the false prophet whom the king had with him, and because he was led astray by the false prophet and ate with him, as he was returning a lion met the prophet on the way and killed him [1 Kings 13:1-34].

From there to Jerusalem, 12 miles.

Total from Caesarea Palestina to Jerusalem, 116 miles, 4 stays, 4 changes.

There are in Jerusalem two large pools at the side of the temple, that is, one on the right, the other on the left, which Solomon made, and further inside the city are twin pools having five porticos that are called Bethsaida [Jn 5:2-3]. There those sick for many years were healed. These pools have water that becomes scarlet when disturbed. There is also a crypt there, where Solomon tortured demons.

There is the corner [590] of a very high tower, where the Lord ascended and the one who was tempting him spoke to him and the Lord said to him, "You shall not tempt the Lord your God but him alone shall you serve" [Mt 4:5-7, 10].

There is also the great cornerstone of which it was said: "The stone that the builders rejected has here been made the head of the corner" [Ps 118:22; Mt 21:42]. And under the pinnacle of this tower are very many rooms, where Solomon had his palace. There also stands the room in which he sat and wrote [the book of] Wisdom; that room is roofed with a single stone. There are also large cisterns of underground water and pools constructed with great labor.

And [591] in the sanctuary itself, where the temple was that Solomon built, the blood of Zachariah on the marble there before the altar you would say had been shed today [2 Chr 24:20-22; Mt 23:35; Lk 11:51]; also visible are the marks of the hobnails of the soldiers who killed him throughout the floor so that you would think they were impressed in wax.

Also there are two statues of Hadrian; there is also not far from the statues a pierced stone to which Jews come each year and anoint it and lament with groaning and rend their garments and then depart. Also there is the house of Hezekiah, King of Judah.

Then, coming out from Jerusalem in order to go up to Sion, on the left side [592] and below in the valley beside the wall is a pool that is called Siloam [Jn 9:7, 11]; it has four porticos; and another large pool outside it. This spring runs for six days and nights, but on the seventh day is the Sabbath: it does not run at all either by night or by day.

On the same side one goes up to Sion and [the place] where the house of Caiaphas the priest was visible [Mt 26:3, 57-68], and the column is still there at which they fell on Christ with scourges. Inside, within the wall of Sion is visible the place where David had his palace. And of the seven synagogues that were there, only one remains and the rest are plowed and sown, as Isaiah the prophet [593] said [Isa 1:7-8; cf. Mic 3:12].

From there as you go out of the wall of Sion, going toward the gate of Neapolis, on the right side down in the valley are walls where the house or praetorium [Mt 27:27; Mk 15:16; Jn 18:28, 33] of Pontius Pilate was; there the Lord was tried before he suffered. On the left side is the little hill of Golgotha [Mt 27:33; Mk 15:22; Jn 19:17], where the Lord was crucified.

[594] About a stone's throw from there is the vault where his body was laid and rose on the third day; there by order of the emperor Constantine a basilica has now been built, that is, "a house of the Lord [*dominicum*]," of extraordinary beauty, having at the side cisterns from which water is raised, and a bath [baptistery] behind, where infants [the newly baptized, i.e., those reborn] are washed.

Then, going to the gate of Jerusalem that is toward the east, in order to ascend the Mount of Olives, [is] what is called the Valley of Jehoshaphat [Joel 3:2, 12]; on the left side, where there are vineyards, is also the rock where Judas Iscariot betrayed Christ; and on the right side [595] is the palm tree from which the children took branches and strewed them as Christ was coming [Mt 21:8; cf. Mt 21:15].

Not far from there, about a stone's throw, are two memorial tombs of extraordinary beauty: in one, which is a true monolith, is laid Isaiah the prophet and in the other Hezekiah, King of the Jews.

From there you ascend the Mount of Olives, where the Lord taught the apostles before his passion [Mt 24:3f.; Mk 13:3f.]: there has been built a basilica by order of Constantine.

Not far from there is a little hill where the Lord went up to pray and Moses and Elijah appeared there when he took Peter [596] and John with him [Mt 17:1-8; Mk 9:2-8; Lk 9:28-36].

From there 1500 paces to the east is the estate that is called Bethany; there is there the vault in which was laid Lazarus, whom the Lord raised [Jn 11:38-44].

Then from Jerusalem to Jericho, 18 miles.

Going down the mount on the right side behind a tomb is the sycamore tree into which Zacchaeus climbed to see Christ [Lk 19:2-4].

1500 paces from the city there is the spring of Elisha the prophet. Before, if a woman drank from that water, she did not bear children. An earthenware vessel was brought to Elisha; he threw salt in it and came and stood over the spring and said: "Thus says the Lord: He has healed these waters. If a woman drinks from it henceforth, she will bear children" [2 Kings 2:19-22].

Above the same spring [597] is the house of Rahab the harlot, to whom the spies came and she hid them when Jericho was overthrown and she alone escaped [Josh 2:1-21; Heb 11:31].

There was the city of Jericho, the walls of which the children of Israel encircled with the ark of the covenant and the walls fell down [Josh 6:1-20]. Nothing is visible of it except the place where the ark of the covenant was and the twelve stones that the children of Israel lifted up from the Jordan [Josh 4:1-9]. There Joshua the son of Nun circumcised the children of Israel and buried their foreskins [Josh 5:2-9].

Then from Jericho to the Dead Sea, 9 miles.

Its water is extremely bitter, where there are no fish of any kind at all and no boats, and if anyone dives into it in order to swim, the water itself turns them over.

[598] From there to the Jordan, where the Lord was baptized by John [Mt 3:13-17; Mk 1:9-11], 5 miles.

There is a place above the river, a little hill on the far bank, where Elijah was caught up into heaven [2 Kings 2:1-11].

Then going from Jerusalem to Bethlehem, four miles along the road on the right side is the tomb where was laid Rachel, the wife of Jacob [Gen 35:19-20]. Two miles from there on the left side is Bethlehem, where the Lord Jesus Christ was born [Mt 2:1-12; Lk 2:1-7]; there a basilica has been built by order of Constantine. Not far from there is the tomb of Ezekiel, Asaph, Job, and Jesse, David, Solomon, and it has on the wall going down into the vault itself the names written above, written in Hebrew letters.

[599] From there to Bethasora, 14 miles, where there is the spring in which Philip baptized the eunuch [Acts 8:26-40].

From there to Terebinthus, 9 miles, where Abraham lived and dug a well under a terebinth tree and spoke with angels and ate food with them [Gen 18:1-8]; there a basilica of extraordinary beauty has been built by order of Constantine.

From Terebinthus to Hebron, 2 miles, where there is a square tomb made of stone of extraordinary beauty, in which are laid Abraham, Isaac, Jacob, Sarah, Rebecca, and Leah [Gen 23; 25:7-10; 49:29-33].

Appendix B:
The Letter of King Abgar[1]

Copy of an epistle written by Abgarus the ruler to Jesus, and sent to him at Jerusalem by Ananias the swift courier

Abgarus, ruler of Edessa, to Jesus the excellent Savior who has appeared in the country of Jerusalem, greeting. I have heard the reports of you and of your cures as performed by you without medicines or herbs. For it is said that you make the blind to see and the lame to walk, that you cleanse lepers and cast out impure spirits and demons, and that you heal those afflicted with lingering disease, and raise the dead. And having heard all these things concerning you, I have concluded that one of two things must be true: either you are God, and having come down from heaven you do these things, or else you who do these things are the Son of God. I have therefore written to you to ask you if you would take the trouble to come to me and heal the disease which I have. For I have heard that the Jews are murmuring against you and are plotting to injure you. But I have a very small yet noble city which is great enough for us both.

The answer of Jesus to the ruler Abgarus by the courier Ananias

Blessed are you who have believed in me without having seen me. For it is written concerning me, that they who have seen me will not believe in me, and that they who have not seen me will believe and be saved. But in regard to what you have written me, that I should come to you, it is necessary for me to fulfill all things here for which

---

[1] See 17.1; 19.8-17 above. Quoted by Eusebius, *Hist. eccl.* 1.13.6-9, who rendered the original Syriac into Greek; ET adapted from *NPNF* 2:1, 100–101.

I have been sent, and after I have fulfilled them thus to be taken up again to him that sent me. But after I have been taken up I will send to you one of my disciples, that he may heal your disease and give life to you and yours.

Appendix C:
Fragments of Egeria's Text

Although we know of only one fairly complete manuscript of the work, there are a number of fragments of the text in two other manuscripts. In 1909 the Benedictine scholar Donatien de Bruyne published a set of eleven very short quotations from the *itinerarium* beginning on folio 8 of a ninth-century manuscript from Toledo that was in the Biblioteca Nacional in Madrid, the *Codex Matritensis Toletanus* 14.24, which were apparently intended to form a series of topographical notes.[1] Most of these simply provide some variant readings of no great significance, but two evidently come from the lacuna between 16.4 and 16.5:

> *In that place* where Job sat on a dunghill there is now a clear space surrounded by iron railings and a large glass lamp burns there from night to night.

> *The spring* where he scraped his sores with a potsherd, it changes color four times a year, first so it has the color of pus, next of blood, next of gall, and next it is clear. [see Job 2:8]

Much more recently the paleographer Jesús Alturo discovered two further somewhat larger fragments in a manuscript in a private collection in Madrid that he dated from around the year 900.[2] The first

---

[1] Donatien de Bruyne, "Nouveaux fragments de *l'Itinerarium Eucheriae*," *Revue bénédictine* 26 (1909): 481–84.

[2] Jesús Alturo, "Deux nouveaux fragments de l'*'Itinerarium Egeriae'* du IXe–Xe siècle," *Revue bénédictine* 115 (2005): 241–50.

of these covered, on one side, the last word of chapter 15 and the first few lines of chapter 16. On its reverse was a passage evidently from somewhere in the lacuna between 16.4 and 16.5. The other fragment similarly had another passage presumably from that same part of the text, with the final section of chapter 16 on its reverse side. The text is difficult to make out in several places, but the material from within the lacuna reads something like this:[3]

> . . . not large . . . is Dennaba . . . city . . . Ausitis within the boundaries of Arabia. . . . Where the dunghill . . . we saw the bishop . . . we entered into the church that is in that city. Prayer having been done, we asked that he would show us every place, just as also . . . he deigned to do. For he immediately led us to that place where the dunghill was, that is, where holy Job sat, which was then in front of the gate of the city. But now four walls have been added in . . . of the city with a gate for this reason, so that the dunghill could be enclosed within the city. That place of the dunghill is now indeed quite clear; for they look after it carefully . . . four columns that support the roof around. . . .
>
> . . . with the help . . . we would have come . . . we entered . . . will be an area . . . an area . . . from beyond that . . . the same joined together exceedingly . . . we marveled greatly at this. There were all the parts that . . . also had a large porch. And its whole building was completely roofed without wood. For, as if beams have been made from the hardest stone, they support the whole building with firm strength from arch to arch, as it has supporting arches such that those arches have twelve feet between them. We entered about the tenth hour; prayer and everything was done that we had been accustomed to do wherever we came to places that we desired. And as it was the sixth day of the week, at night. . . .

---

[3] Amended version of the Latin text and German translation in Brodersen, 138–41.

Select Bibliography

Editions (in chronological order; for a more complete list, see Gingras, 135)

Gamurrini, Gian Francesco. *S. Hilarii tractatus de mysteriis et hymni et S. Silviae Aquitanae peregrinatio ad loca sancta*. Biblioteca della Academia storico-giuridica 4. Rome: Cuggiani, 1887.

———. "S. Silvae Aquitaine: Peregrinatio ad loca sancta." *Studi e documenti di storia e diritto* 9 (1888): 97–147.

Pétré, Hélène. *Éthérie. Journal de voyage*. Sources chrétiennes 21. Paris: Cerf, 1948.

Maraval, Pierre. *Égérie. Journal de voyage (Itinéraire)*. Sources chrétiennes 296. Paris: Cerf, 1982; reissued with additions and corrections, 1997, 2002.

Arce, Agustín. *Itinerario de la Virgen Egeria (381–384)*. 2d ed., Madrid: Biblioteca de Autores Cristianos, 1996.

Brodersen, Kai. *Aetheria/Egeria, Reise ins Heilige Land*. Sammlung Tusculum. Berlin: De Gruyter, 2016.

English translations (in chronological order)

Bernard, John Henry. *The Pilgrimage of S. Silvia of Aquitaine to the Holy Places circa 385 A.D.* London: Palestine Pilgrim's Text Society, 1891.

McClure, M. L., and Charles Lett Feltoe. *The Pilgrimage of Etheria*. Translations of Christian Literature, Series 3. London: SPCK/New York: Macmillan, 1919.

Gingras, George E. *Egeria: Diary of a Pilgrimage*. Ancient Christian Writers 38. New York: Newman Press, 1970.

Wilkinson, John. *Egeria's Travels*. London: SPCK, 1971; 2d ed., Jerusalem: Ariel Publishing House, 1981; 3d ed., Warminster: Aris and Phillips, 1999.

Bibliographies

Devos, Paul. "Egeriana." *Analecta Bollandiana* 105 (1987): 159–66, 415–24; 109 (1991): 363–81; 112 (1994): 241–54.

Janeras, Sebastià. "Bibliografía egeriana recent." *Revista Catalana de Teologia* 28 (2003): 231–40, 507–10.

Starowieyski, Marek. "Bibliograffia egeriana." *Augustinianum* 19 (1979): 297–318.

Egeria's Latin Style and Vocabulary

Bastiaensen, A. A. R. *Observations sur le vocabulaire liturgique dans l'Itinéraire d'Égerie*. Latinitas Christianorum primaeva 17. Nijmegen: Dekker & Van de Vegt, 1962.

Blackman, Deane R., and Gavin G. Betts. *Concordantia in Itinerarium Egeriae*. Hildesheim/New York: Olms-Weidmann, 1989.

Hertzenberg, Mari Johanne Bordal. *Third Person Reference in Late Latin: Demonstratives, Definite Articles and Personal Pronouns in the Itinerarium Egeriae*. Berlin/Boston: De Gruyter, 2015.

Spitzer, Leo. "The Epic Style of the Pilgrim Aetheria." *Comparative Literature* 1 (1949): 225–58.

Swanson, Donald C. "A Formal Analysis of Egeria's (Silvia's) Vocabulary." *Glotta* 44 (1966–67): 177–254.

Väänänen, Veikko. *Le journal-épître d'Égérie (Itinerarium Egeriae): Étude linguistique*. Annales Academiae Scientiarum Fennicae, Ser. B, 230. Helsinki: Suomalainen Tiedeakatemia, 1987.

Vermeer, G. F. M. *Observations sur le vocabulaire de pèlerinage chez Égérie et chez Antonin de Plaisance*. Latinitas Christianorum primaeva 19. Nijmegen: Dekker & Van de Vegt, 1965.

Early Christian Pilgrimage

Bitton-Ashkelony, Brouria. *Encountering the Sacred: The Debate on Christian Pilgrimage in Late Antiquity*. Berkeley: University of California Press, 2005.

Day, Juliette. "Seeing Christ at the Holy Places." In *Spaces in Late Antiquity: Cultural, Theological and Archaeological Perspectives*, ed. Juliette Day, Raimo Hakola, Maijastina Kahlos, and Ulla Tervahauta, 69–88. Abingdon/New York: Routledge, 2016.

Dietz, Maribel. *Wandering Monks, Virgins, and Pilgrims: Ascetic Travel in the Mediterranean World, A.D. 300–800*. University Park, PA: Penn State University Press, 2005.

Elm, Susanna. "Perceptions of Jerusalem Pilgrimage as Reflected in Two Early Sources on Female Pilgrimage (3rd and 4th centuries A.D.)." *Studia Patristica* 20 (1989): 219–23.

Frank, Georgia. *The Memory of the Eyes: Pilgrims to Living Saints in Christian Late Antiquity*. Berkeley: University of California Press, 2000.

Hunt, Edward David. *Holy Land Pilgrimage in the Later Roman Empire AD 312–460*. Oxford: Clarendon, 1982/New York: Oxford University Press, 1984.

————. "The Itinerary of Egeria: Reliving the Bible in Fourth-Century Palestine." In *The Holy Land, Holy Lands, and Christian History*, ed. R. N. Swanson, Studies in Church History 36, 34–54. Woodbridge: Boydell Press, 2000.

————. "Were There Christian Pilgrims before Constantine?" In *Pilgrimage Explored*, ed. Jennie Stopford, 25–40. Woodbridge/Rochester, NY: York Medieval Press, 1999.

Maraval, Pierre. "The Earliest Phase of Christian Pilgrimage in the Near East (before the 7th Century)." *Dumbarton Oaks Papers* 56 (2002): 63–74.

Taylor, Joan E. *Christians and the Holy Places: The Myth of Jewish-Christian Origins*. Oxford: Clarendon/New York: Oxford University Press, 1993.

Walker, Peter W. L. *Holy City, Holy Places? Christian Attitudes to Jerusalem and the Holy Land in the Fourth Century*. Oxford: Clarendon/New York: Oxford University Press, 1990.

Early Ascetic and Monastic Life

Harmless, J. William. "Monasticism." In *The Oxford Handbook of Early Christian Studies*, ed. Susan Ashbrook Harvey and David G. Hunter, 493–517. Oxford: Oxford University Press, 2008.

Stewart, Columba. "Rethinking the History of Monasticism East and West: A Modest *tour d'horizon*." In *Prayer and Thought in Monastic Tradition: Essays in Honour of Benedicta Ward SLG*, ed. Santha Bhattacharji, Rowan Williams, and Dominic Mattos, 3–16. London: Bloomsbury T & T Clark, 2014.

Wimbush Vincent L. and Richard Valantasis, eds. *Asceticism*. Oxford: Oxford University Press, 1995.

On women's experiences in particular, see:

Cloke, Gillian. *This Female Man of God: Women and Spiritual Power in the Patristic Age, AD 350–450*. New York: Routledge, 1995.

Elm, Susanna. *'Virgins of God': The Making of Asceticism in Late Antiquity*. New York: Oxford University Press, 1994.

The Ecclesiastical Buildings of Jerusalem

Biddle, Martin. *The Tomb of Christ*. Stroud: Sutton Publishing, 1999.

Corbo, Virgilio C. *Il Santo Sepolcro di Gerusalemme*, 3 vols. Jerusalem: Franciscan Printing Press, 1981.

Gibson, Shimon, and Joan E. Taylor. *Beneath the Church of the Holy Sepulchre, Jerusalem*. London: Palestine Exploration Fund, 1994.

The Jerusalem Liturgy

Baldovin, John F. *Liturgy in Ancient Jerusalem*. JLS 9. Bramcote: Grove Books, 1989.

————. *The Urban Character of Christian Worship: The Origins, Development and Meaning of Stational Liturgy*. Orientalia Christiana Analecta 228. Rome: Pontifical Oriental Institute, 1987.

Buchinger, Harald. "Heilige Zeiten? Christliche Feste zwischen Mimesis und Anamnesis am Beispiel der Jerusalemer Liturgie der Spätantike." In *Communio Sanctorum: Heiliges und Heiligkeit in spätantiken Religionskulturen*, ed. Peter Gemeinhardt and Katharina Heyden, Religionsgeschichtliche Versuche und Vorarbeiten 61, 283–323. Berlin: De Gruyter, 2012.

————. "Das Jerusalemer Sanctorale: Zu Stand und Aufgaben der Forschung." In *A Cloud of Witnesses: The Cult of Saints in Past and Present*, ed. Marcel Barnard, Paul Post, and Els Rose, Liturgia Condenda 18, 97–128. Leuven: Peeters, 2005.

Day, Juliette. *The Baptismal Liturgy of Jerusalem: Fourth- and Fifth-Century Evidence from Palestine, Syria, and Egypt*. Aldershot/Burlington, VT: Ashgate, 2007.

————. "The Catechetical Lectures of Cyril of Jerusalem: A Source for the Baptismal Liturgy of Mid-Fourth Century Jerusalem." In Paul F. Bradshaw and Juliette Day, *Further Essays in Early Eastern Initiation*, JLS 78, 24–56. Norwich: SCM-Canterbury Press, 2014.

Denysenko, Nicholas. "The Hypapante Feast in Fourth to Eighth Century Jerusalem." *Studia Liturgica* 37 (2007): 73–97.

Frøyshov, Stig Simeon. "The Georgian Witness to the Jerusalem Liturgy: New Sources and Studies." In *Inquiries into Eastern Christian Worship*, ed. Bert Groen, Steven Hawkes-Teeples, and Stefanos Alexopoulos, Eastern Christian Studies 12, 227–67. Leuven: Peeters, 2012.

Jeffery, Peter. "The Earliest Christian Chant Repertory Recovered: The Georgian Witnesses to Jerusalem Chant." *Journal of the American Musicological Society* 47 (1994): 1–39.

Johnson, Maxwell E. "Baptismal Liturgy in Fourth-Century Jerusalem in the Light of Recent Scholarship." In *Inquiries into Eastern Christian Worship*, ed. Bert Groen, Steven Hawkes-Teeples, and Stefanos Alexopoulos, Eastern Christian Studies 12, 81–98. Leuven: Peeters, 2012.

Méndez, Hugo. "Stephen the Martyr (Acts VI–VIII) in the Early Jerusalem Lectionary System." *Journal of Ecclesiastical History* 68 (2017): 22–39.

Moriarty, Rachel. "Secular Men and Women: Egeria's Lay Congregation in Jerusalem." In *The Holy Land, Holy Lands, and Christian History*, ed. R. N. Swanson, Studies in Church History 36, 55–66. Woodbridge: Boydell Press, 2000.

Russo, Nicholas V. "The Distribution of Cyril's *Baptismal Catecheses* and the Shape of the Catechumenate in Mid-Fourth-Century Jerusalem." In *A Living Tradition: On the Intersection of Liturgical History and Pastoral Practice*, ed. David Pitt, Stefanos Alexopoulos, and Christian McConnell, 75–100. Collegeville, MN: Liturgical Press, 2012.

Zerfass, Rolf. *Die Schriftlesung im Kathedraloffizium Jerusalems*. Liturgiewissenschaftliche Quellen und Forschungen 48. Münster: Aschendorff, 1968.

Index of Biblical References

Index of Other Ancient Sources

Index of Modern Authors

(Page numbers in bold indicate where full publication details occur)

Index of Places

Index of Persons and Subjects

Jacob, 57, 100, 118, 120, 123, 144–46, 200, 203, 204

James, bishop of Jerusalem, 180

James the apostle, 100

Jeremiah the prophet, 100

Jeroboam, King, 201

Jerome, 12, 25, 40, 41, 46, 49, 52, 53, 61, 67, 68, 127

Jesse, 203

Job, 19, 55, 127, 128, 132–33, 200, 203, 207–8

John, bishop of Jerusalem, 25, 80, 100

John the apostle, 20, 100, 149, 202

John the Baptist, 20, 100, 122, 130, 131, 203

Joseph, patriarch, 118, 200; husband of Mary, 52, 160; of Arimathea, 178

Joshua, son of Nun, 112, 122, 203

Jovian, Emperor, 144

Judas Iscariot, 171, 200

Julian Saba, 107

Jupiter, temple of, 57, 100–101

Justinian, Emperor, 137

Kyrie eleison, 151

Laban, 144, 146

Laodicea, Council of, 81, 162

Lazarium, 68, 77, 91, 93, 98, 99, 158, 166, 171, 180

Lazarus, 55, 68, 91, 166, 203

Lazarus Saturday, 91–92, 166–67

Leah, 204

Lent, 56, 72–76, 80–86, 88–91, 94, 96, 99, 150, 160–65, 169, 172, 179, 188, 190

litany, 151

Lord's Day, vii, 79, 106, 152, 154–56, 160–61, 164, 167–68, 180–84, 187

Lot, 143

Lot's wife, 126

Lucernare/Lucernarium, 93, 151, 156, 158, 161, 163, 165, 167, 169–72, 179, 181–83, 185, 186, 188

Macarius, bishop of Jerusalem, 65

Maccabees, 100

Magnus, 137, 139

major church, 61–62, 154, 156, 157, 161, 167, 168, 170, 178–81, 183, 184, 186, 188, 189, 191, 194; *see also* Martyrium, the

Manasseh, 122

Mandylion, 137

Marthana, deaconess, 8, 15, 26, 30, 31, 39, 50, 147

martyr(s), 11, 20, 23, 40, 44–46, 49, 62, 75, 99, 100, 142–43, 148, 162

martyrium, 62, 99, 118, 133–36, 142, 146–49, 155, 158

Martyrium, the, 61–62, 66, 77, 79–83, 85, 86, 91–93, 96–99, 101, 155–61, 167–72, 177–81, 183–84, 186–89, 191, 193, 194; *see also* major church

Mary, mother of Jesus, 52, 100, 159–60; sister of Lazarus, 55, 68, 91, 166

Melania the Elder, 8, 9, 12, 30, 32, 41, 49; the Younger, 31, 99

Melchizedek, 20, 47, 51, 128–31

Melito of Sardis, 43

minor orders, 116, 153, 188

missa, 69

monastery, 2, 5, 9, 28, 31, 32, 49, 59, 104, 111, 116–17; *see also* cell(s), monastic

"monastic" prayer, 71–76, 149–52, 156, 159, 183

monazontes, 149–50, 154–57, 159, 194

monk(s), 5–10, 14, 16, 19, 20, 23, 29, 30, 38, 46–49, 52, 54–56, 77, 103, 106–8, 110, 114, 116–20, 122, 124, 125, 128–33, 135, 136, 141–49, 156, 159, 166, 192, 194